EDI LEARNING RESOURCES SERIES

National Assessments

Testing the System

Edited by
Paud Murphy
Vincent Greaney
Marlaine E. Lockheed
Carlos Rojas

Contributors
David Carroll
Vincent Greaney
Erika Himmel
Lynn Ilon
John Izard
Thomas Kellaghan
Marlaine E. Lockheed
O. C. Nwana
Kowit Pravalpruk
Carlos Rojas

The World Bank
Washington, D. C.

The Economic Development Institute (EDI) was established by the World Bank in 1955 to train officials concerned with development planning, policymaking, investment analysis, and project implementation in member developing countries. At present the substance of the EDI's work emphasizes macroeconomic and sectoral economic policy analysis. Through a variety of courses, seminars, and workshops, most of which are given overseas in cooperation with local institutions, the EDI seeks to sharpen analytical skills used in policy analysis and to broaden understanding of the experience of individual countries with economic development. Although the EDI's publications are designed to support its training activities, many are of interest to a much broader audience. EDI materials, including any findings, interpretations, and conclusions, are entirely those of the authors and should not be attributed in any manner to the World Bank, to its affiliated organizations, or to members of its Board of Executive Directors or the countries they represent.

Because of the informality of this series and to make the publication available with the least possible delay, the manuscript has not been edited as fully as would be the case with a more formal document, and the World Bank accepts no responsibility for errors. Some sources cited in this paper may be informal documents that are not readily available.

The material in this publication is copyrighted. Requests for permission to reproduce portions of it should be sent to the Office of the Publisher at the address shown in the copyright notice above. The World Bank encourages dissemination of its work and will normally give permission promptly and, when the reproduction is for noncommercial purposes, without asking a fee. Permission to photocopy portions for classroom use is granted through the Copyright Clearance Center, Inc., Suite 910, 222 Rosewood Drive, Danvers, Massachusetts 01923, U.S.A.

The complete backlist of publications from the World Bank is shown in the annual *Index of Publications*, which contains an alphabetical title list (with full ordering information) and indexes of subjects, authors, and countries and regions. The latest edition is available free of charge from the Distribution Unit, Office of the Publisher, The World Bank, 1818 H Street, N.W., Washington, D.C. 20433, U.S.A., or from Publications, Banque mondiale, 66, avenue d'Iéna, 75116 Paris, France.

Paud Murphy is an education specialist in the World Bank's Economic Development Institute; Vincent Greaney is a senior education specialist in the World Bank's Asia Technical Department; Marlaine Lockheed is principal education specialist in the World Bank's Human Development Department; and Carlos Rojas is an education specialist in the World Bank's Department II for Latin America and the Caribbean.

Library of Congress Cataloging-in-Publication Data

National Assessments : testing the system / edited by Paud Murphy . . .
[et al.] ; contributors, David Carroll . . . [et al.].
    p. cm.—(EDI learning resources series)
  Includes bibliographical references (p.).
  ISBN 0-8213-3679-7
   1. Educational evaluation—Developing countries. 2. Educational
tests and measurements—Developing countries. I. Murphy, Paud.
II. Carroll, David. III. Series
LB2822.75.N375   1996
379.1'54—dc20

            96-25643
            CIP

CONTENTS

Foreword

That basic education contributes to economic growth and the alleviation of poverty is now widely understood; and developing countries are making significant progress in increasing access to school for their children. During the decade 1980–90, the number of years that a typical 6-year-old child in a developing country could expect to spend in school rose from 7.7 to 8.5, and the percentage of the 6 to 11-year-old population in school rose from 69 percent to 76 percent. Given the commitment of more than 150 countries represented at the World Conference on Education for All (WCEFA) to the provision of basic education for all citizens, these figures can be expected to increase further during the current decade. Less widely understood is the type of education that can best support individual and national aspirations. Clearly, providing schools, teachers, and textbooks is not sufficient: Children must also benefit from their school experience. It has been common practice to measure educational outcomes: Numbers graduating or completing different levels. However, these measures of outcome ignore the critical variable: What have children learned? Measuring what children learn from their educational experiences and providing this information to policymakers can improve decisionmaking and promote appropriate cost-effective interventions that improve learning among different groups. Measuring learning achievement over time can also provide important information on the progress (or lack of it) of the education system as a whole.

This book provides background on national assessments: Systematic countrywide measures of learning achievement to guide policymaking. Its origins are in the declaration of the WCEFA which specified the importance of measuring learning achievement. Recognizing the importance of national assessments, an increasing number of developing countries have begun to establish their own systems, and to this end, many have sought World Bank support. As a result, from a zero base in 1988, the World Bank was making loans for national assessments in over 27 percent of its education projects in 1992. This share is likely to continue to increase as more countries seek to improve the quality, efficiency, and equitable provision of basic education.

Vinod Thomas
Director
Economic Development Institute

Acknowledgments

The book came about from a series of seminars held in Asia, Africa, and Latin America in 1992 and 1993, following the 1990 World Conference on Education for All, which underscored the importance of learning acquisition and developing appropriate methods to assess learning achievement. At that time the World Bank became increasingly interested in helping countries monitor progress toward the achievement of national educational goals.

Accordingly, the World Bank's Economic Development Institute and the Population and Human Resources Department planned a series of seminars to provide senior policymakers and technical experts with an opportunity to learn about national assessment systems. The International Association for the Assessment of Educational Achievement was then subcontracted to help prepare and deliver the seminars, three of which took place during 1992 and 1993—one for Asia in Tagaytay city, Philippines; one for Latin America in Santiago, Chile; and one for Africa in Nairobi, Kenya. Most of the chapters in this book were first presented as papers in these seminars. All the authors have been involved with testing and assessment issues in their own countries and internationally.

Contributors

David Carroll is currently British Council adviser to the National Centre for Examinations and Educational Evaluation in Egypt. He has advised governments in three continents on assessment and examinations.

Vincent Greaney is senior education specialist in the World Bank's Asia Technical Department. He was formerly a fellow in The Educational Research Center, St. Patrick's College, Drumcondra, Ireland where his interests were in assessment and reading. He was recently elected to The International Reading Association's Reading Hall of Fame.

Erica Himmel is a professor in the Graduate School of Education, and former Academic Vice Rector, of the Catholic University of Chile. She was technical consultant on the SMICE Assessment of Elementary Education and has advised governments and international agencies on assessment systems throughout Latin America.

Lynn Ilon is assistant professor of the economics of education and international education at the State University of New York at Buffalo. She has been a consultant to the World Bank and USAID on education projects in developing countries on four continents.

John Izard is assistant director of the Australian Council for Educational Research. He has published widely on testing and assessment and has been a consultant to the World Bank, UNESCO, Australian Aid, and the British Council.

Thomas Kellaghan has been the director of the Educational Research Centre in St. Patrick's College Drumcondra, Ireland since 1966. The Centre carries out research for the Irish Department of Education and other agencies on all aspects of education in Ireland. Dr. Kellaghan is author or co-author of nine books and 100 articles.

Marlaine E. Lockheed is principal education specialist in the World Bank's Human Development Department. Before joining the World Bank, she worked for many years at the Educational Testing Service on issues of girls' education. Her current interests are in education decentralization and teacher policy.

Paud Murphy is a general educator in the World Bank's Economic Development Institute. Before joining the World Bank he headed the Irish education agency HEDCO and worked for many years in Africa. His current interests are in distance teaching and girls' education.

O. C. Nwana is in charge of the Educational Research Centre of the Educational Research and Development Council in Nigeria. He served three terms as dean of the faculty of education at the University of Nigeria, Nsukka, and has been an adviser to the Federal Minister of Education.

Kowit Pravalpruk is the deputy director of the Department of Curriculum and Instruction Development in the Ministry of Education in Thailand. He has been a consultant to a number of international agencies across Asia.

Carlos Rojas is an education specialist in the World Bank's Human Resources Operations Division, Department II for Latin America and the Caribbean. Before joining the World Bank he was a principal researcher for Instituto SER de Investigación in Colombia.

1

Introduction

Marlaine E. Lockheed and Paud Murphy

In education, no one questions the importance of monitoring children's learning progress and using the information gathered to assist children who are not performing to their potential. It is equally important to measure the performance of the education system itself. How much are children learning? Are they learning more today than they were five years ago? ten years ago? Are seven-year old children learning as much as the children of another region? Are children in remote rural areas, children from deprived urban backgrounds learning as much as those in the affluent suburbs? Are programs aimed at helping disadvantaged groups actually helping those groups? National assessments—which are systematic, regular measurements of the quality of education provision to guide policymaking—are intended to help answer some of these questions. This book is about these systems; it is aimed at providing policymakers and education practitioners working in developing countries with information about different aspects of these systems and how they work in practice. The book brings together descriptions of a number of different features of national assessments and five country case studies that provide lessons of interest to countries planning national assessments and to individuals interested in studying such systems. We hope the book will encourage discussion of the quality of education provision in countries, how it should be measured and how to use the information gathered to improve quality. While it is aimed mainly at policymakers and practitioners in ministries of education, it is also intended to be of value to those seeking to gain information about various technical aspects of national assessments and how these system function in developing countries.

Importance of Measuring

Two factors underscore the importance of measuring the performance of education systems in developing countries. The first factor is a growing concern with the quality of educational provision within countries. The second is a realization that many of the educational problems a developing country faces may be unique to that country. These two concerns have helped to increase the number of such measurements being carried out by developing countries, and more countries are likely to introduce such measures in the near future.

In the 1960s and 1970s many developing countries, faced with many people who had no access to schooling of any kind, focused on providing places for more children. Because of this, quantitative concerns related to the number of pupils, teachers, classrooms, and textbooks outweighed concerns about the quality of learning in schools. As a number of countries succeeded in meeting their quantitative goals, a movement began in the early 1980s to concentrate on the quality of the education being provided in the schools. Even countries that had not met their quantitative goals realized that attention to quality was necessary. As a result, countries became concerned with measures of educational quality that provided information about system performance, both in relation to fixed targets and over time.

While some problems, such as shortages of resources and high population growth rates, are common to most developing countries, many other problems, such as a historical legacy of segregated schools, may be unique to specific countries, so that importing ideas from other countries may not solve these problems. Throughout the developing world policymakers and educators are considering numerous strategies for enhancing the quality of primary education, including improving the management of education and the supervision of instruction, rehabilitating school buildings, increasing the availability of textbooks, increasing the effectiveness of teacher training, and amending curricula. While each of these strategies has worked in particular situations, the choice for each country will depend on the circumstances peculiar to that country. Making the correct choice is easier when information on the education system's performance is available. Appropriate assessment makes it possible to answer important policy-related questions about large groups of individuals, different types of schools, and the educational system as a whole. Such knowledge provides a basis for policy decisions regarding the goals of education and effective allocation of resources.

National Assessment Systems

Systematic, regular measures of learning achievement in a country that are designed to assist policymaking, are called national assessments. To make decisions about the use of scarce resources to improve the quality of educational provision, developing countries need information about the extent to which the education system is meeting its goals and about the performance of individual schools or groups of schools and analyses of the effects of policies adopted to improve the schools.

Countries can evaluate how well their education system has been performing in a variety of ways. The choice depends on the information desired and the particular questions that need to be addressed. In the past, countries typically used such education indicators as end-of-cycle examination results, repeater and dropout rates, survival rates, and the number of years needed to complete a particular cycle. Much more needs to be done to assess and monitor what children are actually learning at different points in the system and at what level of proficiency. In addition, policymakers need to know about the impact of variables in the learning process on achievement. These include the effect of homework, time spent on teaching and learning, in-service teacher training, teachers' background, and so on.

Assessing students' academic achievement is important for decisions about how to improve educational provision. It is a complex process that requires the consideration of many different factors, including which competencies to assess, how to assess them, and which processes will yield valid and reliable data on student achievement and are possible to implement given local conditions and resource constraints.

Well-designed national assessments can help countries make informed decisions about interventions to improve educational quality. They can also help policymakers to monitor trends in the nature and quality of student learning over time.

The Book

This book focuses specifically on educational assessments that are carried out regularly and systematically with a view to guiding policymaking. As such, it does not contain descriptions of international assessments, such as the many carried out or under way under the auspices of the International Association for the Evaluation of Educational Achievement or studies of science and mathematics carried out by the Educational Testing Service. Typically, these international studies examine samples of students from many different countries and compare the results. The resulting international league tables are of interest to some countries. One valuable benefit for participating countries is that local researchers develop hands-on expertise in designing national assessments and implementing good tests.

The book also does not contain examples of single research studies, many of which have been carried out to very high standards, that provide data of great value to policymakers. However, these studies are intended to provide information on one or other aspect of a system and are not administered again. The book is concerned with educational assessments that are systematic, usually sample-based, collections of data that include a measurement of student achievement to guide policy.

The book is organized in four parts. Part I develops a framework for placing national assessments in the context of various testing purposes, examines the origins of educational assessments and describes national assessments, including their purposes and characteristics. It concludes by looking at the uses of data from public examinations for educational assessment. Part II is concerned with the stages in establishing national assessment systems, their costs, and the development of the test formats required. Part III provides five country case studies of national assessment systems. The book concludes with a review of the lessons learned from these five studies.

In chapter 2, Lockheed provides a global overview of the origins and current interest in educational assessments. She presents a framework for examining the different purposes of measuring learning achievement and places national assessment within this framework. She discusses the three types of information needed by education managers and policymakers and describes the educational assessments needed to get this information. She also discusses costs and institutional settings for educational assessments. Nwana concentrates on describing national assessment systems in chapter 3. He discusses the different elements, characteristics, and limitations of these systems. He also examines experiences in some developing countries, particularly in Africa, and makes the case for establishing more national systems. Part I concludes by answering the key question: can data from public examinations be used in national assessments? Because public examinations are conducted in most developing countries, using the data from these to answer policymakers' and managers' questions would save considerable resources. Kellaghan examines the purposes of public examinations and national assessments, the achievements of interest to each, the types of test used, the test scoring and reporting, the populations of interest to each, the importance of monitoring, the importance of collecting contextual information, and the "stakes" for individuals in taking the tests for each purpose. His conclusion is that examinations cannot serve the same purpose as national assessments.

Part II is concerned with the process and technical aspects. In chapter 5, Greaney argues that a good deal has been written about the technical aspects of national assessments but little about the management and political aspects. He goes on to discuss the stages in the development of a national assessment system, from the formation of a steering committee, through the choice of an implementation agency, identification of target population and assessment approaches, to administration, analysis, and reporting. He concludes that participation by all concerned groups is vital. In chapter 6, Ilon provides a framework within which each stage can be costed. She uses a process approach and illuminates her discussion of the cost elements of each stage by examples from Jamaica. Part II concludes with chapter 7 on designing tests for national assessment purposes. Izard's basic proposition is that tests used in national assessments should have wide and relevant coverage of the curriculum, should provide information to appropriate audiences in a meaningful format, and should be cost-effective. His discussion shows how to achieve these desirable characteristics.

Part III contains case studies of national assessments in Chile, Colombia, Egypt, England and Wales, and Thailand. In chapter 8, Himmel gives a brief history of national assessments in Chile and describes in detail developments since 1988. Of particular interest is the interdisciplinary approach taken, the use made of the results, and Himmel's identification of "success" factors. Chile's experience in using a partnership between a university and the Ministry of Education to develop and administer the national assessment system in its early years is likely to be of great interest to education policymakers in other countries planning to introduce national assessments. Kellaghan's description in chapter 9 of the system introduced in England and Wales prior to 1992 provides evidence of the importance of participation and consultation. Another lesson is that by trying to collect too much information through national assessments, countries may end up by not getting the important information needed to monitor the quality of education. In chapter 10, the Thailand case, Pravalpruk traces the development of the system from its original planning, through the first assessments in 1981 and subsequent assessments, to plans for the future. Of particular interest is that the national assessment was established to measure progress in teaching the broad curriculum, given the concentration on those parts tested by the university entrance examinations. One of the more striking outcomes of this assessment was the introduction of a new curriculum in 1988 to emphasize more process skills. In chapter 11, Rojas describes the recently introduced Colombian system of national assessment. The principal purpose of the national assessment is to aid improvement in the quality of education. Rojas describes the establishment of a division within the Ministry of Education in 1988 with responsibility for assessing the quality of the service being provided, and details the characteristics of the first assessments carried out in 1991 and 1992. As in Chile, a body outside the Ministry of Education is used to assist the national assessment: in Colombia's case a private research institution. The importance of political factors is reinforced in chapter 12, Carroll's description of the introduction of national assessments in Egypt. The difficulties faced by national ministries in assessing the performance of autonomous regions are clearly described.

And finally, chapter 13 illustrates the many lessons that emerge from the experiences in the five countries described in this book and from the expert knowledge of the contributors to Parts I and II. Perhaps the most important message is that countries need to test their education systems regularly to see if the systems are meeting national goals. Clearly, the establishment of a national assessment is one way of doing this. However, simply establishing the national assessment is not sufficient. As the book points out, consultation is vital at all stages, selecting the appropriate information to collect (and not collect) has ramifications for costs and effects, deciding which agencies need to be involved, getting the technical aspects right, and providing the information collected in a succinct, accessible way for those who can improve the education system is key.

It is appropriate to end on this note. Whatever valid reliable and useful information is collected, the information is useless unless it gets to those who can improve the system. A great deal of attention must be paid to this. Parents, teachers, school principals, education specialists, researchers, and policymakers all need to have key relevant information so that the improvements in quality can be made.

Part I: Overview

2

International Context for Assessments

Marlaine E. Lockheed

The 1990 World Conference on Education for All (WCEFA) catalyzed international commitment to ensure that all children be given an equal opportunity to achieve and maintain an acceptable level of learning. This explicit emphasis on the outputs of education was new. To assess progress toward this goal and to facilitate the development of appropriate policies to achieve it, the WCEFA World Declaration on Education for All identified two essential activities: (a) defining acceptable levels of learning acquisition for education programs, and (b) improving and applying systems to assess learning achievement (WCEFA 1990, p. 5). The WCEFA *Framework for Action* called for increased international funding and long-term partnerships to help countries reach their national goals.

Economists now recognize the importance of monitoring student learning, the key education output, and education inputs. However, for many years they assumed that educational inputs were adequate proxies for educational outputs, which were considered too difficult to measure. This assumption is no longer accepted. International evidence has demonstrated that inputs differ so widely in their effectiveness across countries that they are very poor proxies for outputs (Fuller 1987). Furthermore, recent concerns with improving educational efficiency (the ratio of inputs to outputs) and with selecting wisely the most cost-effective educational inputs require separate measures of each (Hanushek 1986; Lockheed and Hanushek 1988). The new emphasis on educational quality and the search for good output indicators are bringing tests into focus.

Tests are the most common measure of student learning and are typically used to monitor learning. Tests are defined as "any series of questions or exercises or other means of measuring the skill, knowledge, intelligence, capacities or aptitudes of an individual or group" (Anderson, Ball, and Murphy 1975, p. 425). Education achievement tests focus on skills, knowledge, and capacities that students acquire through education (schooling). They do not seek to measure intelligence or aptitude.

Psychometricians construct educational achievement tests for many different purposes, of which the most common are (table 2-1):

- Monitoring achievement trends over time
- Evaluating specific educational programs or policies
- Holding schools, regions, and other administrative sub-units accountable for student achievement

Table 2-1. Purposes of Measuring Learning Achievement

Category	Monitoring progress toward national education goals	Evaluating effectiveness and efficiency of specific policies	Holding schools accountable for performance	Selecting or certifying student	Teacher assessment of individual student performance
Example	National Assessment of Educational Progress, United States	Evaluation analytique de l'enseignment Primaire, Benin	National Grade 7 Evaluation, Thailand	Certificate of Primary Education, Kenya	National Assessment, England and Wales
To whom administered	Sample of students in selected age or grade cohorts	Sample of students in sample of schools	Sample of students in sample of schools	All students in terminal year	All students in selected age cohorts
When administered	Periodically (annually, biannually)	One time	One time	Annually	Annually
Content objective	Selected domains (e.g., mathematics, science)	Selected domains	Seletected domains	All domains of curriculum	Selected domains
Behavioral objective	Knowledge and higher order thinking skills	Knowledge and higher order thinking skills	Knowledge and higher order thinking skills	Knowledge and higher order thinking skills	Knowledge and higher order thinking skills
Format					
Objective	Yes	Yes	Yes	Yes	Yes
Performance	Yes	Yes	Yes	Yes	Yes
Standardized					
Content	Yes	Yes	Yes	Yes	Sometimes
Administration	Yes	Yes	Yes	Sometimes	Sometimes
Scoring	Yes	Yes	Yes	Sometimes	Sometimes
Reference					
Norming group	Yes	No	No	No	No
Performance criteria	Yes	No	Yes	No	Yes
Supplementary measures					
Student background	Limited	Yes	Limited	No	No
Classroom/school inputs	No	Yes	No	No	No
Classroom/school processes	No	Yes	No	No	No

Source: Author's information.

- Selecting students for further education
- Certifying student achievement
- Diagnosing individual learning needs.

The behavioral objective of a test is the type of skill being tested. In 1956 Benjamin Bloom classified cognitive behavioral objectives into six elements: knowledge, comprehension, application, analysis, synthesis, and evaluation. Educators have used Bloom's taxonomy widely during the past thirty-five years to characterize both curricula and tests. Testing "knowledge" typically requires students to recall the meaning of terms and specific facts. Testing the higher order skills of comprehension, application, analysis, synthesis, and evaluation requires students to demonstrate that they understand the material, can use information in a concrete situation, can break down material into its parts, can assemble material into a whole, and can judge the value of a thing for a given purpose using definite criteria (Bloom 1956). Most tests in developing countries concentrate on recalling facts, rather than on any of the higher order skills.

Test format refers to the physical design of the items on the test. Test items can be developed in a wide variety of formats, which are often classified into objective test formats and performance test formats. Objective test items can be written in several different formats, not only the multiple choice items often employed in mass testing. Some other types of item formats are matching, question and short answer, rank ordering, statement, and common (short essay). Objective test formats are comparatively expensive to develop, but inexpensive to score.

Performance tests, which are increasingly becoming the format of choice among educational theorists, require students to demonstrate knowledge and skills through an actual or simulated performance. Thus, students may submit a videotape of a dance performance or a portfolio of their works of art. They may be asked to carry out a short science experiment to demonstrate scientific understanding, to write an essay on a specific topic to demonstrate writing skills, or to repair an automobile engine. The closer the performance is to reality, the more authentic it is considered. The cost of developing performance tests varies widely, but they are uniformly expensive to score reliably.

The purpose of the test determines its overall design, for example, the purpose of selection tests is to discriminate between individuals, and hence the test will include many items of a difficulty known to discriminate between those who should be selected and those who should not. As a consequence, the range of competencies tested will be highly constrained. By comparison, the purpose of a test designed to monitor national achievement is to assess a large number of competency areas, but to provide little information about specific individuals. It will include items covering many competencies, but its power to discriminate among individuals will be constrained. Tests designed to monitor trends over time will repeat at least some items, whereas tests designed only to select once need not be equated. In some cases educational achievement tests designed for one purpose can be used for another purpose, but this is more often the exception than the rule. In most instances, the use of tests designed specifically for one purpose (such as selection) for another purpose (such as monitoring achievement trends over time) is inappropriate.

Using tests for more than one purpose can also be unproductive and costly (LeMahieu and Wallace 1986). For example, using tests designed for evaluative purposes (monitoring achievement or evaluating specific educational programs or policies) as diagnostic instruments is unproductive because evaluative testing instruments are not relevant, timely, or brief enough to make for good diagnostic instruments. It is more costly because using evaluative tests for diagnostic purposes implies testing every student in the population, thereby increasing the costs of a test that only requires a good sample to obtain an accurate estimate of students' performance.

Table 2-1 compares the characteristics of tests for monitoring achievement, evaluating policies, school accountability, selection, certification, and individual diagnosis. Tests designed for these six purposes are, or can be, similar in terms of their content, behavioral objectives, and format, although selection tests are likely to be more difficult than tests for management purposes. They are significantly different, however, in terms of the number of students tested, the degree to which the tests are standardized, their use of external reference criteria, and the extent of supplementary measures collected. Tests for management purposes can be administered to samples of students; tests for selection, certification, or individual performance assessment need to be administered to all students. Tests for management purposes need to be standardized with respect to their content, administration, and scoring; tests for selection are frequently not standardized for either administration or scoring (and sometimes not even for content). Tests for monitoring progress must refer to external criteria; other types of tests often do not. Tests to evaluate the effectiveness or efficiency of specific educational policies must include measures of these policies, as well as measures of other student and school characteristics; tests for other purposes use supplementary measures only to a limited extent.

Monitoring Trends

Tracking progress requires having tools capable of monitoring trends over time. For test scores to be meaningful over time, student performance must be measured against an inelastic yardstick of achievement, such as a norm reference group or specific criteria (Anastasi 1988; Berk 1984). In addition, tests must be standardized with respect to content, behavioral objectives, format, administration procedures, and scoring. Standardizing the content requires that the same or equivalent questions or performance tasks be posed for all students. Standardizing test administration requires uniformity in the written and verbal instructions given to examinees, in the length of time afforded them, in the materials provided to them, and in the physical testing environment. Standardized scoring requires explicit, impartial procedures for correcting tests or judging performance. One of the biggest obstacles to monitoring student learning over time in developing countries is the lack of such tests.

This is not to say that countries are inexperienced with testing. They are not. However, most countries are experienced with two types of unstandardized tests: (a) those used for selection or certification, which are created new each year only to certify academic accomplishment or to select students in a single age or grade cohort for secondary or higher education (examinations); and (b) those teachers use to assess the performance of individual students over the course of the year (continuous student assessment).

Examinations

Binkley, Guthrie, and Wyatt's (1991) survey of assessment systems in seventeen countries reported that 80 percent of the tests were used for certification or selection. A recent World Bank survey of five anglophone and fourteen francophone African countries found that virtually all tests were designed for selection and certification purposes (Kellaghan and Greaney 1992). Selection examinations are useful for rationing scarce places and can influence instruction, but they are not designed to provide meaningful measures of accomplishment from one year to the next. Instead, because of the need to maintain test security, the items on the tests are completely different from one year to the next. This has implications for the extent to which they can refer to an inelastic yardstick of performance. For example, it means that a norm reference group, that is, a group that was administered exactly the same items at some earlier time period, cannot be employed to provide the standard. It also means that performance or criterion referenced selection or certification tests may be unable to provide a measure of change over time.

While many countries attempt to create tests that are of similar difficulty each year, most countries do not test this equivalence empirically, because standard psychometric techniques rely to some extent upon the reuse of at least some items. Instead, countries must rely on subjective judgment. These judgments are often less accurate than empirically-based equating procedures. As a result, wide fluctuations in test scores are often reported. For example, in one anglophone African country, the proportion of students who passed the grade 7 mathematics test dropped from 83 percent in one year to 55 percent the following year, undoubtedly because of differences in the difficulty of the test, not differences in what cohorts of students only one year apart actually learned. Given their strong security needs, selection and certification tests are not likely to be standardized with respect to content and behavioral objective, and are often not standardized in other respects as well. They are therefore not useful for monitoring trends.

Continuous Student Assessment

Regular monitoring of student performance is an essential teaching tool. It can be accomplished in two ways. First, the teacher can regularly assess student performance through such informal or unstandardized devices as quizzes, written assignments, and projects. Second, the teacher can administer formally developed tests of the kind often prepared by testing agencies and publishers. In most developing countries, formally developed tests for monitoring individual student progress are nonexistent, and the only type available are those teachers develop. Because these tests are completely unstandardized, they are unable to provide useful data for monitoring trends.

Assessments for Education Management

Education managers need three types of information to inform decisionmaking: (a) general information on how well the education system is doing with respect to achieving its goals; (b) specific information about the performance of individual schools or groups of schools, for example, school districts or geographic regions; and (c) analyses of the implementation and effects of policies adopted to improve schools. General information provides the global picture, school or regional information helps managers hold schools or regions accountable for their performance, and the analytic work helps to guide future investment decisions. How well can existing types of examinations and tests provide these types of information?

Educational assessments differ from individual diagnostic, selection, or certification examinations in several ways. First, educational assessments typically provide information about the system as a whole, not about individual students. They are low stakes, sample-based tests not subject to the distortions caused by such high stakes tests as selection examinations.[1] Second, they include not only measures of student learning, but also of student background and school inputs and processes that enable the assessment data to be used for policy analysis. Many researchers have sought to identify the minimum set of information that should be collected. Most recommend the collection of basic intellectual, socioeconomic, and cultural background data on students. Examples include the students' sex, age, nutritional status, socioeconomic status, language, attitudes, expectations, and ability. Theory, research, and experience suggest four areas about which data on classroom inputs should be gathered: the curriculum, instructional materials, adequate time for learning, and effective teaching (Lockheed and Verspoor 1991). Beyond these inputs are (a) managerial processes at the schools and within the classroom, such as tracking, school structure, and autonomy; and (b) school context conditions such as student access to knowledge, organizational press for achievement, and professional teaching conditions (Oakes 1989). Third, to be useful for monitoring the performance of the educational system over time—that is, determining whether or not the system is making progress toward its goals—educational assessments use standardized measures of student learning achievement, school inputs, and processes. Fourth, the results of educational assessments are typically disseminated to a variety of audiences: educators, parents, and the public in general.

At least eight of the Organization for Economic Cooperation and Development (OECD) countries currently undertake education assessment as described above. In most cases, the educational assessments supplement existing programs of student certification and selection (Binkley, Guthrie, and Wyatt 1991). Some developing countries, including Mexico and Thailand, have also undertaken sample-based assessments. Other countries routinely measure the learning of all students at various points in the education cycle (Chile is an example), but programs in which all students in a particular grade are tested can be subject to some of the distortions caused by high stakes testing.

Total recurrent costs for tests are determined largely by the number of students that are tested and the type of test items used (objective items or performance items). To monitor progress, one can obtain reliable measures with scientifically drawn samples of as few as 2,000 students. Evaluations often use a small sample of schools (say 1 percent) and of sample students within schools. School performance accountability requires testing samples of students at all schools. Selection and certification examinations typically test all students in all schools scoring the students' last year of study. Teacher assessments involve all students in all grades. Thus, assessments that monitor progress and studies that evaluate policies involve only relatively few students and schools, while

---

1. Shepard (1991) identifies six distortions from high stakes tests: such tests can become inflated without actual improvement in learning, narrow the curriculum, misdirect instruction even for the basic skills, deny students opportunities to develop thinking and problem solving skills, result in hard-to-teach children being excluded from the system, and reduce teachers' professional knowledge and status.

school accountability schemes, selection and certification examinations, and teacher assessment of student performance involve much larger numbers of schools and students.

Assuming the development costs of an objective test (multiple choice or short answer) to be about US$100,000 and those of a performance test (requiring students to demonstrate knowledge and skills) are half that (Horn, Wolff, and Velez 1991), with estimated recurrent costs of US$1 and US$10 per student, respectively, it is possible to estimate what it would cost to carry out different types of tests in average low-income (excluding China and India), lower-middle income, and upper-middle income countries. Table 2-2 presents these estimates, which are bases on the average number of students and schools in countries at three levels of economic development. While these figures are hypothetical, they give an idea of the order of magnitude involved.

Recurrent costs associated with teacher assessment of student progress are the highest, assuming that all primary students are tested annually and that the tests are neither produced nor scored by teachers as part of their regular work. In the average developing country (other than India and China), testing all students with formally developed tests would cost between US$1.6 and US$4.0 million to produce and score tests having objective items, and between US$16 and US$41 million to produce and score tests having performance items. Tests for selection or certification are next in costs, amounting to up to US$700,000 for objective tests and up to nearly US$7 million for performance tests in the average developing country. Tests for school accountability cost approximately the same as tests for selection and certification in low-income countries. Tests for monitoring the progress of the education system and for evaluating education policies are by far the least expensive activities, costing less than one-tenth of 1 percent of the cost of testing all students in all grades. By using samples of students to monitor national progress, more expensive test formats could be employed. Developing countries could afford to use performance tests for monitoring progress or for evaluation exercises, and they would cost less than one-fifth of 1 percent of the cost of administering and scoring objective tests for selection or certification.

Given the figures in table 2-2, many developing countries find that testing all children annually is infeasible. However, sample-based surveys and specially designed standardized tests for monitoring progress can provide education managers nearly all the same information as tests administered to all students, but at a fraction of the recurrent cost.

Assessment Institutions

Worldwide, educational assessment is a new idea that deviates significantly from previous experience with high stakes testing for individual diagnosis, selection, and certification purposes. A specialized unit of the central ministry of education runs most of the latter types of examination programs. Assessments are a different undertaking. Most countries with educational assessment programs have located these programs outside the government. Of the OECD countries that currently employ educational assessments, 75 percent house this program in a single institution, located outside the government, with which the government contracts to provide the assessment service. These are typically independent research institutions (see table 2-3). The implicit rationale for locating assessment activities outside the government is that the government is providing the service (that is, operating the schools) and should not be its own auditor.

Table 2-2. Average per Country Total Recurrent Costs for Each Test for Five Testing Purposes in Developing Countries, 1990

Test and country type	Average number of primary schools/country (1985)	Cost (US$ per country)				
		Monitoring progress toward national educational goals	Evaluating effectiveness of specific policies	Holding schools accountable for performance	Selecting and/or certifying students	Teacher assessment of individual student performance
Objective tests at US$/test						
Low income	7,812	2,000	1,562	156,240	172,233	1,578,024
Lower-middle income	15,828	2,000	3,165	316,560	557,614	3,323,880
Upper-middle income	19,160	2,000	3,862	386,200	692,059	4,119,400
Performance tests at US$10/test						
Low income	7,812	20,000	15,624	1,562,400	1,722,330	15,780,240
Lower-middle income	15,828	20,000	31,656	3,165,600	5,576,140	33,238,800
Upper-middle income	19,160	20,000	38,620	3,862,000	6,920,590	41,194,000
Typical number of students and schools tested	n.a.	2,000	1% sample of schools; 20 students per school	All schools; sample of 20 students per school	All schools; all students in terminal grade	All schools; all students

n.a.   Not applicable.
Source: Calculated from Lockheed and Verspoor (1991).

Table 2-3. Institutional Base for the Control of Various Elements of Elementary and Secondary School Assessements in Eight OECD Countries

Country	Finance	Program development	Item development	Administration	Scoring
Canada	Provincial central government	Developed by multiple shareholders	Multiple shareholders	Classroom teachers to specified procedures	Externally scored or scored to external standards
Finland	Central government agency	Research institute working party (officials, teachers subject specialists)	Research institute	Classroom teachers to specified procedures	Externally scored by staff trained by the research institute
France	Central government ministry	Centrally constituted working groups inspectors, teachers, administrators, researchers, subject specialists)	Centrally constituted working groups, (inspectors teachers, administrators researchers, subject specialists)	Classroom teacher following centrally issued guidelines	Classroom teacher following strict coding procedures, rechecked externally
Netherlands	Central government	Research institute	Research institute	Trained data collectors provided by research institute	Externally scored by staff trained by the institute
Spain	Central government agency	Central government research agency advised by teachers, subject specialists, officials	Central government research agency advised by teachers, subject specialists, officials	Trained data collectors provided by private sector contractor	Externally scored by staff trained by the contractor
Scotland	Central government agency	Research institute advised by teachers, Her Majesty's Inspectorate, etc.	Research institute advised by teachers, Her Majesty's Inspectorate, etc.	Classroom teachers to specified procedures, externally trained observers	Externally scored by staff trained by the research institute
Sweden	Central government	University research institutes	University research institutes	Classroom teachers	Classroom teachers and research institutes
United States	Central (national) government agency	Central government agency/private sector contractors	Private sector contractors	Trained data collectors provided by contractor	Externally scored by contractor

Source: Binkley, Guthrie, and Wyatt (1991).

In developing countries, the trend has been to retain the auditing function within ministries of education. A review of twenty-four World Bank–supported assessment systems in developing countries found that 75 percent of the systems were located in a ministry of education, while 21 percent of the systems were located in semi-autonomous or private institutions under contract to the ministry of education (Larach and Lockheed 1992). In some cases an auditing function has been established in an institution outside the ministry of education, but subsequently has been brought inside the ministry. For example, the precursor of the Chilean national assessment system was established by professionals at the Pontificia Universidad Catolica de Chile in 1978, but was brought into the ministry of education in 1992 (Himmel, chapter 8 in this book).

There are three important reasons for housing the assessment function outside the ministry of education: (a) both delivering and auditing a service creates a conflict of interest that could compromise the auditing function; (b) the complex technical skills needed to implement all aspects of an assessment may be in limited supply, and hence in great demand, and may exceed the government's ability to afford full-time personnel with these skills; and (c) sample-based assessments undertaken periodically may not require the services of full-time government personnel. Thus, in most industrial countries the government provides the finances for the assessment, while different nongovernmental organizations are contracted to provide the different technical skills required: program development, item development, administration, and scoring. In many cases, the government retains the responsibility for disseminating the results.

World Bank Support for National Assessment

Many developing countries have sought donor support to strengthen their testing systems or to establish national assessment capability. World Bank support for educational testing increased significantly in the early 1990s, catalyzed by growing evidence regarding the poor performance of educational systems in developing countries, the desire by countries to manage their education systems better and more efficiently, the 1990 World Conference on Education for All's call for national systems for monitoring learning, and the need to monitor the impact of education reforms supported by the Bank and other donors on student learning. A review of education projects supported by the World Bank showed a dramatic increase in the number of projects that included support for testing related activities, from 5 percent of education projects in 1975 to nearly half of all projects by 1991 (Larach and Lockheed 1992).

Ministries of education have received donor support for all test purposes described in Table 2-1. For example, of 450 World Bank supported education projects, 1963–92, 33 percent supported tests for student certification and selection, 21 percent supported tests for monitoring student progress toward national educational goals, 19 percent supported tests for teacher diagnosis of student learning; the remainder of the projects supported testing for multiple purposes.

Support for national assessment systems has risen most sharply, from zero projects prior to 1988 to 27 percent of projects in 1992, the most recent year for which data are available. This increase reflects the Bank's greater attention to strengthening national capacity for evaluating the impact of education policy reforms.

References

Anastasi, A. 1988. *Psychological Testing*, 6th ed. New York: Macmillan.

Anderson, S., S. Ball, and R. Murphy. 1975. *Encyclopedia of Educational Evaluation*. New York: Jossey-Bass.

Berk, Ronald A., ed. 1984. *A Guide to Criterion-Referenced Measurement: The State of the Art*. Baltimore, Maryland: The Johns Hopkins University Press.

Binkley, Marilyn, James W. Guthrie, and Timothy J. Wyatt. 1991. *A Survey of National Assessment and Examination Practices in OECD Countries*. OECD: Lugano, Switzerland.

Bloom, Benjamin S. 1956. *Taxonomy of Educational Objectives: Cognitive Domain*. New York: David McKay.

Fuller, B. 1987. "Raising School Quality in Developing Countries: What Investments Boost Learning?" *Journal of Educational Resources* 57:255–91.

Hanushek, E. A. 1986. "The Economics of Schooling: Production and Efficiency in Public Schools." *Journal of Economic Literature* 23:1141–77.

Himmel, E. (1992). *A Case Study of the Use of National Assessment in Chile*, Santiago, Chile. Processed.

Horn, Robin, Laurence Wolff, and Eduardo Velez. 1991. *Developing Educational Assessment Systems in Latin America: A Review of Issues and Recent Experience*. Regional Studies Program. Report No. 9. Washington, D.C.: World Bank, Latin America and the Caribbean Technical Department.

Kellaghan, Thomas, and Vincent Greaney 1992. *Using Examinations to Improve Education: A Study in Fourteen African Countries*. Washington, D.C.: World Bank.

Larach, Linda, and Marlaine E. Lockheed. 1992. *World Bank Lending for Educational Testing*. Background Paper 92/62R. Washington, D.C.: World Bank, Population and Human Resources Department.

LeMahieu, Paul G., and Richard C. Wallace, Jr. 1986. "Up Against the Wall: Psychometrics Meets Praxis." *Educational Measurement: Issues and Practice* (spring):12–16.

Lockheed, Marlaine E., and Eric Hanushek. 1988. "Improving Educational Efficiency in Developing Countries: What Do We Know?" *Compare* 18 (1):21–38.

Lockheed, Marlaine E., and Adrian M. Verspoor. 1991. *Improving Primary Education in Developing Countries*. New York: Oxford University Press.

Oakes, Jeannie. 1989. "What Educational Indicators? The Case for Assessing the School Context." *Educational Evaluation and Policy Analysis* 11 (2):181–99.

Shepard, Lorrie A. 1991. *Will National Tests Improve Student Learning?* Paper presented at the American Educational Research Association Forum, Washington, D.C., June.

WCEFA. World Conference on Education for All. 1990. *Meeting Basic Learning Needs: A Vision for the 1990's*. New York: Inter-Agency Commission for World Conference on Education for All.

3

What Are National Assessments and Why Do Them?

O. C. Nwana

The countries of developing Africa and other developing countries differ in many significant ways from the industrial nations of America, Asia, and Europe. To cite a few examples of these differences, consider the developing countries' general level of education (their low levels of literacy and numeracy); their level of economic development (low gross national products); the general state of health of their citizens (low life expectancy, high infant and maternal mortality, high birth rates, and high incidence of endemic and epidemic diseases); and their level of democratic political development (high incidence of autocratic, theocratic, aristocratic, and military regimes).

These and other factors have created the circumstances causing most countries of Africa, Asia, and Latin America to lag behind in exploiting to the fullest the resources (human and material) with which they have been naturally endowed. This is related to their status as exporters of raw materials to the factories of Europe, Japan, and North America and their position as consumers rather than as producers of finished products.

With the introduction of education of the Western type into these countries, they have come to realize more than ever that any effort to improve the quality of life of their citizens, and possibly to attempt to bridge the development gap between themselves and the Western world, with which they have to co-exist and interact, can only be achieved by liberalizing and popularizing secular education. Indeed, the developing countries' commitment to education as a means of development is demonstrated by their signing of the 1990 World Education Conference's declaration of Education for All by the Year 2000. If indeed the developing world is to achieve high quality education by the year 2000 or thereabouts, then a consideration of the assessment strategies that will monitor this global commitment becomes extremely important.

Assessment and Its Purposes

Some years ago, the U.S. National Council of Teachers of Mathematics used an input-output model similar to the one shown in figure 3-1 below to explain assessment. The rectangular figure is the student. As inputs we have the teacher, educational technology, and the curriculum. The output is the same student. Or is it?

Figure 3-1. Input-Output Model of Assessment

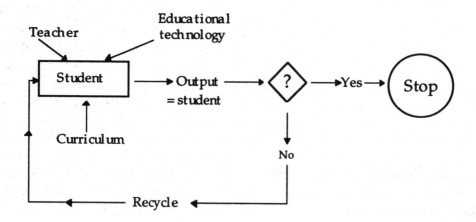

Yes, physically it is the same student, but the diamond box contains a question mark. The question is whether the student's behavior has been sufficiently modified in a desired direction. The expectation of the curriculum designer is that as a result of the interaction with the curriculum, the teacher, and the educational technology the student's behavior will have changed. But has it? To determine the answer an evaluation is conducted. If the answer is yes, the inputs have done their work. If the answer is no, the student is recycled through the system until the desired behavior changes are attained.

Assessment answers the question: how and to what extent have we succeeded in changing the learner's behavior by means of the instruction offered? Unfortunately, in the traditional classroom the question is usually asked at a point when it is too late to use the results meaningfully. That is, it is asked on conclusion of the instruction, and therefore cannot be useful to modify it. This type of assessment is known in the literature as summative assessment.

A more useful type of assessment is known as formative assessment. In this approach the question is asked several times during the instruction. What is more important, the answers obtained are used to modify the instruction to try and ensure that the objectives of the educational program are more likely to be realized. Many instruments are used to carry out such assessment. The most popular are tests, examinations, assignments, projects, questionnaires, interviews, and observations.

Assessment serves many purposes, including:

- Motivating students to study
- Diagnosing students' problems
- Promoting students
- Selecting students
- Certificating students
- Providing students with guidance and counseling
- Differentiating among students
- Determining the effectiveness of teachers

- Determining the effectiveness of instructional programs
- Maintaining standards
- Making administrative decisions in the education sector
- Carrying out research on education.

Many people are familiar with the promotion, selection, and certification examinations given by the various educational systems in Africa. These are of two types: internal examinations given by individual educational institutions and external examinations normally administered by public examining bodies. In English-speaking West Africa, the West African Examinations Council has existed as a public examining body for about forty years. It carries out examination functions for The Gambia, Ghana, Liberia, Nigeria, and Sierra Leone. Its examinations are mostly at the secondary school level in both conventional subjects and business, technical, and vocational subjects. A similar setup existed in East Africa, and the body involved was the East African Examinations Council. The areas covered were similar to those in West Africa. In Africa as a whole, including the francophone countries, the focus of public examinations has been individual student performance, which leads to decisions about selection for further study and/or certification on completing different stages of the school cycle.

The Concept of and Rationale for National Assessment

A relatively new concept is that of national assessment, which is only about two decades old. Let me try to explain it by first examining examples of questions that a national assessment may address:

- Do students living in urban, semi-urban, and rural areas receive the same quality of education?
- Do primary school teachers need more training in some curriculum subjects than in others?
- Do students taught by qualified teachers, that is, those who hold the nation's teaching certificate, perform better than those taught by unqualified teachers?
- How does the performance of students in one state or province compare with that of students in another state or province within the same country?
- Does students' performance differ by gender in the major school subjects?
- Is students' performance in key subject areas improving over the years or declining?
- How well does the education given in educational institutions relate to the world of work?
- Is the national standard of education rising or falling?
- Have the attitudes of school leavers improved in regard to a number of noncognitive objectives of education, for example, national consciousness or traits needed to get along well in society?

The answers to such questions will help the policymakers and administrators of any nation's education system as they try to make cost-effective decisions for the benefit of the system. The major objective of any national assessment program is to design appropriate instruments and to administer them rigorously to obtain the answers to questions of this type.

Thus a national assessment program differs from existing promotion, selection, and certification testing. It is not merely a testing program. Rather, it is an information gathering system that facilitates the making of cost-effective decisions. National assessment is a survey of the performance of a nation's students that reveals changes in such performance over time. One question that stands out when any assessment is being planned is "What do we need to know?" Each of the nine example questions listed earlier clearly indicates what we need to know or to what we are seeking solutions.

In Nigeria education is big business. As of December 1992, approximately 15 million pupils were in primary schools, just under 3 million in secondary schools, and about 300,000 in tertiary institutions. Such a huge venture cannot and should not be run blindly: running it properly requires making many important decisions that should be made based on information gathered and appropriately analyzed. In other words, the decisions must be informed. Hunches will not do, as has tended to be the case over the years.

The rapid expansion of educational opportunities in Nigeria is echoed throughout developing Africa. The belief that education is the best instrument for achieving optimal development in the least time is a gospel held by all of developing Africa (and the developing world as a whole). It is the rationale for the huge financial investments countries have made and will continue to make in education, reverses in their economies notwithstanding. Thus decisionmaking in education must be based on sound empirical information if countries are to achieve the maximum benefit from it. If African children are to be properly educated despite the scarcity of available resources, then cost-effective techniques must be applied and wastage must be eliminated. This is what national assessment is all about.

The Elements, Characteristics, and Limitations of a National Assessment Program

Collecting information for making cost-effective systemwide decisions necessarily demands a significant investment of time by both students and teachers. It also requires adequate funding. The instruments used to collect the information must be both valid and reliable if they are to be of use. Let us consider the concepts of reliability and validity before taking the discussion further.

An instrument is reliable if it measures whatever it measures accurately and consistently, but it is valid if it measures what it is expected to measure and does so accurately and consistently. Consider the following example. Suppose a country's ministry of education has the following telephone numbers:

Minister	042-770-504, 042-771-345
Permanent secretary	042-771-640
Secretary to the minister	042-771-500

Suppose that when you dial the minister's number 042-770-504 each time you reach the minister's secretary at 042-771-500. The telephone has not given you what you wanted, but it has been accurate and consistent in what it has given. It is a reliable phone. However, it is not valid because it has not delivered what you wanted, namely, getting through on the minister's line. If, however, each time you dial 042-770-504 the phone on the minister's desk rings, then it is valid because it is giving you what you wanted in an accurate and consistent manner. Observe also that, in this case, the phone is also reliable because it is accurate and consistent. In general, if an instrument is valid, it is necessarily reliable. If, by contrast, when you dial 042-770-504 and reach 042-771-345, 042-771-640, 042-771-720, 042-771-250, or 042-771-550 at various times, then the phone is neither reliable nor valid.

Reliability is usually established by using such methods as test-retest, equivalent forms, split half, and the Kuder-Richardson formula. As for validities, these may be of different types, for example, concurrent, predictive, face, content, and concurrent. This chapter will not explain the variety of methods available to determine reliability and validity in the assumption that readers will already be familiar with them.

An important aspect of any national assessment is that the utmost care is taken to ensure the acceptability and accuracy of the outcomes. For this and other reasons, a national assessment system should possess the following elements (Lapointe 1990):

- *An independent governing board.* Establishing a national assessment unit within a testing body that already exists, while meaningful, will not give it the status it requires in a developing African country. Its activities will tend to be overshadowed by personal assessment and certification. It should be established legally as a corporate body.

- *A technical advisory committee.* This committee should be made up of scholars and educational practitioners who have the relevant qualifications in educational measurement and evaluation, psychometrics, statistics, and so on, but more important, who are familiar with and loyal to their country's major educational goals and aspirations. It is gratifying that developing Africa now has a large pool of such people, many of whom were trained in Australia, Canada, the United Kingdom, or the United States and have taken courses run by agencies such as the U.S. Educational Testing Service, the National Foundation for Educational Research (NFER) of the United Kingdom, and the Australian Council for Educational Research (ACER) of Australia. In the last twenty years, a few universities and colleges of education in Africa, such as the University of Ibadan, Nigeria, and the University of Nigeria, have established postgraduate courses in this field.

- *Broad involvement and consensus building to ensure widespread support in the planning and design of assessment.* In most developing countries, where ethnic and geographical as well as ideological differences exist, the need for consensus in planning cannot be overemphasized if the national assessment exercise is to take off and continue.

- *Careful development of tests and questionnaires.* In many developing countries, expertise on test development may be in short supply. An additional problem is how to involve a broad range of practitioners.

- *Rigorous administration and standardized procedures.* These are particularly difficult to ensure in remote rural areas.

- *Scientific data analysis.* Analysis should be carried out by means of modern computing facilities, which are now available all over Africa.

- *Clear and objective reports for different audiences.* In Africa, where governments are the principal owners of education systems, national assessment reports must provide them with information about the direction in which the education effort is moving and the extent to which their financial investment is bearing fruit and why. The next level of audience is the operatives of the school systems: teachers, administrators, and managers. Another audience is parents and the general public, all of whom should receive reports appropriate to their level of education.

As for the characteristics of a national assessment: only a sample of students need to be tested; all students in the sample are given identical or equivalent tests or questionnaires; and because only a sample is required, participating schools, districts, provinces, states, and students may remain anonymous (Lapointe 1990).

As one would expect, any national assessment program has its limitations, which include the following:

- Given its design and characteristics, a national assessment can only yield group data.

- A national assessment cannot help a teacher to assess the strengths and weaknesses of individual students.

- The results of national assessment are unlikely to help motivate individual students.

Other Issues Involved in National Assessment

As noted earlier, in a national assessment the schools and students surveyed are usually samples of identified populations. For instance, in a particular year a given country such as Kenya may decide that its national assessment will cover the subjects English, mathematics, science, and social science in years three, six, and nine of schooling.

Given the cost of national assessment and the demands on students and teachers, it is probably best to think of it in terms of two- or three-year cycles covering some three or four subjects per cycle. The governing board of the national assessment body, in consultation with the relevant national entities, will decide which subjects will be covered during any particular national assessment cycle. The board also sets in motion the machinery for determining the subject matter content and the process objectives, and uses the technical advisory committee to achieve this objective.

As for the assessment questions themselves, the approach of the U.S. National Assessment of Educational Progress is to measure a broad spectrum of content in each subject area and to keep track of innovations in curricula. Care is also taken to ensure that items are free from cultural, racial, religious, gender, and locational bias. This is extremely important because research has shown that seemingly neutral achievement test items may actually favor one subcultural group or handicap another. In multi-ethnic and geographically diverse situations, as is the case in developing Africa, this factor does operate and test developers must recognize it and guard against it. This can be done through detailed item critiques and revisions.

Another important matter is the analysis of the results of any national assessment. The first aspect of analysis is scaling, which is the conversion of scores from various student groups, school subjects, and test instruments over different time periods to equivalent values to enable later comparison. The second aspect is the analysis of the scores in such a manner as to relate them to various background variables. This is related to the data collection issue. In addition to achievement measures, the national assessment will gather background data to facilitate the interpretation of the achievement results. Such background data would include information about students, teachers, and school principals. From the students it is usual to elicit such information as the home environment, ethnic background, mother tongue, parents' level of education, school attendance, academic aspirations and expectations, usefulness of the subject being assessed, courses taken so far, and any special experiences. Such background information enables better interpretation of the results of national assessment, in particular, it will reveal what inputs other than classroom intervention will be required to achieve national educational goals.

Usually information is sought from teachers about their background, training, and classroom experience, including their gender, ethnicity, credentials, teaching experience, in-service and workshop experience, types of students taught, and experiences given to the students. The questionnaires to be completed by the principal usually seek information on the school and its on-site administrators.

As already noted, national assessment reports are prepared for various audiences. They are also more elaborate than the reports from standardized testing. Within each subject area assessed, the assessment provides information on students' knowledge and understanding as a group and their achievement across school levels and subpopulations.

The concept of national assessment is not new to developing Africa. Educators across the continent have thought about it, and indeed, some efforts have been made to give it a trial; however, none of the efforts come close to those in the United Kingdom or the United States, neither do they possess all the necessary characteristics. Nigeria, for instance, has undertaken a number of isolated studies that have tried to map progress in a number of school subjects. However, these efforts were not sustained. Recently, however, the National Council on Education has directed the Nigerian Educational Research and Development Council to undertake the monitoring of students' performance in public examinations over time. The program is in place, and if enough progress is made, the various efforts to monitor performance nationally intended to inform decisionmaking may well pave the way for establishing a proper program of national assessment of educational progress. Perhaps the body best constituted for national assessment in Nigeria is the Nigerian Educational Research and Development Council. This body was established by law as an independent entity. Its functions include promoting, coordinating, initiating, and advising on research and curriculum development and documenting, storing, and disseminating information about education for decisionmaking purposes.

National Assessment Projects in Africa

The World Bank and other agencies, such as the U.S. Agency for International Development, are currently supporting the establishment or promotion of national assessments in a number of African countries, for example:

- Burkina Faso (1991): to compare students' performance across the country and to identify problem areas within the curriculum;
- Cape Verde (1988): to create student assessment examinations that would be used to monitor and evaluate the education system's efficiency;

- Lesotho (1992): to measure the quality of instruction across classes and schools (financed by the U.S. Agency for International Development);

- Madagascar (1990): to enhance the country's capacity to improve the quality of education at the primary and secondary school levels;

- Mali (1989): to assess the qualitative improvements expected from an education sector consolidation project and to make adjustments as necessary;

- Mozambique (1991): to measure the impact of a proposed intervention to enhance quality and to enable comparison with worldwide data;

- Nigeria (1991): to develop national primary education norms and standards for student achievement;

- Uganda (1993): to ascertain national levels of achievement in targeted subject areas and to monitor changes in achievement over time.

In general these projects have only been in place for two or three years. They have all received technical personnel support to establish the administrative framework, run training programs for staff, and start the development of testing instruments. It is too early for them to have made any appreciable impact on the education systems of the countries in which they have been established, but the expectations are high.

The Zimbabwe Project

A major case study of national assessment was that undertaken by the International Institute for Educational Planning in Zimbabwe in 1991 (Ross and Postlethwaite 1991). The major aim of the project was to develop a mechanism for accurate and quick collection and analysis of data and rapid reporting of the results to the Ministry of Education and Culture. During the study period Ministry of Education officials generated a number of crucial policy questions, data collection instruments were developed, and data were collected across the country employing probability sampling techniques. The data were analyzed by computer and interpreted, and the results were made available in good time for appropriate decisionmaking.

The major areas covered in the report under baseline indicators of inputs to schools included school buildings, toilet facilities, pupil/teacher ratios, teacher absenteeism, teachers' qualifications, libraries, teacher housing, school furniture, and distribution of supplies. Under indicators of learning outcomes, the project adopted reading comprehension performance using an instrument developed for the purpose. In an effort to relate educational inputs to output indicators, the project correlated the performance in the reading comprehension test with such variables as teachers' qualifications and availability of classrooms, textbooks, space, and toilets.

The project demonstrated clearly that data required for decisionmaking can be quickly and cooperatively generated if the will and the support to do so are present. Aside from the benefit to rational decisionmaking, the project was of immense benefit in building up the capacity of local staff in the various skills and strategies required to execute such national surveys.

National Assessments in Latin America: The Chilean Experience

As in developing Africa, Latin American countries such as Chile, Colombia, Costa Rica, and Venezuela have attempted to establish national assessment systems. Perhaps the most typical and successful of the efforts is that of Chile, which undertook the National Program for Quality Assessment of Basic Chilean Education from 1988 to 1991 (Himmel, chapter 8 in this book).

The project, which was centered at the Pontificia Universidad Católica de Chile, adopted an interdisciplinary approach to educational assessment. Central to the study was that the results should give indications of educational progress and direction, as well as inform on the desirability of decentralizing the management of the educational system. The instruments developed covered both the cognitive (Spanish, writing, mathematics, natural sciences, social sciences) and the affective domains (self-concept, attitude to school and learning, peer and social relationships, vocational orientation, value acquisition). The Chilean example demonstrates a case of where a previously highly centralized education system gave way to regional and subregional educational authorities in the interests of improving efficiency.

The project was temporarily discontinued because of funding problems. This is a situation that is likely to recur in externally funded NAS efforts in Africa whenever the funding contracts end and the consultants depart unless the necessary precautions are taken.

Political Structure and Effectiveness

The recommendations regarding initializing national assessment notwithstanding, a variable that can affect the effectiveness of the system is the national educational structure (as derived from the country's general political setup). For predominantly unitary political systems such as those in Kenya, Ghana, and Uganda (which have only one ministry or department of education), there will be relatively few administrative and bureaucratic bottlenecks. There is only one education authority and the entire country operates a single education system and teaching service. The vast majority of developing African countries belong to this class. However, in federal systems such as Nigeria, where there are many education authorities (which in some cases use different curricula), a national assessment body may have more problems establishing the consensus required to ensure its acceptability.

Fundamental Questions

Early in this chapter we asked nine questions typical of what national assessments can address. Having now reviewed the characteristics and deliberated on some examples in action, especially in the developing world, how can national assessments answer these and similar questions? In an effort to provide a response, we shall take three of the questions raised earlier as examples.

A comparison of the physical, human, and operational educational resources available to urban, semi-urban, and rural schools in a country can enable assessment of the relative quality of the education made available to pupils in these areas. The Ross and Postlethwaite (1991) study cited earlier is a good example of this. There is also a comprehensive national survey of the 200 best-administered secondary schools in Nigeria (Federal Inspectorate Service 1993).

Administering the same standardized tests (or their psychometric equivalent forms) to pupils in the same grade across varying geopolitical locations and different cultural backgrounds will yield results that can help compare the relative performance of these groups, thereby permitting corrective action or adjustment in the educational delivery system. The World Bank-sponsored project of the Nigerian National Primary Education Commission has obtained preliminary results that show significant variations in achievement. The same holds true for the Chilean NAS project cited earlier.

Administering standardized achievement tests in key school subjects (such as writing and mathematics) over a number of years will yield results that will enable comparison of the performance of, say, primary school leavers in these subjects over time. It is common to hear in the developing world (and perhaps also in the industrial world) that standards of public education are falling, especially in comparison with those of the colonial period. Answers to the issue of falling or rising educational standards cannot be reasonably addressed until empirical evidence collected from equivalent and equated groups or both is systematically obtained, analyzed, and interpreted. It is the hope of the World Bank-assisted projects in Africa, as well as of the program in Latin America, that they will address this issue. The National Assessment of Educational Progress of the United States has carried out this type of comparison within the U.S. education system and revealed interesting trends in pupils' performance in such disciplines as reading, writing, mathematics, and science.

Summary and Conclusions

This chapter discussed national assessment, which enables us to make cost-effective decisions on educational systems. By its nature, a national assessment is elaborate and uses a combination of achievement tests and other indicators of the quality of education. The data generated are scientifically processed and reports are produced for different audiences.

African countries have made progress in promoting appropriate skills and strategies in the assessment of pupils' achievement in the basic school subjects for promotion and certification purposes. Equally important, however, if not more so, is the need to determine how the entire educational system is performing and in what direction it is going. Efforts should now be made to establish those assessment structures that will keep an eye on national performance in a regular and systematic manner to determine whether the scarce resources being invested in education are yielding good results. National assessment programs have therefore become necessary in the African education context, and the experiences of the industrial world in this regard can be of help.

References and Bibliography

Asher, J. William. 1976. *Educational Research and Evaluation Methods.* Boston, Mass.: Little Brown.

Federal Inspectorate Service. 1993. *Quality Assessment Inspection of 200 Good Nigerian Secondary Schools.* Lagos, Nigeria: Federal Ministry of Education.

Lapointe, Archie E. 1990. *Why A National Assessment?* Princeton, New Jersey: National Assessment of Educational Progress.

Koffler, Stephen, and others. 1991. *The Technical Report of NAEP's 1990 Trial State Assessment Program.* Princeton, New Jersey: The National Assessment of Educational Progress.

Mullis, Ina V. S. 1991. *The NAEP Guide,* revised edition. Princeton, New Jersey: The National Assessment of Educational Progress.

Nwana, O. C. 1979. *Educational Measurement for Teachers.* Sundbury-on-Thames, U.K.: Thomas Nelson.

————. 1981. *Introduction to Educational Research.* Ibadan, Nigeria: Heinemann.

————. 1992. *Performance of Nigerian Students in Public Examinations.* Abuja, Nigeria: Nigerian Educational Research and Development Council.

Ohuche, R. O., and S. Akeju. 1988. *Educational Measurement and Evaluation.* Onitsha, Nigeria: Africana FEP Publishers.

Ross, Kenneth N., and T. Neville Postlethwaite. 1991. *Indicators of the Quality of Education: A National Survey of Primary Schools in Zimbabwe.* Paris, France: International Institute for Educational Planning (UNESCO).

4

Can Public Examinations Be Used to Provide Information for National Assessment?

Thomas Kellaghan

Insofar as both public examinations and national assessments provide information about the achievements of students in education systems, it is reasonable to ask if a public examination system, where it exists, can be used to obtain the kind of information that national assessment systems are designed to collect. Performance on public examinations might seem appropriate for assessing the outputs of schools for a number of reasons. Because the examinations are geared to school curricula and because students, teachers, and the general public regard them as important, schools are under strong pressure to teach the subject matter and skills that are examined. Furthermore, as public examinations are provided in many subject areas, obtaining information on a much wider range of achievements than is usually included in national assessments should be possible.

Is it possible to capitalize on this situation to provide information on the performance of the educational system? Eight major issues seem relevant in attempting to answer this question: the purposes of public examinations and of national assessments; the achievements of interest to the two activities; the tests, scoring, and reporting procedures used; the populations of interest to the two activities; the monitoring capabilities of the two activities; the need for contextual information in interpreting assessment data; the implications of attaching high stakes to assessments or tests in terms of effects on schools, students, and test validity; and finally, efficiency and cost-effectiveness in obtaining the information needed. Before discussing these issues, I will first consider some of the basic concepts involved in public examinations and national assessment.

Concepts

Public examinations are formalized procedures, normally separate from the classroom situation, in which candidates have to answer questions, usually based on externally devised syllabuses, to demonstrate that they possess certain knowledge and skills. Examinations may be offered in a large number of subject areas, although individuals students will take only a limited number of them. The examinations generally require written, essay answers, but they may also assess practical and oral skills. In some countries, multiple choice questions are used for part or all of the examination.

33

Public examinations are an important aspect of education in Africa, Asia, Europe, and the Caribbean. In developing countries they are usually offered at the end of primary schooling, at the end of the junior cycle of secondary schooling, and again at the end of the senior cycle of secondary schooling (Kellaghan and Greaney 1992). European countries do not hold public examinations before the end of the junior cycle of secondary schooling, which usually coincides with the end of the compulsory period of education at about sixteen years of age (Madaus and Kellaghan 1991).

While public examinations are concerned with measuring the knowledge and skills of individual students, national assessment is a form of parameter estimation for a whole education system or part of it (for example, a region or a district). The aim of parameter estimation is to provide precise information about the nature and extent of existing conditions in the education system. Estimates may focus on the education system's inputs, for example, the numbers of students enrolled, student-teacher ratios, or the availability of science laboratories in schools, or on its outputs. It is to the latter activity that the term national assessment is applied. The activity involves assessing students' achievements, for instance, how well they can read or how well they can solve mathematical problems or understand scientific concepts.

A logical extension of parameter estimation, whether of inputs or outputs, is monitoring. Monitoring involves following trends over time. The index used to identify such trends is sometimes termed an educational indicator, which is a form of social indicator, which in turn was a term inspired by the use of economic indicators such as gross national product and consumer price index. Although the intellectual roots of the educational indicator system are to be found in the social indicator movement of the 1960s and 1970s, the focus of the educational indicator system today is clearer and its policy linkages much stronger than social indicators ever were (Odden 1990).

Indicators are used to provide a general overview of the state of an educational system; to reveal something about its performance or health (Oakes 1989). A number of points may be made about indicators and their use. First, they are quantifiable, that is, they represent in numerical form some aspects of the system. Second, as a particular value of an indicator will apply to only one period or point in time, several observations are required if one wants to observe trends over time (Johnstone 1981). Third, indicators in themselves do not judge the quality of performance. Other information is required to define satisfactory levels of performance. Finally, background contextual information relating to students' home and community backgrounds and to the curricula and facilities in schools is useful to interpret indicators and to make policy decisions.

While education authorities routinely collect some kind of information on the operation of their education systems that relates, for example, to the number of students enrolled and student-teacher ratios, and perhaps to progression and retention rates, obtaining data on the outputs of systems is uncommon. That situation is changing, however, as authorities in many countries realize that having students in school is pointless if the students are not benefiting from the experience. Furthermore, some students probably benefit while others do not. To identify the extent to which students benefit, output information is required in the form of students' achievements.

The document adopted by the World Conference on Education for All, which was convened jointly by the executive heads of the United Nations Children's Fund (UNICEF), the United Nations Development Programme, the United Nations Educational, Scientific, and Cultural Organization (UNESCO), and the World Bank in Jomtien, Thailand, in

March 1990, notes the importance of school outputs. Recognizing that the provision of basic education is only meaningful if students actually acquire useful knowledge, reasoning ability, skills, and values, Article 4 of the World Declaration on Education for All (1990, p. 5), which the conference adopted, states that the focus of basic education must be "on actual learning acquisition and outcome, rather than exclusively upon enrollment, continued participation in organized programs and completion of certification requirements." Following on this, the UNESCO/UNICEF Joint Committee on Education, at its meeting on October 26–27, 1990, recommended that a priority area of cooperation should be "to build a monitoring system linked to education-for-all goals, paying attention to . . . learning achievement, and focusing especially on building up national capacities in this field."

Several countries now operate systems of national assessment that periodically measure the achievement levels of students in the education system. The best known systems are those that have operated in the United Kingdom since 1948 and in the United States since 1969. Several other countries also have national assessment systems, including Australia, Chile, Costa Rica, Canada, Egypt, France, Finland, the Netherlands, and New Zealand. In Africa, Lesotho and Uganda are currently establishing systems.

Several of the countries that have established national assessment systems already have public examination systems, including France, Finland, the Netherlands, and the United Kingdom. Thus the authorities in countries in which information was already available from public examination performance perceived a need for national assessment. Note, however, that information from public examinations is not available in any of these countries for students during the earlier stages of their schooling.

While we can give many reasons for examining what goes on in our education systems, one reason that is very much to the fore is accountability. Accountability can be described as "a process which involves the duty both of individuals and the organizations of which they are part to render periodically accounts for tasks performed to a body having the power and authority to modify that performance subsequently" (Neave 1985, p. 19). This definition does not reflect the complexity of the concept or the variety of ways in which accountability can be interpreted. It does not say, for example, who should be responsible to whom or for what functions. The chain of responsibility may be complex. Teachers and schools may be held responsible to a local or central government authority that, in turn, may be held responsible to parliament that, in turn, may be responsible to the general public or taxpayers. Further issues relate to where in this chain one should place the responsibility for improving conditions, to whom sanctions should be applied and by whom, and what standards should be used to determine whether or not to apply sanctions.

Purposes

The purpose of public examinations is to assess the performance of individual students. National assessment, by contrast, is concerned with assessing the performance of the whole education system or a part of it. Given this difference, we can ask whether aggregating data from individual assessments to obtain information on the system is possible. To answer the question we have to consider the more specific purposes of individual assessment and the implications of these purposes for the kind of test that is used.

In the case of public examinations, decisions about certification and selection are made on the basis of students' performance. Of these purposes, selection has tended to be more important (Kellaghan and Greaney 1992; Lockheed 1991). This is not surprising when places at the next stage of education are limited, whether in secondary school or at university. Given the importance of the decision that is made on the basis of students' examination performance, in the interests of equity every effort must be made to design a test that will reliably distinguish between students who are likely to perform well in the next stage of education and those who are likely to perform less well.

A consequence of this concern is that the test or examination will attempt to achieve maximum discrimination for those students for whom the probability of selection is high. The procedure for doing this is most transparent when standardized tests are used. In any standardized test in which the major interest is the grading of students, following a try-out of items, those items that all students get right are excluded along with items that none of them gets right, because retaining such items in the final test would not contribute to discrimination between students. Items of intermediate difficulty provide the best discrimination throughout the distribution of achievement. However, in a test that is designed for selection purposes, the bias in item selection is likely to be greater, as even items of an intermediate level of difficulty may not be very functional. Thus, if 25 percent of students are to be selected, items that maximize discrimination around the seventy-fifth percentile will be selected for inclusion in the test.

The procedure in nonstandardized tests is less transparent, but obviously test designers must also try to select questions and establish scoring criteria that will discriminate between students around the point of selection, probably based largely on experience. Clearly, tests comprised of such items or questions will not cover the whole curriculum, or even attempt to do so. However, as the purpose of national assessment is to find out what students know and what they do not know, the instrument used must cover the curriculum adequately.

A further problem relating to purpose arises from the use of information on student performance for accountability purposes. While the major purposes of national assessment are to provide information about education standards, to use that information to improve the quality of education provision, and to demonstrate to the public that this is being done, issues of accountability also enter the picture. The location of responsibility is an important political issue that is as likely to be influenced by political ideology as by research or professional opinion and, in turn, is likely to affect the nature of national assessment (see Black 1992). In this context, using public examinations to provide information for national assessment gives rise to two issues. The first relates to how notions of accountability surrounding public examination systems might affect notions of accountability related to national assessment, and the second to how notions of accountability underlying national assessment might affect the public examination system.

Accountability in the case of public examinations seems to focus primarily on individual schools and teachers. At least, this would seem to underlie the publication of examination results for schools in some systems, often, one may note, without any consideration of the social and economic circumstances in which schools are working. Automatic adoption of this practice in the case of national assessment would be unfortunate, and might happen if a national assessment system were to be built on the public examination system. Before taking such action, an important step would be to debate the political pressures that support accountability and to consider the location or locations of responsibility, which might include government, and even the general public who provide the resources for education, as well as those more directly involved in the education process.

Using the same testing procedure to provide information for the selection and certification of students' as well as for national assessment might also embroil the public examination system in debates on accountability that might not have any relevance for their selection and certification functions. To date, national assessments have developed out of much more complex views of accountability than the one on which public examination systems seem to operate. Furthermore, these views are often quite diametrically opposed. This debate should not be allowed to have an adverse influence on the conduct of public examinations.

Achievements of Interest

There is obviously some overlap between public examinations and national assessments in the achievements of students that are of interest to the two enterprises. During the period of basic education, one would expect both certification and national assessment to be based on information about basic literacy, numeracy, and reasoning skills. If we look at primary certificate examinations, we find that many do focus on a number of core subjects, and a glance at several national assessments indicates that they do the same. For example, many national assessment systems include students' first language and mathematics (Canada, Finland, France, the Netherlands, Spain, Sweden, the United Kingdom, and the United States). Some countries also test in a number of other areas, especially science achievements. A number of countries include art and music (Sweden, United Kingdom), while some include a second language (Spain, Sweden).

However, no national assessment attempts the coverage that one finds in public examinations at the secondary level. The range of subjects on offer varies from one examination authority to another, but finding syllabuses and examinations in twenty, thirty, or even more subject areas is not unusual.

The gap between public examinations and national assessments in their achievements of interest brings us back to the purposes of the two enterprises. While public examinations respond primarily to the needs of individual students who, as they progress through the system, begin to specialize in areas of interest, national assessment is concerned with the functioning of the system in general. Given this concern of national assessment, its focus on core elements of the curriculum such as literacy and numeracy, which are regarded as important for all students, is not surprising.

So far, national assessments have focused on cognitive areas of development. However, in some countries education authorities are talking about extending assessments to students' attitudes and aspirations, which, of course, are not assessed in public examinations. They are also debating the possibility of assessing higher-order and transferable cognitive skills that might apply across a range of curricular areas. If these developments take place, they will further separate the areas of interest of public examinations and national assessments, because public examinations are likely to remain subject bound.

Tests, Scoring, and Reporting

The requirements for national assessment differ from those for public examinations for a number of aspects of tests, scoring, and reporting. The first relates to the quality and structure of tests. In all testing, some standardization has to be imposed on the student behavior sample that is used and on how it is interpreted if performances are to have a comparable meaning for different students, in different places, and at different times. Public examinations often appear relatively unstructured (at a superficial level at any rate), and their scoring procedures often lack clear specification, relying heavily on the judgments of individual markers. Another obvious deviation from standardization in public examinations is found in students' freedom to choose the questions they want to answer in an examination. This may be desirable insofar as it allows students to choose areas of specialization in which they feel they can excel. While the scoring in public examinations assumes that different questions that are answered by different students can be regarded as equivalent, that assumption may not be good enough for the purposes of national assessment.

The fact that lack of structure might not be satisfactory from the point of view of generalizability and reliability (that is, dependability or replicability) should not be taken to mean that an overstructured approach to testing should be adopted, as this could lead to artificiality in what is measured. What is required is some balance between the structure embodied in standardized tests and the reality that obtains in direct or performance-based testing methods. It is not possible to say at what precise point on the continuum between structure and nonstructure the best balance is obtained. Indeed, the point may vary for different testing purposes. For example, as generalizability and comparability are so important in national assessment, testing for that purpose cannot tolerate the degree of nonstructure that is often found in public examinations and that might not be good to change.

A second major area of divergence between tests used in national assessments and those in public examinations lies in their content coverage. Extensive content coverage is not required to produce selection tests that will predict later student performance, although adequate content coverage is required in certification tests if the tests are to reflect accurately the curriculum that the students have covered. However, the coverage cannot be as thorough as that required in national assessment tests if for no other reason than that it would place an unduly heavy burden on examination candidates. A national assessment should provide a detailed picture of important areas of the curriculum if it is to indicate its particular strengths and weaknesses as reflected by students' test scores. Fortunately, this can be achieved without placing too great a burden on individual students by having them take different parts of a test.

Here we should note that in a national assessment we may be interested in what students do not know as well as in what they know. While including items that were not covered in the curriculum in a test of certification might not be fair, items that demonstrate students' lack of curriculum coverage could be included in a national assessment and could be very informative for policymakers.

Other points relating to testing concern scoring and reporting. Scoring and reporting in public examinations usually follow norm referenced procedures. The crucial topic of interest in a selection test is how a candidate performs with reference to other candidates. The same kind of norm referencing is often implicit in how certification results are reported. The main information conveyed by a grade of say B is not that the student has acquired a particular body of knowledge or skills, but rather that he or she performed better than students who were awarded C or D grades.

On the basis of national assessments, by contrast, we usually want to be able to say something about students' level of knowledge and skills. Because of this, assessments tend to be criterion referenced rather than norm referenced, and the results are often reported in terms of certain performance criteria, for example, that a certain percentage of students can perform a particular mathematical operation. While criterion referenced performance can be turned fairly readily into norm referenced results, norm referenced performance does not usually provide sufficient information to allow the results to be presented in criterion referenced terms.

A final issue relating to testing that might be treated differently in public examinations and in national assessments is bias. Bias occurs when successful task performance depends on an ability (or abilities) other than those that it is intended to measure and when that ability is not universal among the students being tested (Wiley and Haertel forthcoming). Thus, for example, if the examiner's intent is to measure mathematical achievement (the target ability), but some of the students taking the test have poor proficiency in the language in which the test is written (the ancillary ability), the assessment may not reflect the students' knowledge of mathematics accurately. Furthermore, some students will have an advantage, not because their knowledge of mathematics is superior, but because of their knowledge of the testing language. This is a problem for tests of certification or selection because it may have serious consequences for students. Hence, public examination systems try to eliminate bias, for example, by pretesting items, or they ignore it. Bias, if it occurs in national assessment, will also be a problem of course, because it means that the picture of mathematical achievement obtained will not reflect the true level of achievement of students in the system. However, rather than just trying to reduce or ignore bias in its test instrument, a national assessment system could well direct its efforts toward identifying its extent and then taking steps to deal not with the symptoms of the problem, but with its source, which is likely to lie in unequal opportunities for students in the education or social system. Contextual information, which I will deal with later, could help in the task of identifying factors associated with bias.

Populations of Interest

If public examinations are to be used for national assessment, then they should provide information for those populations of students that are of interest to policymakers. The first public examination is usually not held before the end of primary schooling. However, all national assessments that I am aware of (with the exception of Spain, which tests at the lower secondary level) test pupils during the course of primary school. In Canada, pupils are tested from kindergarten up. In the United Kingdom, they are tested at ages seven and eleven. In Sweden, pupils are tested in grades 2 and 5, in Finland and in France in grades 3 and 6, in the United States at grade 4, and in the Netherlands at grade 5. Thus, there is almost a consensus among national assessments that information is required before the age at which students sit for a public examination.

The reason for the consensus is fairly clear. Information for national assessment should lead to decisions that might be required to improve the quality of education. It seems reasonable to assume that during the rapid period of development in the primary school years pupils are particularly vulnerable, and that if children make a poor start at school they are unlikely to succeed later. We also know that repetition and dropout rates are serious problems during primary schooling. Information obtained at the end of primary schooling comes too late for effective action in these cases. If information is needed while children are still at primary school, and practice in most countries suggests that it is, then one would either have to institute public examinations at this stage or set up a national assessment program. The institution of public examinations, however, would not be cost-effective if the results were not required for selection or certification. More cost-effective procedures are available if the information is required only for national assessment.

Monitoring

Monitoring is an important aspect of national assessment. To be able to say that student achievements are improving over time (perhaps as a result of education reforms) or are deteriorating, the authorities need to obtain information at different points in time. The question is whether public examination data can be used for this purpose.

We have to acknowledge that any information obtained about standards over time will, of course, be limited to those students who take examinations and to the subjects that they take. As public examinations are voluntary, as the subjects students choose at certain levels may also be, they are unlikely to provide information about a complete population of students.

If we accept this situation, can we at least be confident that monitoring the performance of those students who take public examinations would provide reliable information on changes in standards over time, even for limited populations? We must consider two issues in answering this question. One relates to changes in the characteristics of the population taking examinations over time and the second relates to changes in examinations.

As educational provision expands and as more students sit for public examinations, two things that are happening in many countries, the examinees' characteristics change over time. However, this might not be obvious from a consideration of examination results. For example, one often finds that the percentage of students who pass an examination or obtain a particular grade remains fairly constant over a number of years. This would seem to suggest consistency in standards. In this case we have to ask: does a pass (or a particular grade) in different years really represent equivalence in achievement over time, or is the consistency primarily a function of a decision to keep the proportion of passes (or of particular grades) fairly constant? If the latter situation is the case, the fact that a greater number of students are obtaining particular grades could indicate a lowering of standards of achievement rather than stability over time.

A study of public examinations carried out in the United Kingdom some years ago addressed this issue (Willmott 1977). In addition to taking public examinations (the Certificate of Secondary Education and General Certificte of Education examination), candidates also took a standardized test of general ability, and the scores on this test were used as a reference or common standard against which to assess examination performance on two occasions, five years apart. Differences between years in grade were estimated after taking into account differences in the test ability of the examination candidates. With one exception, the quality of entry for all subjects, as assessed by the general ability test, was found to have fallen during the five years. Furthermore, in all school subjects except two, grades were awarded more leniently in the later of the two years. Obviously, an examination of grades awarded would not have revealed any of this information.

As well as changes in the populations taking public examinations, changes also occur in the examinations themselves from year to year. The authorities release public examinations after they have been taken so that upcoming examinees can use them as guides. A consequence of this is that in the absence of a clear definition of the standards to be maintained when a new examination is constructed, making meaningful comparisons of performance at different times will be extremely difficult. By contrast, tests for national assessment are not usually made public. While parts of them may, so that schools know what is expected in the tests, other parts are generally not released so that they can be used again. Not releasing complete tests is a response to the difficulty experienced in public examinations of building tests or examinations that are exactly equivalent, and thus permit comparisons of performance from one occasion to another.

Even when the same test is used over a period of time, it may not have an equivalent meaning for students on different occasions. In British national assessments, in which the same measure of reading was used from the 1950s to the 1970s, the authorities noted that changes in curricula and language usage over time meant that students in the 1970s may have been at a disadvantage in taking a test that had been designed for students in the 1950s (see Kellaghan and Madaus 1982).

More recently, findings from the National Assessment of Educational Progress in the United States indicated that reading proficiency had decreased between 1984 and 1986 at ages nine and seventeen, particularly at seventeen. When questions were raised about the validity of these findings, which did not concur with people's judgments about what was happening in the schools, detailed studies suggested that the findings were an anomaly created by changes in the order in which items were presented in the tests and in the context in which the items had been embedded (Beaton and Zwick 1990). As a result Beaton, one of the investigators of the problem, has advised that "when measuring change, don't change the measure."

To deal with the difficulty of constructing two tests that will be exactly equivalent, a statistical procedure called item response theory (IRT) is sometimes used. IRT models assume that a single latent trait underlies performance on the items of a test, and that it is possible to describe mathematically the relationship between a person's trait level and performance on an item. If these assumptions are met, then establishing the equivalence of items and of tests should be possible. Item response theory has been used in public examinations (for example, in the Primary School Leaving Examination in Singapore) to equate performances from year to year. It is also used in the American National Assessment of Education Progress to establish proficiency scales.

Another practice that can be used on its own or in conjunction with IRT to establish comparability from test to test is to have some students take the same items on both tests and not publish those items. The performance of these students is then used to place scores from tests in different years on a common scale. Some national assessments use this procedure. There is no reason why it could not be used in public examinations except that the form of some examinations, for example, written essays or practical examinations, would not lend itself readily to the practice.

The controversy about standards following the release of the contents of a report by Her Majesty's Inspectorate on the 1992 General Certificate of Secondary Education

(GCSE) public examination results in Britain supports this view. The inspectors said that the improvement of almost 29 percent in the number of students receiving A to C grades since the last year of General Certificate of Education Ordinary Levels in 1987 could be taken to indicate a gradual erosion of standards since the introduction of the GCSE in 1988. They went on to say that the quality of GCSE papers was uneven, and they were particularly concerned about the lack of suitable challenges for the most able students. They concluded that the criteria for awarding different grades needed to be more objective, and that the different examination boards should adopt more consistent procedures. In particular, they noted that the assessment of spelling, punctuation, and grammar was inconsistent and that coursework, which was graded by teachers, needed to be monitored more closely. While the inspectorate was expressing these views, the chairman of the Joint Council for the GCSE was saying: "We take great care to ensure consistency and I have no reason to doubt this year's gradings, which were much as I expected" (*Times* 1992, p. 1). When such markedly different conclusions can emerge from a study of changes in standards on public examinations, one could reasonably conclude that the available evidence is too ambiguous to accept that public examination performance can be used for monitoring purposes. Indeed, the system of public examinations may be so complex that they must be regarded as unlikely sources of unambiguous and clear evidence about changes in national standards of achievement (Kellaghan and Madaus 1982).

The Collection of Contextual Information

Information other than data on students' achievements should be obtained in national assessments for several reasons. First, for many people the quality of physical resources, staff, and activities in school is important in itself. Second, as only a small range of educational outputs can be measured, the use of contextual information may prevent schools from placing undue emphasis on the outputs that are measured to the exclusion of other important factors. Third, by allowing an examination of the interactions of inputs, processes, and outputs, contextual information may provide policymakers with clues about why schools get the outcomes that they do (Oakes 1989).

Several kinds of information are likely to indicate the determinants of achievement to policymakers, particularly determinants that might be alterable through changes in educational policy (Lockheed 1991; Messick 1984; Oakes 1989; Odden 1990). First, what students bring to school from their family and community backgrounds that may contribute to their success or poor performance at school is of interest. Many studies point to the importance of these background factors for students' school learning (Kellaghan and others 1993). However, one cannot assume that factors that are important in one cultural context will be of similar importance in other contexts. For example, the fairly consistent finding from industrial countries in Europe and North America that family size is negatively related to educational achievement has not been found in studies in Kenya (Bali and others 1984) or in Tanzania (Drenth, van der Flier, and Omari 1983). In these countries the investigators found a positive rather than a negative relationship between family size and educational achievement as measured in a variety of ways (standardized tests of ability and public examinations at primary and secondary levels).

A second area of contextual information, and one that is more relevant to decisions about the distribution of educational resources, relates to provision in schools, that is, to what extent schools provide access to knowledge and opportunities to learn various domains of knowledge and skills. In concrete terms, we can ask about the physical facilities in schools, the range of curricula offered, and the availability of learning support materials such as libraries and laboratories. The evidence suggests that variation in provision in these areas is more closely related to educational achievement in developing countries than in industrialized countries (Levin and Lockheed 1991).

Third, policymakers should know how school resources are used. It is one thing to have libraries or science laboratories. Whether or not students use them extensively is another matter. The less material aspects of schools are also important, in particular, the quality of the instructional leadership and the institutional pressure that the school exerts to get students to work hard (see Cohen 1987).

Finally, as teachers are the key component in any educational system, information should be obtained on the conditions in a school that may enhance or constrain teachers' ability to implement instructional programs.

In theory, contextual information could be collected in conjunction with public examinations. However, this would place an enormous burden on examination authorities, which in many cases are already greatly overstretched. Furthermore, it would not be cost-effective to collect and process information for all students taking public examinations.

High Stakes and Low Stakes Testing

Attaching high stakes to performance on examinations or tests, whether public examinations or national assessments, has two important consequences. One is that the effects of high stakes testing on students, curricula, and teaching can be considerable. The second concerns the validity of measurement.

An examination or test is said to have high stakes attached to it when sanctions are directly linked to performance on the examination or test. Obviously high stakes are attached to performance on public examinations, because students' performance can have important consequences for their future educational and occupational options. However, an examination or test can take on the characteristics of high stakes tests even if sanctions are not explicitly attached to individual student performance. Thus, for example, if test results are used to rank school districts or schools in terms of performance on an examination, schools will perceive the results as an important indicator of what is to be valued in education (Madaus and Kellaghan 1992). Because of this, in many countries proposals for educational reform have been put forward to use examinations and assessment to improve instructional practices in schools (Madaus and Kellaghan 1992). This view underlies what has come to be known as measurement-driven instruction, which is based on at least three propositions: tests or examinations will have a positive impact on teaching and learning if (a) they provide a clear concept of what students and teachers should work toward, (b) they measure accurately the attainment of these goals, and (c) they attach high stakes to students' performance.

This may seem an eminently satisfactory scenario if one has good examinations (see World Bank 1988). If the objectives and skills to be measured are carefully chosen and if the tests truly measure them, then the goals of instruction will provide well-defined targets for teachers and students on which they can focus their efforts. Furthermore, the examinations will provide students and teachers with standards of expected achievement. Given this situation, there should be no reason why students should not work for marks, and good reason why they should (Fredericksen 1984).

While evidence indeed exists that public examinations and tests to which high stakes are attached affect learning and teaching, the effects are not always positive (Madaus and Kellaghan 1992; Shepard 1991). First, as curricula and examination objectives become aligned, schools will teach things that are examined and will not teach things that are not examined. This often results in the neglect of important knowledge and skills. Second, curricula will become more standardized across schools. This may be good, but it also may result in schools becoming less sensitive to the needs of students experiencing difficulties (Giroux 1992). Third, examinations tend to encourage the use of a transmission model of teaching, in which what is taught is equivalent to what is learned. This approach has little room for a constructivist model, which views students as actively constructing knowledge and understanding for themselves, and sees what is taught as only one factor influencing what is learned (Gipps 1990; Giroux 1992). Fourth, considerable effort will be put into test preparation by teachers and students. This can include training in test skills, choosing objectives based on items on the test and teaching accordingly, and presenting students with items similar to those on the test (Haladyna, Nolan, and Haas 1991). Fifth, the effects of high stakes testing will not be limited to the students at the grade at which the tests are administered, but are likely to trickle down to lower grades. For example, teachers may use the multiple choice format of public examinations not only in their classroom tests, but also in their teaching methodology in the early grades of primary school (Kellaghan and Greaney 1992). Finally, strategies to improve test scores that some schools resort to are to exclude students likely to get low scores from the test population on the day of the examination or to retain them in a lower grade so that they are not eligible to take the examination (Madaus and Greaney 1985).

While high stakes are more usually associated with public examinations, there are examples of national assessment to which high stakes are attached and that set out to lead instruction. For example, the national assessment system in the United Kingdom is designed to influence what goes on in schools. In the United States, by contrast, national assessment provides an unobtrusive measure of the educational system, focusing on what students know and can do, and does not try to influence directly what goes on in schools. In this situation, of course, the danger exists that teachers, administrators, policymakers, and the public may not see the results of national assessment as relevant to their immediate concerns.

Before deciding that attaching high stakes to national assessment might be appropriate, policymakers should consider a number of issues. First, is there a possibility that a high stakes situation will have negative consequences on school curricula and practice, such as narrowing the curriculum and the adoption of a particular model of teaching? Second, if the country already has public examinations, policymakers should examine their relationship to national assessment. Obviously, problems would be likely to arise if two separate systems that were not closely coordinated were operating to influence educational practice in the direction of certain objectives.

This last point might sound like a good basis for arguing that national assessment should be assigned to a public examination system that would be modified to take the concerns of national assessment into account. Before reaching this decision, policymakers should consider one other issue: the effect this would have on the validity of the national assessment information. Given that teachers will direct their efforts toward teaching topics and skills covered in tests to which high stakes are attached and toward familiarizing students with the test format, the research evidence that indicates that the test performance of students will improve on such tests is hardly surprising (Cooley and Leinhardt 1980; Le Mahieu 1984). However, are we then justified in concluding that students' actual achievement in terms, for example, of problem solving skills, as distinct from their test performance, has also improved? The answer would seem to be no, at least until we have satisfied ourselves that some of the variance in test scores is not attributable to the content and format of the test rather than to an improvement in actual achievement.

Recent studies in the United States have highlighted the extent of the problem of the invalidation of test results when instruction focuses on boosting scores on a particular test. In one study, the fact that standardized tests to which high stakes were attached showed larger average yearly gains in mathematics at ages nine and thirteen than did data from the National Assessment of Educational Progress led to the conclusion that the gains on the standardized tests could be attributed to increasing familiarity with a given test form and more focused instruction on the content of that specific form (Linn, Graue, and Sanders 1990). Thus, raising test scores without increasing learning was possible (Shepard 1991).

In another study, investigators compared the test results of third grade pupils on a high stakes test that had been used for several years in a large urban school district with results on comparable tests covering the same content that had not been used in the district for several years. The students' scores were higher on the high stakes test that was regularly used than on either an alternative form of the test or an alternative test (Koretz, Linn, Dunbar, and Shepard 1991). The degree of distortion on the district's test results was 15 to 25 percent for reading and 30 to 39 percent for mathematics (Haney, Madaus, and Lyons 1993).

The evidence from these studies indicates that when students are taught in such a way that the match between instructional processes and test items is very close, making inferences about students' actual skills and knowledge is difficult. Furthermore, the problem may be particularly acute if we want to test whether a student can apply skills and knowledge to solve new problems, because in this case the problems must be new to the student and not ones that were taught in class. Practice on a problem may improve students' test scores; however, not only will it eliminate the possibility of drawing unambiguous conclusions about students' ability to solve problems, it may actually interfere with the development of understanding by students (Linn 1983).

The lesson as far as public examinations, which inevitably invite test preparation, and national assessment are concerned would seem clear. If our concern is with finding out if real improvements in achievement have occurred in the educational system, which should be the concern of national assessment, then national assessment procedures must be independent of public examinations and must be protected from the possibility of test corruption or test score pollution that seem to accompany high stakes tests.

Efficiency and Cost-Effectiveness

The final issue I want to consider in the context of public examinations serving as vehicles for national assessment relates to efficiency and cost-effectiveness. Three ways in which national assessments differ from public examinations are relevant in this context. First, while public examinations are held annually, the frequency of national assessments varies from once every year (in France and the United Kingdom) to once every ten years (in Finland). Once every four or five years would seem a reasonable compromise and should provide adequate monitoring information.

Second, not every student has to take a test in a national assessment. All that is required is a sample of students that adequately represents the total population of students and that is large enough for the proposed analyses.

Third, every student who participates in a national assessment does not have to respond to all the items. The use of matrix sampling in which a total test is divided into several components means that comprehensive content coverage can be achieved without placing an undue burden on individual students.

Only the last of these issues would preclude the use of public examinations for national assessment on the grounds of efficiency. If other conditions were satisfactory, national assessment data could be extracted from public examination data for a sample of students at appropriate intervals (for example, every third or fifth year) in a cost-effective way.

Conclusion

In conclusion, we may return to the question posed in the title of this chapter: can public examinations be used to provide information for national assessment? I think the clear answer to that question must be no. I do not know of any existing public examination system that meets all the objectives of national assessment systems.

If we rephrase the question to ask if a public examination system could be modified to provide information for a national assessment, the answer may be more qualified. A public examination used for certification might be modified to provide adequate curriculum coverage, although this might have adverse effects on the public examination system by, for example, making examinations too long. Furthermore, policymakers may want national assessments to go beyond curriculum-specific areas of knowledge, skills, and attitudes that would not be appropriate in a public examination. The emphasis on norm referencing in public examinations would also be a problem, but could possibly be dealt with. As far as the population of interest is concerned, information about younger students than those taking public examinations could, of course, be obtained in a public examination, but this would not seem to be a cost-effective procedure. Besides, introducing public examinations at an early stage in the educational process might not be beneficial to pupils. Contextual information to help interpret student performance could be collected in the context of a public examination, perhaps on a sample basis.

The issues that create what I believe to be insuperable problems in using a public examination system for national assessment relate to selection and accountability, the monitoring of standards, and attaching high stakes to performance. Public examinations lack the basis for comparability that is required for monitoring because, on the one hand, examination populations change over time in a unknown way, and on the other hand, methods of scoring are often not known, or at any rate cannot be demonstrated to be sufficiently consistent. Indeed, problems of comparability can emerge even under the highly controlled conditions under which national assessments are carried out.

Public examinations are high stakes tests and will inevitably remain so as long as selection decisions are based on performance. National assessment should not be associated with such high stakes for a number of reasons. First, such an association would probably lead to negative effects on teaching and learning, and second, if the instrument of measurement becomes corrupted, this is likely to defeat the very *raison d'être* of national assessment, which is to obtain an accurate picture of students' achievements in the system.

References

Bali, S. K., P. J. D. Drenth, H. van der Flier, and W. C. Young. 1984. *Contribution of Aptitude Tests to the Prediction of School Performance in Kenya: A Longitudinal Study.* Lisse: Swets and Zeitlinger.

Beaton, A. E., and R. Zwick. 1990. *The Effect of Changes in the National Assessment: Disentangling the NAEP 1985–86 Reading Anomaly.* Princeton, New Jersey: Educational Testing Service.

Black, P. 1992. "The Shifting Scenery of the National Curriculum." Presidential address to the Education Section of the British Association, University of Southampton.

Cohen, M. 1987. "Improving School Effectiveness: Lessons from Research." In V. Richardson-Koehler, ed., *Educators' Handbook. A Research Perspective.* New York: Longman.

Cooley, W. W., and G. Leinhardt. 1980. "The Instructional Dimension Study." *Educational Evaluation and Policy Analysis* 2:7–25.

Drenth, P. J. D., H. van der Flier, and I. M. Omari. 1983. "Educational Selection in Tanzania." *Evaluation in Education* 7:95–209.

Fredericksen, N. 1984. "The Real Test Bias: Influence of Testing on Teaching and Learning." *American Psychologist* 39:193–202.

Gipps, C. V. 1990. "National Curriculum Assessment: A Research Agenda." Paper presented at the annual conference of the British Educational Research Association.

Giroux, H. A. 1992. "Educational Leadership and the Crisis of Democratic Governments." *Educational Researcher* 21(4):4–11.

Haladyna, T. M., S. B. Nolan, and W. S. Haas. 1991. "Raising Standardized Achievement Test Scores and the Origins of Test Score Pollution." *Educational Researcher* 20(5):2–11.

Haney, W., G. F. Madaus, and R. Lyons. 1993. *The Fractured Market Place for Standardized Testing.* Boston, MA: Kluwer Academic.

Johnstone, J. N. 1981. *Indicators of Education Systems.* Paris: UNESCO.

Kellaghan, T., and V. Greaney. 1992. *Using Examinations to Improve Education. A Study in Fourteen African Countries.* Washington, D.C.: World Bank.

Kellaghan, T., and G. F. Madaus. 1982. "Trends in Educational Standards in Great Britain and Ireland." In G. R. Austin and H. Garber, eds., *The Rise and Fall of National Test Scores.* New York: Academic Press.

Kellaghan, T., K. Sloane, B. Alvarez, and B. S. Bloom. 1993. *Home Environments and School Learning. Promoting Parental Involvement in the Education of Children.* San Francisco, California: Jossey Bass.

Koretz, D. M., R. L. Linn, S. B. Dunbar, and L. A. Shepard. 1991. "The Effects of High Stakes Testing on Achievement: Preliminary Findings About Generalization Across Tests." Paper read at annual meeting of the American Educational Research Association, Chicago, April 1–5.

Le Mahieu, P. G. 1984. "The Effects on Achievement and Instructional Content of a Program of Student Monitoring through Frequent Testing." *Educational Evaluation and Policy Analysis* 6:175–87.

Levin, H. M., and M. E. Lockheed. 1991. "Creating Effective Schools." In H. M. Levin and M. E. Lockheed, eds., *Effective Schools in Developing Countries.* Washington, D.C.: World Bank.

Linn, R. L. 1983. "Testing and Instruction: Links and Distinctions." *Journal of Educational Measurement* 20:179–89.

Linn, R. L., M. E. Graue, and N. M. Sanders. 1990. "Comparing State and District Test Results to National Norms: The Validity of Claims that 'Everyone is Above Average'. " *Educational Measurement Issues and Practice* 9(3):5–14.

Lockheed, M. E. 1991. "Multi-Dimensional Evaluation: Measures for both Right and Left Sides of the Equation." Paper prepared for the International Symposium of Significant Strategies to Ensure the Success of All in the Basic School, Lisbon, Portugal, May 13–18.

Madaus, G. F., and V. Greaney. 1985. "The Irish Experience in Competency Testing: Implications for American Education." *American Journal of Education* 93:268–94.

Madaus, G. F., and T. Kellaghan. 1991. "Student Examination Systems in the European Community: Lessons for the United States." In G. Kulm and S. M. Malcolm, eds., *Science Assessment in the Service of Reform.* Washington, D.C.: American Association for the Advancement of Science.

————. 1992. "Curriculum Evaluation and Assessment." In P. W. Jackson, ed., *Handbook of Research on Curriculum.* New York: Macmillan.

Messick, S. 1984. "The Psychology of Educational Measurement." *Journal of Educational Measurement* 21:215–37.

Neave, G. 1985. "Accountability in Education." In T. Husen and T. N. Postlethwaite, eds., *The International Encyclopedia of Education.* Oxford, U.K.: Pergamon.

Oakes, J. 1989. "What Educational Indicators? The Case for Assessing the School Context." *Educational Evaluation and Policy Analysis* 11:181–99.

Odden, A. 1990. "Educational Indicators in the United States: The Need for Analysis." *Educational Researcher* 19(5):24–29.

Shepard, L. A. 1991. "Will National Tests Improve Student Learning?" Paper presented at the American Educational Research Association Public Interest Invitational Conference, Accountability as a State Reform Instrument: Impact on Teaching, Learning, and Minority Issues and Incentives for Improvement, Washington, D.C.

Times (London). 1992. "GCSE Doubts Force Pledge from Patten." September 2.

Wiley, D. E., and E. H. Haertel. Forthcoming. *Extended Assessment Tasks: Purposes, Definitions, Scoring, and Accuracy.*

Willmott, A. S. 1977. *CSE and GCE Grading Standards: The 1973 Comparability Study.* London: Macmillan.

World Bank. 1988. *Education in Sub-Saharan Africa. Policies for Adjustment, Revitalization, and Expansion.* Washington, D.C.

World Declaration on Education for All. 1990. Adopted by the World Conference on Education for All, Meeting Basic Learning Needs. New York: UNICEF House.

Part II: Planning

5

Stages in National Assessment

Vincent Greaney

National assessment (NA) is designed to give government and other policymakers objective information on the operation of some facet of the education system. In addition to obtaining information on pupil achievement levels at the regional or national levels, policymakers need to identify the relative importance of some factors that could help account for variations in pupil achievement. The scope, and consequently the costs, of the assessment can vary considerably depending on the objectives or the agenda of the ministry of education.

Much has been written about the psychometric properties of achievement tests, questionnaire design, sampling and analysis, and report writing, all of which are components of a comprehensive national assessment. Many of these writings, however, fail to emphasize procedures that might provide useful and timely information likely to have an impact on policymaking. In particular, the literature has paid insufficient attention to the political and management dimensions of national assessments. These dimensions include questions about establishing an effective steering committee, selecting an implementing agency, developing instruments that address important policy issues, assessing costs, and reporting so as to maximize impact.

The following pages describe the sequence of activities associated with national assessment. The list is not meant to be exhaustive. Neither should it be considered mandatory. It merely represents a list of activities that those planning a national assessment might take into account. Expense as well as logistical and manpower requirements will dictate the range of assessment options they may select.

An NA exercise should not be undertaken unless all those concerned agree its results are likely to have an impact on policymaking in the education sector. In other words, a strong government commitment to NA is required at the outset. In developing countries in particular, if NA is to be introduced and subsequently institutionalized within educational systems, it must address issues of concern to the minister of education.

Countries can undertake NA through participation in comparative international studies or through independent national assessment programs. The nature, relevance, and utility of the information derived is likely to vary depending on whether a country opts to participate in a national or an international assessment.

Participating in International Studies

Reasonable arguments can be advanced for opting to participate in a reputable international assessment exercise, such as those undertaken by the International Association for the Evaluation of Educational Achievement (IEA) or the International Assessment of Educational Progress (IAEP). Manpower requirements and costs will certainly be less than those of a national assessment because much of the instrumentation and the sampling design will already have been developed. Also, by participating in advance meetings and in the conduct of the actual assessment, educators in developing countries can benefit from training from some of the leading practitioners in the field of assessment and become familiar with the technology of survey research. These educators are also introduced to state-of-the-art issues related to curriculum coverage and achievement testing. Experience to date suggests that many developing country educators are concerned primarily with the need to develop basic reliable tests in the key subject areas (Loxley 1993).

Despite the level of support available from the international coordinating agency, international studies also require considerable support at the national level. The IEA, for instance, estimates that the minimum national requirement is a full-time researcher and a data manager. Further personnel requirements will vary according to the nature of the assessment. Developing countries that wish to participate must pay a nominal annual fee and make a contribution to the overall costs of the international study based on their economic circumstances. Local funds have to be obtained for printing, data processing, and attendance at IEA meetings. In general, costs may be covered by a ministry of education, from university operating budgets, or from a direct grant from the ministry of education to a university or research center. IEA experience suggests that government-owned institutes rather than universities have a better track record in conducting assessments (Loxley 1993). A lack of meaningful contact between university researchers and government ministries is particularly noteworthy in a number of Latin American countries.

When national assessments are designed to address national issues and national curriculum objectives, international achievement tests, rating schedules, or questionnaires are unlikely to be sufficiently specific to meet design objectives. Items covered in an international test represent a common denominator of the curricula of the participating countries (Greaney 1980) and may not cover key aspects of the curriculum (Greaney and Close 1989). Also the importance assigned to curricular objectives is likely to vary from one country to another. Thus, important policy-related information is more likely to be obtained from a national than from an international assessment.

Participation in an international assessment involves curriculum comparisons. Information gleaned from the initial comparative activity may prompt ministries of education to review the content area covered in light of evidence from other countries. The results of the IAEP assessment in Ireland suggested to the Irish education authorities that the mathematics curriculum may have placed too much emphasis on familiar or routine aspects of mathematics and not enough on tasks presented in a somewhat unfamiliar format. Also, while national assessments suggested that pupils were achieving satisfactory levels in interpreting charts and graphs, the IAEP results showed that they were doing particularly poorly in this aspect of the mathematics curriculum. An examination of the items used in the different assessments indicated that the IAEP measured a higher level of pictorial understanding than did the national Irish assessments (Greaney and Close

1989). Subsequently, policymakers used these findings to support changes in this aspect of the mathematics curriculum.

In many developing countries, national public examinations tend to dominate school life, dictating not only what is taught, but also how it is taught. The results of such examinations can provide limited information on the functioning of the education system, for example, the number of pupils taking particular subjects, regional disparities in examination performance, and gender differences. Public examinations are generally considered high stakes tests and as such are subject to a series of constraints that limit their suitability for NA. They are not the subject of this chapter.

The Steering Committee

At the outset those involved should address the political dimension of the NA. The ministry of education should establish a politically heavyweight steering committee to provide status for the NA to help ensure that it responds to the needs of the powerful national groupings in the education establishment, especially those of the minister of education, and to help remove the administrative and financial stumbling blocks that can jeopardize or paralyze the NA effort. The interests represented in a national steering committee will obviously vary from country to country, depending on the educational-political power structures. In the United States, for instance, the National Assessment of Educational Progress (NAEP) Steering Committee included two governors and teacher union representatives. In some developing countries representatives of major ethnic, religious, and linguistic groups might be included in the steering committee.

The steering committee should identify the audience that is to be involved in or affected by the NA so that their needs and concerns can be addressed (Joint Committee on Standards for Educational Evaluation 1981). Such an audience should include representatives of those responsible for administering the NA, considering the results for policymaking, and funding the exercise as well as those who will be entrusted with the policy reforms that may arise from the NA, such as school administrators and teachers. The information needs of these various stakeholders should be addressed to ensure that the exercise does not result in a report that is criticized or ignored because it failed to address the "correct" questions.

From a minimalist perspective, the inclusion of key groups in the steering committee can help neutralize opposition that may arise at the end of the exercise. In a more positive vein, it can provide insights that the committee might otherwise have overlooked; help key stakeholders appreciate the constraints under which other agencies, including the ministry of education, have to operate; and provide a sense of ownership over the proposed reforms, thereby increasing the likelihood that the stakeholders might consider subsequent policy initiatives to be acceptable.

As addressing the concerns of all stakeholders is impossible, some prioritization will be necessary. Issues that the steering committee will have to consider include identifying the purpose and rationale of the NA, deciding on the content and on the grade levels to be targeted, developing a budget and assigning budgetary control, selecting an agency or agencies to conduct the NA and providing the terms of reference, setting up reporting procedures, and determining publication rights over the contents of the report(s) and other papers that may be prepared based on the NA's result.

The steering committee is likely to be at its most active at the start of the assessment exercise. During the instrument development stage it should receive draft copies of questionnaires and tests so that committee members can see whether these drafts are adequately addressing the information needs that prompted the assessment in the first instance. The implementing agency selected by the steering committee is responsible for most of the detailed work related to instrument development, sampling, administration, and reporting. However, a strong steering committee can help ensure cooperation from the various stakeholders that the implementing agency will have to deal with by helping to open doors that might otherwise have remained closed.

The Implementing Agency

Who should be assigned responsibility for the day-to-day conduct of the national assessment? Should it be an internal agency, an external agency, or some other entity?

Internal Agency

Many ministers of education may wish to look no further than their own personnel. Some of a country's most knowledgeable educators may be employed within the ministry of education. Ministry personnel would also have ready access to up-to-date information for sampling purposes, while such people as school inspectors or members of curriculum textbook units would have considerable insights into key aspects of the system. Ministers might argue that no extra budgetary allocation would be required because the NA could be charged to the ministry of education's operating budget.

On the negative side, many ministries simply lack the technical competence in areas such as instrument development, sampling, and data analysis to carry out an NA exercise. Depending on the government's educational and political priorities, it can too readily withdraw government employees to tackle "more pressing" issues, and thus subject the NA to frequent delays. Also, compared to an external agency, ministry of education personnel would have a more vested interest in the outcome. They might be less likely to focus on potentially awkward issues or to make public unpalatable findings, thereby limiting the utility of the assessment for policy change.

Many ministries of education in both developing and industrial countries traditionally do not share information with others involved in education or with the public. The concept of the public's right to know does not exist. The ministry's unwillingness to share its results is understandable. Results that show poor delivery of an education service or failure by the formal education system to achieve a particular sensitive goal (for example, helping to revive a national language) can embarrass ministry officials, and their political masters even more.

Lastly, the ministry would have to pay for some of the direct costs associated with NA (printing, travel, possible use of external consultants, processing), and should take account of the opportunity costs of ministry personnel who are delegated to work on the NA.

External Agency

One can make a strong case for assigning the responsibility for administering the NA to a nongovernmental agency. The Chilean assessment described elsewhere in this book adopted this approach for some time, as have Colombia and Costa Rica. In Colombia, for instance, the Ministry of Education asked its test development center to develop the achievement measures and contracted a research institute to conduct the other aspects of the assessment. Information gleaned from a respected nongovernmental agency may be considered more objective, and thus more acceptable to other major stakeholders in education. Technical competence, especially in instrument development, sampling, psychometrics, and data processing, is more likely to be found within university departments and independent research institutes than with ministries of education.

If penalty clauses are written into contracts with external agencies, they may be more likely to complete the NA on time. However, adequate funding must be provided at the outset to complete the task. Unlike government departments, universities may have little flexibility once the budget has been used up.

If an agency other than the ministry of education undertakes the NA exercise, it is advisable that a memorandum of agreement about funding, the timetable, relations with the steering committee, and permitted data uses be signed before any work commences. In some instances competent researchers who are denied the conventional right to publish may decide not to participate in the NA. Where university personnel are entrusted with the NA, they need to take care to avoid an overacademic treatment of the data and issues.

Internal and External Agencies

An alternative is to entrust the NA to a team of ministry of education personnel and outside technical and curriculum experts. Such an arrangement can capitalize on the strengths of both groups, and possibly increase the likelihood of general acceptance of the NA's findings.

Foreign Experts

Where the necessary professional competence is not available locally, foreign experts may have to be hired. In such cases, the development of local capacity (especially in the areas of sampling, instrument development, analysis, and report writing) to conduct NA should be a priority. In other words, the foreign experts should also provide training. The foreign consultants should answer to the steering committee and their work should be directed primarily by the need to supply policy-related information. Although in some instances the findings of foreign experts may carry greater weight with the government than those of local consultants, entrusting the entire NA to an external source is not recommended. If the process is entrusted solely to foreign technical experts, local capacity will not be developed. There is also a danger that policymakers may ignore the findings of foreign experts because of the assumption the foreigners would be unfamiliar with the local educational context.

Irrespective of which type of agency the steering committee selects, the implementation agency must have a reputation for competence. In this instance competence includes quality work, technical skills, and integrity. The agency will need expertise or access to expertise in project management, research design, curriculum analysis, test and questionnaire development, sampling, printing and distribution, data collection, processing and analysis, and report writing. Perceived competence is essential for gaining admission to schools and for getting key individuals and organizations to respond to questionnaires and requests for interviews.

Building Support

Attitudes to participation in a national assessment exercise may vary across developing countries. Teachers in countries that have strong traditions of high stakes assessments in the form of public examinations may need to be convinced that the NA exercise is nonthreatening in nature, and not an instrument of accountability. The education authorities need to give and honor firm commitments that schools will not be held accountable for their pupils' results. Teachers who feel threatened may undermine the process by refusing to participate in the NA or invalidate the results by helping their students during the assessment. Failure to take teachers' reservations into account contributed to the major modifications in the original British Scholastic Attainment Targets Assessment System. The Chilean project informed principals, teachers, and parents of the assessment. The organizers distributed sample tests and gave some 100 talks to interested parties to explain the project.

To ensure that a national assessment reaps long-term dividends, whoever has the overall responsibility (either the ministry if it assumes the role or the steering committee), care must be taken to ensure that a broad level of consensus exists among the key stakeholders about objectives, and that the key policy issues are assessed and reported in time to effect the policy dialogue. Throughout the entire development, data gathering, analysis, and report writing periods, this body should also recognize the power structure within the education system. Lines of communication with key interest groups, such as the inspectorate or its equivalent, school managerial authorities, teachers' representatives, and teacher training authorities, should be kept open.

The Target Population

The ministry of education's information needs will dictate the age or grade levels that are to be assessed. If reading comprehension standards are of interest, then early grades during which pupils are acquiring prereading and initial reading skills are probably inappropriate. However, if a country is having a problem with a high rate of early school leavers, the later the assessment is left, the fewer the number of students and teachers that will be effected by policy changes prompted by the NA. As a result, its potential impact, for instance, in providing useful information for preservice and in-service teacher education, is diminished. In many developing countries an NA in the final primary grade may be inappropriate, because the requirements of the all-important primary leaving examination often dominate learning and teaching at this level. Thus the level of pupil application and teacher cooperation may be less than satisfactory.

Unless the NA has been designed to provide detailed feedback to individual pupils, teachers, and schools, as in the case of the British Scholastic Attainment Targets assessment model (Gipps 1993), assessing all pupils is unnecessary. A number of Latin American countries have tested populations rather than less expensive samples (Horn, Wolff, and Velez 1991). A random sample of schools should be selected, controlling for key variables of interest, such as region and school type. Efficiency and validity considerations should dictate the sample size. Sampling pupils of a particular age may cause unnecessary school disruption, especially in developing countries. Given different ages of initial school enrollment and class repetition practices, nine-year old pupils, for example, might be found in at least five different grade levels. The IEA Reading Literacy Study (Elley 1992) overcame this problem by testing students in the grade level containing the most pupils at a particular age level.

The authorities might consider using matrix sampling. This permits the coverage of an extensive array of items by administering different items to different students. In the U.S. NAEP, for instance, samples of pupils in grades 4, 8, and 12 were administered one-seventh of the total number of test items developed for each grade. Chile also used matrix sampling as part of its grade 4 assessment. While matrix sampling permits the coverage of much larger sections of the curriculum and may prove less time-consuming than conventional standardized tests, the technical and logistical requirements of printing many different forms of the same test, packaging and administering them, and combining test results may be daunting, especially for a country's first NA.

Sampling assistance may be available outside the ministry of education or the universities, for instance, from the government department responsible for the national census.

Instrument Construction

The first NA exercise should not be overly ambitious in terms of subject areas to be covered, assessment procedures, sample complexity, or demands on personnel. Even the 1986 U.S. NAEP, which was implemented by the vastly experienced Educational Testing Services, was confined to two subject areas, mathematics and science. By keeping the scope of the NA manageable, the steering committee and the implementation agency increase their chances of succeeding during this initial capacity building exercise. Valuable assessment experience and useful policy-related information can be obtained from assessments confined to one or a few regions of a country. This is particularly true in large, diverse countries such as China, India, and Indonesia.

The technical aspects of developing assessment instruments (multiple choice tests, written assignments, practical exercises, and oral and aural tests as well as attitudinal scales) are beyond the scope of this chapter. However, in developing these instruments it is essential that they are consistent with the overall objective of the assessment. A persistent focus on the policy objective is required at all stages. If, for instance, the objective is to monitor the language competence (expressed in terms of reading, writing, and oral skills) of final-year primary school pupils, the NA's design must ensure that each of the three elements of language are assessed, analyzed, and reported. In particular, technical personnel need to be reminded that pertinent data must be available on time if they are to influence policy.

Once terms of reference have been agreed, instrument construction can commence. The implementing agency is likely to be charged with the task of measuring achievement. In all likelihood, the lack of a match between the national curriculum and the test items in commercially produced tests or in tests used in international studies will require the construction of new instruments or tests.

Subject matter specialists normally carry out much of the basic work in developing a NA focused on achievement assessment. Such specialists need not, indeed, should not, be limited to university personnel. Classroom teachers should be seconded for this purpose on account of their insights into current practice, their familiarity with teaching priorities, and their knowledge of the curriculum as implemented in the classroom. With instruction in the basics of table of specification construction, subject matter specialists can assign relative weights to individual curricular areas.

Irrespective of who develops them, all instruments have to be pretested on samples similar to those in the target population. This exercise helps provide estimates of the time needed to take the test and to identify items that prove either too difficult or too easy or that fail to discriminate adequately among pupils (in the case of norm referenced tests), ambiguous questions and diagrams, and inadequate instructions for test administrators. Selection of final items or tasks usually requires some knowledge of basic psychometrics, and even more important, careful checking to ensure that the final selection adequately reflects the curriculum being assessed.

What Is to Be Assessed?

Policy needs will dictate the issues and subjects to be assessed. The NA may be limited to one subject area or may encompass other subjects as well as other aspects of the education system of interest to policymakers. In Mauritius, the NA tested word knowledge, reading comprehension, and English as a second language on 5 percent of the targeted population (Chinapah 1992). In Chile (see chapter 8 by Himmel in this book), the grade 4 NA included Spanish, writing, and arithmetic (taken by all), while 10 percent of the students took natural science, history, and geography. Tests of pupil self-image and self-esteem and parent and teacher questionnaires were also administered. Thailand (Chinapah 1992) attempted to identify factors related to the scholastic achievements of grade 3 pupils, such as socioeconomic status, school size, grade repetition, and access to preschool. Both teachers' and parents' perceptions were also obtained.

In recent years, the IEA has assessed an extensive array of subjects in separate assessments. In mathematics, items related to knowledge and information, techniques and skills, capacity to analyze problems and to follow reasoning, attitudes toward mathematics, and home support for mathematics. In literacy, the items measured word recognition, attitude to reading, and perceptions of the value of reading, while written composition has focused on pragmatic, descriptive, persuasive, and reflective tasks as well as on perceptions of the value of writing.

In the United States, future assessments in the area of language are likely to differ substantially from current practices, which have tended to emphasize reading, written vocabulary, and comprehension skills (University of Illinois 1993). Consistent with recent developments in the area of language, assessments will probably focus on how well students can speak, listen, write, and read.

Ministries of education should require feedback on the extent to which important aspects of the official curriculum are being achieved. Information of this type is essential for planners, for the providers of preservice and in-service teacher training, for the school inspectorate, for members of curriculum and textbook bodies, and especially for teachers. To provide this information, the education authorities might consider one or a few of the assessment approaches dictated by policy priorities (described in the following section) in any one NA exercise. Expense, and logistical and manpower requirements will dictate the range of assessment options considered.

Assessment Approaches

From the outset, the steering committee will have to decide whether to use a norm or criterion referenced approach toward assessment. Norm referenced tests determine a student's status with respect to the performance of other individuals who took the test. The widely-used Scholastic Aptitude Test is an example of such a test. Norm referenced tests allow for statements such as, " X is twenty points above the national average" or "Y's performance placed her on the eightieth percentile."

Criterion referenced tests, by contrast, determine a student's status with respect to a specified domain. The qualifying times for Olympic races and the stages used to prepare a seed bed are examples of criteria used in criterion referenced approaches. In the field of education, the emphasis on mastering specific, clearly described behaviors, for example, writing two paragraphs with less than six spelling errors or correctly multiplying three out of four computations involving pairs of two-digit numbers, tends to appeal to teachers and to be more readily understood by the public than norm referenced data.

Despite their widespread use in some Western countries and their usefulness for statistical analysis, norm referenced tests are subject to a number of serious limitations, especially in the context of developing countries. First, they are difficult to construct. Second, pretesting and national norming adds considerably to their cost. Third, norms may be limited to a particularly linguistic group or to a few geographical regions. Finally, up-to-date lists of schools, a key sampling requirement, are frequently not available. Furthermore, norms can become outdated quickly. As countries build schools in poorer districts, the original norms are likely to be pitched at too high a level. Thus comparisons over time become suspect. Similarly, the rapid increase in the population of school age children, a conspicuous demographic feature in many developing countries, renders norms unsuitable for longitudinal comparisons. During these periods of rapid change true national achievement levels may also be changing rapidly.

Type of Test

Validity considerations suggest the authorities weigh the use of other forms of assessment in addition to multiple choice. In the United States the authorities have apparently realized that they have overemphasized standardized multiple choice tests (Cizek 1991; Darling-Hammond and Lieberman 1992). Students' classroom activities have tended to "consist of listening, reading textbook sections, responding briefly to questions, and taking short-answer and multiple-choice quizzes" (Darling-Hammond and Lieberman 1992, p. B1). The American Educational Research Association has urged alternative assessment approaches to assess schools' effectiveness. Multiple choice tests cannot assess important aspects of the curriculum, such as oral fluency and writing and practical skills. Neither can they measure a student's understanding or appreciation of a novel. A sharp shift has occurred away from multiple choice tests to alternative assessment procedures (Rothman 1991, p. 11), especially to more "authentic" measures of pupil assessment, including portfolios of students' work, scientific experiments, and tasks that require higher-order thinking skills.

Performance Tests

Performance tests or tasks can assess competencies in such areas as practical measurement skills in mathematics or ability to conduct a scientific experiment or to cultivate a plot. While the costs associated with this form of assessment are considerably larger than those incurred in conventional multiple choice assessment because of the high labor input, they can be reduced considerably by careful selection of a small representative sample of the targeted population. In the United Kingdom, for instance, the Assessment Performance Unit administered practical assignments in mathematics to a sample of approximately 1,000 students as part of its assessment during the 1980s (Foxman and others 1980 a.b.). Students were required to weigh and measure objects as part of a series of practical tasks. As the curricular dimensions likely to be measured by performance tests are the same ones that teachers preparing pupils for important conventional public examinations are likely to ignore, they need to be assessed periodically to determine if the objectives of the official curriculum are actually being achieved.

ORAL AND AURAL TESTS. Oral and aural tests represent a particular form of performance assessment. In oral assessment the emphasis is on children's use of language rather than on their knowledge of its use. Fluency ratings are obtained usually in one-to-one situations. Students might be required to read a brief passage aloud followed by a series of oral questions based on the reading matter. Aspects of oral fluency, such as command of vocabulary and use of idiom, could be assessed in a structured discussion. Aural assessment may be administered to relatively large groups in conventional examination settings. Students may respond to tasks presented on a tape and their responses are usually written. Competency in a second language and in music can be assessed in this manner.

WRITING ASSESSMENT. Students vary in their ability to perform various writing tasks. Therefore, as part of the NA, instead of undertaking one relatively lengthy task, students might be asked to write a paragraph about a particular event, write a set of instructions, or describe a common object. In this manner an improved sampling of writing skills might be obtained. Students' writing portfolios (a collection of their writing during the school year) might also be rated by independent assessors using predetermined criteria.

PRACTICAL ASSESSMENT. Classroom practice does not reflect the emphasis on practical skills in many national curricula, particularly in developing countries, partly because the public examination system rarely, if ever, formally assesses these skills. Skills that are not tested tend not to be taught. Practical assessment allows for the assessment of process as well as product, for instance, students who are asked to prepare a seed bed may be rated for the procedures they use and their use of implements as well as on the quality of the completed bed.

Performance tests tend to be more difficult and time-consuming to score than multiple choice tests. Satisfactory reliability indices are also difficult to achieve with performance tests. Careful pretesting and modification of instruments and procedures may be required to achieve the desired reliability level.

Nonachievement Variables

Achievement data should not be interpreted in isolation from the environment that contributes to pupils' performance. The identification of factors related to pupil achievement can be particularly useful for policymakers, who can influence the allocation of scarce financial resources so as to maximize their impact. Cognitive psychologists have made us aware of the relationship between human cognition and context (Lieberman 1992). Questionnaires and rating schedules can provide valuable contextual and policy-related information and can be obtained at the same time as the achievement data are being gathered at relatively little additional expense. These data might include information about teachers, for example, qualifications, frequency of attendance at courses; class size; length of school day; teaching time; school facilities, for example, the number and condition of desks and books; the amount of the textbook covered during the school year; the time devoted to different subjects; the amount of homework assigned; the percentage of students being tutored outside school; and attendance, completion, and promotion rates.

Attention to some of these contextual variables can forestall policymakers' tendencies to focus only on those subject areas assessed by national public examinations or international assessments. It can also help them to identify manipulable variables, for example, school timetables, the nature of preservice and in-service teacher training, and student promotion rates, that appear to be positively related to pupil achievement.

Frequently, the desire to get as much information as possible about a system at the design stage of a national or an international assessment exceeds the evaluation team's capacity to analyze the information. Clarity of purpose at the outset can help avoid unnecessary expense attributable to developing, pretesting, printing, distributing, and scoring lengthy questionnaires much of whose content will never be analyzed or reported. In addition, policymakers and steering committee members may be justifiably disappointed if some of the variables assessed in the questionnaire are not analyzed and reported.

The Review Process

In addition to pretesting achievement tests to identify faulty or misleading items, all materials, including questionnaires and rating schedules, should be screened separately to ensure that no advantage is conferred on any particular group, whether ethnic, linguistic, religious, or regional. Similarly, the material should be screened to eliminate typographical errors or inappropriate wording. In the United States, for example, all items used in the NAEP have to be scrutinized to ensure that they are free from racial, cultural, gender, and regional bias. The review should extend to artwork. Most experienced educational researchers can probably recall typographical or layout errors that were not picked up at the review stage, and that subsequently resulted in some important items having to be dropped at the analysis stage.

The review process should place a high priority on validity. Validity involves professional judgment. Teachers might be asked to estimate the extent to which the final selected test items represent an adequate and balanced sampling of the objectives of the national curriculum (curriculum validity) or of the material covered in the classroom (instructional validity). When an evaluation is being conducted to assess the effectiveness of an educational program, referring to the validity of a test is insufficient. In this instance, validity also refers to how the test is used, the conditions of data collection, and the interpretation of the results (Joint Committee on Standards for Educational Evaluation 1981).

To avoid ambiguity, confusion, and subsequent disappointment, both the steering committee and the implementing agency should review tests, questionnaires, other instruments, and administrative procedures to ensure that the following are available:

- A detailed description of the constructs and the content to be measured;
- An analysis of what each instrument or procedure purports to assess;
- A precise specification of how the instrument is to be administered, scored, and interpreted in the proposed NA;
- A set of supportive quantitative and qualitative evidence to justify the use of the particular instrument or procedure;
- An overall assessment of the validity of the use and, in particular, of the interpretation of the instrument or procedure.

The challenge is to reduce the likelihood that the authorities will consider the conclusions inappropriate. For instance, arguing that students' command of a foreign language had improved because of increased scores on a written vocabulary test might be inappropriate. Other factors, such as written and oral fluency and the extent to which there had been "teaching to the test" would have to be taken into consideration before such a conclusion might be justified.

The implementing agency should select the instrument and procedures used to ensure reliability, that is, to provide consistent indicators of the subject matter or trait that is being measured. A pupil's score on a particular performance task should not vary substantially from one assessor to another. Detailed guidelines on administration and scoring, coupled with pretesting, can help minimize unreliability. In NA the concern is with the reliability (or amount of error) associated with the overall mean or average score, which is quite different from the error associated with individual pupils' scores.

As a final stage of the review process, to help check that the key objectives of the NA are being covered, the steering committee and the implementing agency might develop a mock-up version of the final report that lists chapter and table headings. This can help ensure that there is no disagreement between the steering committee and the agency as to what should be included in the report.

Administration

The logistical requirements of administering national assessments are substantial. They include corresponding with targeted schools to secure their cooperation; supervising the printing, packaging, and distribution of materials; recruiting and training those who will administer the assessment exercises; organizing supervisory visits to the schools selected to participate in the NA; collecting assessment materials (important because of the need to ensure that the same procedures are used to collect materials to prevent access to them by those who may wish to do some creative editing of responses); and matching and scoring answer sheets or scripts. Administrative, personnel, and financial management skills are required for this aspect of the assessment.

The designers of the assessment instruments should prepare a detailed instruction manual to ensure that administrative procedures are standardized. To standardize test administration conditions as much as possible, each assessor and administrator should have appropriate letters of introduction, the name and precise location of school, the number of students to be tested, the methods of selecting students within schools, instructions on how to establish appropriate conditions for testing, a work schedule, precise details for administering tests and other instruments or tasks, and sufficient supplies of materials.

In many developing countries the inadequacy of the mail service may require local ministry of education officials to visit schools to alert them to the date and format of the NA and to elicit their support. Frequently complete lists of schools and teachers are not available; "phantom" schools and teachers may be unearthed at the important initial stage.

Ideally, as much as possible of the actual test administration should be entrusted to the teachers of the pupils being assessed, which can significantly reduce administrative costs. Scoring and interpreting results can provide valuable professional enhancement. At another level, teacher involvement can contribute to the assessment's political viability and increase the possibility that reforms prompted by the assessment might be acted on. On the negative side teachers may feel that their work is being evaluated. This perception, whether groundless or not, can result in a low stakes assessment being regarded as high stakes assessment, with serious consequences for both pupils and teachers. Experience with public examinations in many developing countries indicates that this may lead teachers to influence the level of student performance, thereby invalidating the assessment. As an alternative, teachers from neighboring schools could be recruited to administer the assessment.

Where the implementing agency has serious concern that the validity of the assessment may be jeopardized by assigning test administration to teachers, it should adopt alternative strategies. Use of the ministry of education's inspectorate and/or curriculum and advisory staff to administer tests and other instruments can help reduce the cost of the NA. The involvement of ministry personnel can also help ensure that the exercise has status and increase the likelihood that the tests will be administered correctly and that the results will be used to formulate policy changes. It will also ensure that ministry personnel actually visit schools and see what goes on and the conditions under which schools operate for themselves. The ministry must take the opportunity costs of this strategy into account.

Analysis

Once the assessors have collected the achievement test and other data, the implementing agency should establish a data management system to monitor the quality of scoring, recording, data entry, and analysis. It should recheck unanticipated results. Many education systems that operate annual national public examinations have established procedures to minimize the amount of human error in their procedures.

The key policy issues that need to be addressed should direct the types of analysis undertaken. In the United States, for instance, the NAEP has measured achievement differentials between ethnic groups. As a result, U.S. authorities can claim that in 1990, for reading at age seventeen, the average proficiency of whites was twenty-nine points higher than that of blacks. The existence of trend data has allowed the authorities to state that this differential is down from a fifty-three-point gap in 1971 (Elliot 1993). Harried policymakers are badly served when researchers present them with volumes of crosstabulations within which (somewhere) are the relevant findings.

Statistical competence is required at this stage. The analyst must be able to advise policymakers on the interpretation, limitations, and implications of the results. Frequently data other than achievement data are collected to help policymakers assess the effects on achievement of various factors such as language of instruction, level of teacher training, home background, class size, school facilities, and type of school management (public or private). The analyst might help establish how much of the variability in student achievement can be attributed to these factors. Attention to these kinds of questions can help avoid simplistic conclusions such as private schools are better than public schools in mathematics achievement when most of this difference can be accounted for by differences in the students' home backgrounds, or that large classes produce better results than small ones.

Results in the form of league tables, in which the test scores of various schools and subgroups (for example, racial, religious, geographic) are ranked, often appeal to policymakers. However, they should interpret them with considerable caution because they generally fail to take into account the context in which the subgroup data were collected. For instance, in comparison with urban pupils, pupils in poor rural areas may be considered to have performed poorly. Simple, crude comparisons that do not allow for the adverse circumstances in which some schools operate may be misleading. The added value achieved by these latter schools may actually be greater than that achieved by those operating under more favorable circumstances. The danger of contributing to a defeatist attitude in these schools is obvious. As league tables inevitably cause anxiety the possibility of low-scoring groups not participating in a subsequent NA should be considered.

Reporting

Assessment results should be reported as soon as possible after data collection. Lengthy delays in producing the final report diminish the utility of the exercise. The written report should be concise, simply written, and devoid of educational jargon (Shephard 1980). It should use simple graphs and bar charts. The timely and well-presented and illustrated reports produced by the NAEP, and recently by the IEA, might serve as models. The report should document the procedures and criteria used so that readers can assess the significance of the conclusions drawn. Conclusions should be based on unambiguous evidence derived from the data. The implementing agency can prepare press releases to reduce the possibility of misinterpretation by the media. Representatives of the steering committee or, with the approval of the steering committee, of the implementing agency, should present oral reports to key interest groups, such as senior ministry of education officials, inspectors, teacher training authorities, teachers' and school managers' representatives, curriculum authorities, and textbook publishers. Seminars could be organized to discuss the results of their implications.

Cost-Effectiveness of the NA

NA can lead to greater economic efficiencies in the education system. It can help pinpoint aspects of the curriculum that are too easy or too difficult, thereby prompting a curriculum revision. By linking teacher questionnaire and achievement data it can provide feedback to the ministry of education to help it organize in-service training in response to established teacher needs. In the area of materials, for instance, it can recommend that textbooks be provided or that textbooks be shortened if the NA establishes that pupils consistently do not finish the text.

The costs of an NA will vary and will reflect the level of support provided by the ministry of education and local economic conditions. Against a background of competing demands for scarce resources, the costs of the NA have to be justified and kept as low as possible. The quality of the data produced should be of sufficient value to justify the resources expended.

Test and questionnaire development and other technical components of the NA may account for relatively small percentages of the overall budget. Indeed, experience to date suggests that other elements of the NA may prove much more expensive. In Chile, for instance, the technical components accounted for 10 percent of the overall SIMCE budget, while the remaining 90 percent was spent on logistic and management items such as printing, distribution, data gathering, data processing, and distribution of the report (see chapter 8 by Himmel in this book). Although not directly comparable, U.S. costs for data collection, processing, analysis, and reporting were considerably larger than those for instrument development and sampling as shown below (Koeffler 1991):

Item	Percentage of total costs
Instrument development	15
Sampling and selection	10
Data collection	30
Data processing	10
Data analysis	15
Reporting and dissemination	15
Governance (meetings and other administrative costs)	5

Although he was referring to international assessment, Loxley's advice to set aside a contingency fund for emergencies is relevant in the context of NA. Recommending a figure of 10 percent of the budget for this purpose, he notes that "it is never a question of whether emergencies will arise, but rather of when and how many" (Loxley 1992, p. 293).

Conclusion

National assessment can provide a country with a valid indicator of the health of some aspects of its educational system. Given the percentage of central government expenditure devoted to education (more than 10 percent in many developing countries), the need to monitor this investment scarcely needs to be justified. A high level of technical competence and administrative and political skill is required to conduct an effective assessment.

Assuming that the results of even a well-administered national assessment would bring about immediate changes in the educational system would be naive. In bringing about change, the ministry of education needs to take the values of the various educational pressure groups into consideration. These include the religious, ethnic, and language groups; teachers' unions or organizations, representatives of school management; parents; school inspectors; curriculum specialists; and textbook publishers. Given the role of values on decisionmaking, pertinent data on functioning of the school system must be available if the selection of educational priorities is not to depend on the values of the politically more powerful groups. Data obtained at regular intervals can help ensure that educational reform is not dictated by purely whimsical political considerations, but is informed by objective, valid, and reliable data.

References

Chinapah, Vinayagum. 1992. *Monitoring and Surveying Learning Achievements: A Status Report.* Paris, France: UNESCO.

Cizek, Gregory J. 1991. "Innovation or Enervation." *Phi Delta Kappan* 72 (May):695–99.

Darling-Hammond, Linda, and Ann Lieberman. 1992. "The Shortcomings of Standardized Tests." *The Chronicle of Higher Education* 29(January):B1–B2.

Elley, W. B. 1992. *How in the World Do Students Read? IEA Study of Reading Literacy.* The Hague, Netherlands: IEA.

Elliot, Emerson J. 1993. "National Testing and Assessment Strategies: Equity Implications of Leading Proposals for National Assessments." Paper presented at the Equity and Educational Testing and Assessment Seminar, Washington D.C., March 12.

Foxman, D. D., M. J. Creswell, M. Ward, M. E. Badger, J. A. Tuson, and B. A. Bloomfield. 1980a. *Mathematical Development, Primary Survey Report No. 1.* London, U.K.: Her Majesty's Stationery Office.

Foxman, D. D., R. M. Martini, J. A. Tuson, and M. J. Creswell. 1980b. *Mathematical Development, Secondary Survey Report No. 1.* London, U.K.: Her Majesty's Stationery Office.

Gipps, C. V. 1993. "National Curriculum Assessment in England and Wales." Paper presented at the International Centre for Research and Assessment Conference, University of London Institute of Education, July 7–9.

Greaney, Vincent. 1980. "Developing National Measures of Attainment." *International Review of Education* 26:3–16.

Greaney, Vincent, and John Close. 1989. "Mathematics Achievement in Irish Primary Schools." *The Irish Journal of Education* 22:51–64.

Horn, R., L. Wolff, and E. Velez. 1991. *Developing Educational Assessment Systems in Latin America.* Regional Studies Program, Report No. 9. Washington D.C.: World Bank, Latin America and the Caribbean Technical Department.

Joint Committee on Standards for Educational Evaluation. 1981. *Standards for the Evaluations of Educational Programs, Projects, and Materials.* New York: McGraw-Hill.

Koeffler, Stephen. 1991. "Assessment Design." Paper presented at the Seminar on Measurement/Assessment Issues, Educational Testing Service, Princeton, New Jersey, November 17–22.

Lieberman, Ann. 1992. "The Meaning of Scholarly Activity and the Building of Community." *Educational Researcher* 21:5–12.

Loxley, William. 1992. "Managing International Survey Research." *Prospects* 22:289–96.

———. 1993. Personal communication.

Rothman, Robert. 1991. "Supply of New Assessment Methods Said Trailing Behind Strong Demand." *Education Week* March 20.

Shephard, Laurie. 1980. "Reporting the Results of State-Wide Assessment." *Studies of Educational Evaluation* 6:119–25.

University of Illinois. 1993. *The Standards Project for English Language Arts*. Champaign-Urbana, Illinois: Center for the Study of Reading.

6

Considerations for Costing National Assessments

Lynn Ilon

Developing and implementing national assessments is a process rather than the more traditional good or service usually costed in educational settings. Thus, costing national assessments carries with it particular challenges. First, because it is multifaceted, it is likely to involve a variety of instruments and measures. Second, the effectiveness of the final product derives primarily from the quality of the development process. Without the involvement of the right people at the right stages, an otherwise sound instrument can prove useless. Third, the assessment process can involve a seemingly endless combination of inputs. No established formula or production function is available for national assessment systems. Each has its own variations and characteristics, which make it unique.

The costing of such an assessment is also a process. Assessment specialists, policymakers, educators, and an economist need to establish the parameters through a process of collaboration. Unless the original design happens to fit within a predetermined budget limit (an unlikely and rare event), the costing process will involve an iterative process of modifying specific inputs until costs fit within the budgeted amount. Maximizing the benefits derived from expenditures on national assessments depends inextricably on the planning and budgeting process (see Coombs and Hallack 1987 for an overview of how cost analysis fits in the overall educational planning process).

This chapter is organized around this process. First, it proposes a general framework for costing the process (Ilon 1992). Because costing is a process rather than a one-time activity, a framework is needed to support it, otherwise it can become enormously messy and complicated.

The second part of the chapter is organized around the assessment process described by Greaney in chapter 5. Each step in the assessment process involves taking some critical decisions that weigh costs against quality and determine specific groups of inputs. I posed these decisions as questions wherein a discussion of major cost considerations, problems, and issues takes place.

In some cases, Jamaica is used as an example. An assessment team used a detailed version of this framework in Jamaica. Although Jamaica required a test rather than an assessment system, it did involve several subtests, including the evaluation of students, class work, two performance tests, and three objective tests. The assessment team costed a full process including the development process, a documentation process, and a reporting process.

Establishing a Framework for Costing

At the outset, establishing basic parameters for costing is important. Such an approach establishes a general working framework that permits the big picture to emerge from the minutia of finely detailed unit costs and quantities. This is in keeping with the notion that an assessment is a process and will involve much negotiation between the various parties involved. When faced with a process decision, policymakers require quick estimates of the relative costs of tradeoffs without having to wade through pages of details.

The logical first step in the costing process is to collect unit costs on all likely ingredients. Appendix A presents a possible (although not exhaustive) list of such ingredients. Obviously, unit costs vary substantially between and within countries.

The second step is to establish a relatively small set of modules that can easily be adapted to various stages of the assessment process. These modules each include a limited set of ingredient clusters to which unit prices and quantity estimates are attached for quick cost estimates. Let us consider five possible modules as examples: conceptualizing, producing, data processing, informing, and physical processing (for a more complete description of these modules see Ilon 1992). Each of these modules is described briefly below and assigned ingredient clusters in appendix B.

- Conceptualizing. The assessment framework should include this module whenever a major input involves the creative or analytical work of professionals. The steering committee, instrument construction process, review process, and analysis all involve substantial conceptual processes.

- Producing. This module involves putting ideas into consumable form. The primary production stage is assessment administration, although getting information for various groups is also producing.

- Data processing. In national assessments this module is the mainstay of the analysis step. However, the review process may also depend heavily on data processing, and administration may involve data processing insofar as it involves organizing assessment distribution through computer databases.

- Informing. At various stages throughout the national assessment system process, the implementing agency needs to inform various groups about such items as meetings, examination administration time schedules and procedures, and test results.

- Physical processing. This module involves assembling, shipping and delivering materials, supplies, and equipment. It usually follows the producing module.

Obviously, these modules are not discrete, but the framework facilitates quick estimates of relative costs. The examination planning team should link each of these modules to a specific set of ingredient clusters (see appendix B). The team can devise a worksheet for each module that lists specific ingredients along with their unit prices. Then, for any given activity, a testing expert can estimate the quantity of each ingredient and the team economist can get a general estimate of the total cost of the activity. This framework links each of the national assessment steps discussed above to a specific combination of modules. Table 6-1 shows these relationships.

Table 6-1. Matching Costing Modules with Assessment Steps

Steps	Conceptualizing	Producing	Data processing	Informing	Physical processing
Steering Committee	X				
Implementing Agency	X				
Building Support	X	X		X	
Target Population	X				
Instrument Content & Construction	X	X	X		X
Manuals	X	X			X
Review Process	X	X	X		X
Administration	X	X		X	X
Analysis	X		X		X
Reporting	X	X		X	X

Once the examination planning team constructs a module with its appropriate ingredients and unit costs and conceptualizes the various steps in terms of the modules, it is fairly easy for an experienced testing expert to estimate the quantities of each ingredient required to carry out the steps according to a proposed plan. Some resources may be provided at no budgetary cost. These ingredients may be entered as "0" unit cost for purposes of budget development (see Levin 1983 for a good delineation of various types of costing, including social and budgetary cost analysis). Once an initial cost has been estimated, the testing expert along with the economist enter into an iterative process where either propose reduced-resource modifications and the economist estimates a revised budget. Eventually, some compromise between an optimal assessment and an optimal budget will result.

Costing the Assessment Process

The framework facilitates the actual process of costing the assessment. Costing requires the efforts of many members of the assessment planning team. The economist on the team must work closely with team members to assure that the steps and ingredients have been clearly specified. Also, even when the assessment process has been clearly and accurately delineated, the economist may have to recost the assessment process more than once in order to incorporate proposed modifications. The economist may also suggest modifications if final cost estimates are too high.

Steering Committee

The steering committee provides overall direction for the assessment process. It provides the interface between larger social and political aims of the assessment and the more technical aspects of its implementation.

From where will the members be drawn? Transportation can be the major cost in organizing and facilitating a steering committee. To some extent, costs might vary depending on the type of transportation available. Perhaps a choice exists between ground and air transportation along with a cost difference. Coordinating steering committee meetings with other meetings that most members also need to attend can minimize transportation costs. Members compensation for travel time is an additional cost of transportation.

Selecting members from a relatively small geographic area can minimize costs, but not without incurring some political and effectiveness costs. The assessment planning committee needs to weigh the costs of transportation for distant members against the gains in community commitment, input, and support. Also, narrowing the representation may jeopardize political support. Limiting input from distant (and possibly disparate) areas can jeopardize assessment quality.

Will members be compensated for their time? Depending on the local traditions and the types of members chosen for the steering committee, compensation for the time members spend on committee activities can vary widely. In cases where most members are government employees or work for agencies affiliated with the government, their agency or department may donate their work time free of charge. Some members, for example, clergy or community activists may regard this type of activity as part of their larger civic duty.

In other cases, getting the right mix of people may require substantial outlays of cash. Some professional members may require payment in accordance with their normal professional fees. Others may require only token payments, such as an honorarium. In either case, a particularly difficult decision will be whether to compensate all members equally. Some members who are otherwise willing to donate their time might resent compensation paid to their colleagues.

Who will cover their expenses? Sometimes, even if members require payment for their time, the assessment planning committee arrange for such payments to come from sources other than an assessment budget. Community organizations and government agencies that derive specific benefits from the assessment, or local communities or groups, may be willing to pick up some or all of the costs of a member's participation.

What resources need to be set aside to coordinate meetings and communication? Facilitating the meetings will require minimal time and effort if steering committee meetings are informally convened among a relaxed group of people. Arranging the meeting may only require a call to reserve the room, a quick telephone call or notice of the meeting's time and place, and some relatively minor administrative preparations.

At the other end of the spectrum is a meeting that lasts a couple of days, requires the participation of many members from distant parts of the country, and needs a fairly formal setting and structure. These types of meetings will require substantial time from an administrative assistant or secretary to coordinate transportation, hotels, meals, meeting rooms, refreshments, and materials and supplies. Communicating with members may also be time-consuming in the case of members who live in areas without reliable communication systems. Coordinators will have to make special efforts well in advance to get meeting notices and materials to such members. Follow-up telephone calls may be necessary to be sure that they received the information.

How expensive is it to fund steering committee activities? At any rate, the cost of the steering committee is likely to be small relative to total assessment costs. In the case of Jamaica, the steering committee was composed of members who would donate their time. Had the budget included their compensation, however, total cost would have increased by one-third of one percent.

Implementing Agency

The government must assign some agency to overall authority over the assessment development and administration. The implementing agency may well be the agency that actually administers the test, but it may also contract out various pieces to other agencies or organizations. Costing the various combinations of in-house and contracted services is an important part of the assessment costing process.

How prepared is the implementing agency to do assessment on a national scale? Although one usually thinks about a singular implementing agency for a national assessment examination, the readiness of a variety of agencies affects the cost of implementing an assessment. Unless the country is large and has a well-developed assessment department, dispersed and disparate set of government and nongovernment agencies may require extensive coordination and involvement of an assessment coordinating committee. In addition to the agency that will actually coordinate the national assessment process, the national assessment system may heavily involve departments that handle accounting, printing, travel, facilities, and procurement. Assessment planners must evaluate each of these agencies for their ability to handle the quantity, quality, and administrative issues that are inherent in a large-scale national assessment. A national assessment agency may exist, but many are not large enough or experienced enough to handle all the coordination needed to get an assessment under way. Equally, supplying enough tests, on the quality of paper needed, under the anticipated time constraints may stretch the capabilities of the government printers. Also of concern, the various agencies involved need to be able to devote additional resources to test security.

In addition to actual cost outlays for these agencies, work on a national assessment often means taking time away from other activities. Although these types of costs (opportunity costs) are often not budgetary costs, they are, nevertheless, a loss to the government and ought to be acknowledged, and possibly calculated, if not specifically budgeted.

How prepared are the personnel within the agency to design and carry out such an assessment? Most countries now have someone who has specific training in assessment. A few have a critical mass of personnel who have had the breadth of exposure to national assessment programs that allows them to oversee the development, administration, and scoring of a large-scale assessment. For many, this will be the first time they have actively participated in assessment development on this scale. Substantial monies may have to be set aside for their training. Some may even be sent away to obtain degrees in the field, thereby delaying implementation for several years. Alternatively, outside experts can be contracted either on a long-term basis or for shorter, but critical, periods of time to both oversee the process and train counterparts. Consultants are an expensive proposition, involving the usual consulting fees and the transportation expenses inherent in bringing in outside experts.

Implementing a national assessment involves more people than just professionals. Implementation may require data entry people for test registration (if applicable) and score reporting; secretaries to coordinate meetings, type manuscripts, and distribute information; clerks to sort, count, and package tests before and after their distribution; and drivers to transport assessments. Each of these people need to be in place and may require specific training before fully implementing an assessment process.

What new facilities and equipment will be required to carry out all stages of the assessment process? Unless the implementing agency has been administering large-scale, high-quality assessments on a regular basis, it will probably need to make some change to its facilities. Some countries may not have a tradition of regular national assessments in place. Others may have done regular assessments on a national scale, but relied on a few, modestly trained experts to develop items on an occasional basis. In either case, the agency will have to upgrade its facilities to implement a national assessment of adequate quality. In many cases, data processing equipment may require a rewired block of rooms or additional security measures. Particularly dusty environments might call for climate control equipment.

Storing assessment booklets and materials before their distribution and after they have been returned can be a major expense. Many assessment environments will need a room with a secure lock and to which access is restricted. Packaging, labeling, and counting instruments may require other types of rooms.

Some of these facilities can be rented or otherwise secured for the needed period. For example, clerks can label, package, and distribute instruments in a school gymnasium or a large conference room. The budget must include transportation and communication costs if the facilities do not provide them.

What is the availability and cost of alternative sources of expertise? At an early point in the decision process, examination planners must decide which activities they will ask the government to do and which ones they will give to a contractor. Governments are not cost minimizers but are rather social or political maximizers. Thus, government may sacrifice cost-efficiency for social or political gains (for an excellent review of the political dimensions of testing see Troman 1989). Ideally assessment planners would make these decisions by weighing costs against benefits. Local or regional assessment organizations may employ professionals who have more experience or training than the government can afford to employ. Because such agencies have a variety of assessment activities to carry out over the course of a year, such agencies can spread the cost of the professionals over many projects. The same logic applies to facilities, equipment, and other personnel.

One alternative considered in Jamaica was having an outside assessment specialist come in during specific phases of the process and either advise or oversee the process. The cost of such a specialist added 11 percent to total test costs, primarily at the development stage. Jamaica was to provide all other materials and personnel. The daily cost of one outside expert was seventeen times the cost of the salary of a local educational specialist. In order to contain costs, the assessment team designed an assessment process that supplemented necessary outside expertise with local personnel.

Building Support

National assessments need the support of the larger community. Building support can mean anything from talking with school and community groups to conducting full-fledged media campaigns. Such support requires, at a minimum, informing people as to why an assessment is taking place and how it will be administered. Support building can get much more complex and, with it, the costing process becomes more involved.

Will specialized materials need to be developed? The mix of people, materials, and coverage required for this will determine the primary costs. Countries where substantial understanding of and support for national assessment already exists need only a simple information packet written by an assessment coordinator and photocopied for limited distribution. Depending upon their knowledge of testing and the technical expertise available to explain results to them, some audiences may need relatively sophisticated media packets. Professionals may have to develop videos, slideshows, television commercials, or posters at high cost. Payment for access to television or radio time is another consideration.

What types of people and training will be required? If proposed materials are relatively straightforward information pieces, existing assessment staff may well be able to develop the materials themselves. If, however, they involve computer shows, posters, videos, and so on, the assessment planning team will need to employ specialists. Such specialists can probably be contracted for a specific job and need not be part of the permanent assessment staff. Borrowing existing personnel from government offices may also be possible.

In addition to the people required to develop the materials, the budget may need to include monies to pay people who will "carry the message." If support building requires particular professionals or community members, they may ask for compensation for their time.

How will people, equipment, and materials be transported? Getting the information out to the target audience may well be the most expensive part of the process of building support. If information needs to get to remote locations, transportation costs may be high (see the discussion on transportation in the section on "Steering Committee").

The Target Population

Rarely will a country choose to assess an entire population of students. Rather, the assessment planning committee will chose specific groups and employ specific sampling processes. This reduces overall costs and allows for some of these saved resources to be used to upgrade overall quality.

What type of stratification will be required? For costing purposes, sampling decisions can be thought of as falling into two categories: breadth and depth.

The first category, breadth, involves making decisions about how many groups one wants to sample. How many grades? How many subjects? How many types of population (urban/rural, minority/majority, dominant language/alternative language)? These are frequently the most costly decisions with regard to sampling because they often have implications for assessment development. For example, if the assessment is meant to cover widely divergent cultural groups, this will require a careful process of review and pretesting.

Specialists may have to translate and back-translate the assessment in various languages if the assessment will include different language groups. Adding a subject means a whole new process in parallel with other subjects: sampling, development, manuals, reviews, and analysis.

The other type of decision involves depth. This concerns decisions about sample size. This is a coverage decision and primarily involves transportation and administration costs.

With decisions involving either breadth or depth, a host of decision factors come into play. The tendency is to focus on printing costs. Printing costs, however, are comparatively small in comparison to other costs such as those of assessment development, distribution, administration, and scoring. At this point carrying out cost estimates of various options is desirable and specialists use this information to inform decisions about sampling. A testing specialist will need to examine each step in the assessment process to see how it would change under various options.

Will everyone receive the same assessment? All students need not take all subtests for their cohort. Having each student take a selection of subtests rather than the entire battery may be wise when assessing many subject areas. This reduces the time students need sit for the assessment, but still permits simultaneous assessment of a number of subjects. There is an implicit tradeoff here. The sample must be enlarged if everyone will not take every subtest. Possibly this involves just adding additional students to the testing room—not a major cost factor. It may, however, require adding additional assessment sites and administrators. At any rate, the additional packing, sorting, and distributing assessments will entail some extra costs.

Assessment of some subjects or subtests on a smaller group of students is another possibility. This may be cost-efficient when the scoring process is expensive and necessitates minimizing the number of scored instruments. Given the reliability problems of many handscored assessments (such as essay examinations), a tradeoff will exist between the reliability of scores and costs. This is a case where planners and psychometricians need to work together closely to find a good balance between costs and benefits.

Relative to the total cost of an assessment, adding test takers can result in relatively small additional costs. In the case of Jamaica, the cost of the test was estimated for either 10,000 or 20,000 test takers (table 6-2).

Table 6-2. Cost Comparison of Varying Sample Sizes, Jamaica 1992

Activity	10,000 test takers		20,000 test takers	
	US$	Percentage of total	US$	Percentage of total
Test development	49,460	38	49,460	25
Registration	10,212	8	16,716	9
Production and administration	29,734	22	56,116	28
Scoring and reporting	42,930	32	73,959	38
Total	132,336		196,251	

Source: Ilon and Harris 1992.

Doubling the sample size increased costs about 48 percent. The primary costs were for production and administration, which increased nearly 90 percent, while scoring and reporting costs increased some 72 percent. The main factor contributing to additional production and administration costs was the additional costs of people's time, which accounted for some 70 percent of the added costs in this category. The costs of additional materials, supplies, and test booklets accounted for only 20 percent of the additional production and administration costs.

Instrument Content and Construction

The content is closely linked to the construction of an assessment in terms of costs. Essentially, the choice of content determines the cost of construction. For that matter, costs inherent in scoring various types of items also informed the choice. Thus, a careful weighing of various options should entail cost estimates of both construction and scoring.

The amount of time the education specialists need either to develop or score the tests determines the primary cost difference. Sometimes this can be a relatively even tradeoff. Table 6-3 shows the amount of specialists' time needed for performance and objectives tests in Jamaica. Clearly the tradeoffs were pretty even.

Table 6-3. Comparison of Professionals' Time Required for Objective and Performance Tests, Jamaica 1992 (number of days)

Category	Development	Scoring and analysis	Total
Test of objective items	227	80	307
Test of written performance	30	227	257

In the case of Jamaica, written performance tests were cheaper than objective tests. The case is not clear-cut for other countries, however. Differentiating between fixed and variable costs is critical when comparing the costs of different item types. Development costs are fixed for any given administration. If more people take the test, only scoring costs increase. For the Jamaican test, the per student cost of professionals, time for scoring and analysis was about US$0.48 for written performance tests, but only about US$0.17 for objective tests. Thus, the larger the sample size, the more likely that performance tests will be more expensive than objective tests. Using a framework for costing the process is the only way to sort through these options.

What types of items will need to be constructed? The cost of various types of items involves estimating both their construction costs and their scoring costs. The following paragraphs discuss item types covered in chapter 5:

- **Written performance assessments.** Specialists will usually need to handscore these types of items. Thus, the type of scoring process and the level of scoring expertise needed establishes the major cost differences between item types. (Jesson, Mayston, and Smith 1987 discuss a new technique aimed at getting effectiveness information from performance assessments. They contend that this ability to extract rather more precise indicators from performance tests makes them more cost-effective.) In some cases, item scoring can proceed in a fairly objective manner: a trained paraprofessional can determine whether the answer contains various predefined components or whether a solution to a math problem has been accurately calculated. Only one person need look at a given assessment, and the scoring process might be relatively quick. These are minimum cost performance items.

  By contrast, some types of performance items are extremely expensive to score. In some cases, a reliable score derives from a very specific setting. This may require groups of scorers working together, where each assessment gets at least two independent scores, where a process integrates reliability checks, and where substantial clerical help is available for ongoing monitoring and calculating.

Furthermore, these group scoring sessions often need an extra half day involving the scoring of sample answers, which the group discusses and arrives at a common standard. These types of scoring procedures require travel, accommodation, meeting rooms, and payment compensation.

- **Nonwritten performance assessments.** Written forms are not appropriate for assessing many types of competencies. Such competencies involve some type of specific student action or input. In the case of specific types of nonwritten inputs, the development cost of the specific media largely determine costs. Students record their responses after listening to a tape, watching a video, observing a demonstration, or viewing a particular scene. In such cases, the budget must include the development costs of this type of medium. In addition, the budget must include the costs of transporting and on-site securing of special equipment. Such media may also require spare parts and on-the-spot repairs. Some of these assessments may require raw materials such as those in some vocational or technical fields.

Nonwritten responses require a different set of scoring costs than written responses. When students need to demonstrate their abilities in front of a professional assessor (say, in the example of music or acting mastery or ability to handle specific human interactions), the assessment of each student requires the presence of at least one, and often two or three, professionals who assess on the spot. These are the most expensive types of items to score (a) because such assessment requires the presence of professionals and, (b) because individual assessment takes a necessary block of time for each student. The cost of such professionals parallels the discussion of professional time in the "Steering Committee" section. Their time, transportation, and accommodation may all be expenses. Furthermore, a clerk may need to schedule the sessions, ensure that all equipment and materials are in place, secure a testing site, and arrange for the professionals' participation.

- **Multiple choice and objective assessments.** These types of assessments require a substantial investment in the development phase but their scoring is relatively inexpensive. Multiple choice tests require developing a substantial number of items, initially perhaps four times as many as in the final instrument. Through a process of pretesting and review, specialists may discard or modify many items. The modified items need another round of pretesting. Thus initial development costs are quite high. A cost-effective way to proceed is to develop an item bank for storage of additional items for use in future instruments.

Scoring, however, can be fairly straightforward. The use of scoring keys, templates, or computer scanning equipment can facilitate item hand or machine scoring. Each student's score takes little time to obtain and the results can be very reliable. When sample sizes are large, multiple choice and objective tests are the least expensive of the various test types.

- **Practical assessment.** Some countries incorporate work done outside the assessment setting in the assessment process. Samples of school work are the most common types of work assessed. This incurs few administrative or scoring costs, because students do most of this work during classroom time and a classroom teacher does the supervision. Securing reliable scores is the major cost. Specialists may need to train teachers in the specifics of the assessment and how they should administer such assignments. Teachers may need guidance and monitoring to assure that they have not given their students any special assistance. Teachers may be tempted to positively influence student responses when they think assessment results will be used to judge the quality of their teaching. Educating teachers about the uses of the assessment, being very specific about the type of help they may give students, and monitoring output from specific sites can improve reliability, but all at a given cost. Training costs and payments to professionals for monitoring will be a factor in the final cost.

How will professionals be compensated? Nearly all the types of assessments discussed in the preceding paragraphs require professional involvement in either their development or their scoring, or both. In many cases, the assessment planning team needs to incorporate teachers into the process. In other cases, the examination coordinator employs independent professionals such as university professors and curriculum specialists. The assessment planning team should give some thought as to how these people will be compensated for their time. Will the employers consider the work as part of normal duties? Will an honorarium be enough compensation, or will participants require professional rates? In addition, development and scoring frequently involve group work where people meet collectively, often over the course of several days. The assessment budget needs to include an estimate of transportation, hotel, and food costs.

What types of facilities will be needed? Often, groups can use readily available facilities, such as an office conference room or an auditorium. In other cases, the group must use rental rooms at a hotel or convention site. Sometimes the group needs special equipment: overhead projectors, computers, photocopiers, or computer viewing equipment. The budget should include their purchase or rental and transport costs.

Manuals

All assessments will require instructions for test administration. Even with trained administrators, instructions should reinforce a uniform assessment process. Thus, the minimum assessment manual is a simple set of typed and photocopied instructions. At the other end of the spectrum is a range of technical, results, and administrative manuals, all professionally typeset, designed and printed on high quality paper in bound form.

What types of documentation needs to be compiled into manuals? This is clearly an area where costs can be minimized if necessary. Although the minimal requirement for a set of administrative instructions needs careful development, this can generally be done by one or two professionals and typed by a secretary. The budget may exclude such costs where the staff involved are small or are already on the payroll.

Technical manuals and manuals that accompany results are sometimes optional. In the case of a technical manual, documenting the process and results, making a few copies, and filing them in a secure location for access by those who need to have the information may suffice. Because documentation should be part of the entire process, developing a technical manual that essentially exists only in file form can be relatively cheap. It will be tempting to underestimate the clerical time needed to assure well labeled, documented, easily accessed, and referenced files.

Costs can vary substantially where the planning committee anticipates development of more detailed and widely distributed manuals. If the planning committee anticipates wide access and distribution, it will pay to have the manuals written so that they are not only technically correct, but so that a moderately educated audience can easily understand them. Thus, manual development will involve not only the work of assessment specialists who know the technical aspects of the work, but of editors and graphic artists who can work with the assessment specialists to help make materials more readable.

Printing costs typically involve decisions about paper quality, numbers of printed manuals, use of color, binding, and packaging. Asking the printer about the costs of various options is a good way to start.

How will they be distributed? If the manual consists of administration instructions, clerks can package manuals with instruments, thus incurring few additional costs. In the case of technical manuals, distribution should coincide with the distribution of the results, which again involves few additional costs. The assessment planning committee should give specific attention to the distribution of technical manuals. Who will receive such manuals? District education offices? Universities and colleges? Particular professionals? School principals?

Distribution costs can very substantially. Some countries may have enough computers and computer literate professionals that simply distributing a diskette of technical or results specifications is adequate. In most cases, a specialist will need to design a printed copy. In either case, the assessment planning committee must plan for its distribution. Will manuals be mailed? Can they go with other types of mail? Some countries rely on inexpensive couriers to get their internal mail to its destination.

Review Process

The process of reviewing items before they are put in the final instrument is a crucial step in assuring a quality assessment. Since the quality of this process is largely hidden in the final instrument, it is tempting to cut cost corners here where they seemingly go unnoticed. To avoid this temptation, the testing expert needs to keep the assessment planning committee constantly informed about the consequences of proposed cost-cutting modification.

Who will conduct the review? The main cost in the review process is people. A computer cannot be used to scrutinize some types of items. The input from professionals can be extensive at this stage. The review process requires expertise. The main cost is professionals' time, although data processing will incur some costs and (depending upon how extensive it is) costs could be high for pretesting. Often, more than one professional at a time is involved. Thus, the budget may have to include the costs of scheduling, transportation, and hotel accommodation.

The implementing agency can partially or completely contract this process to outside experts because particular expertise is required at this stage. The process might involve extensive telephone or electronic communication and minimal travel if all parties have access to such equipment and are comfortable with using it for this purpose.

Thus, the final costs will involve all the variables discussed in the "Steering Committee" section. What process will be employed? The review process may well entail pretesting the instrument(s). If testing experts expect substantial variation between and among groups—urban/rural dwellers, ethnic groups, male/female students, or geographically defined groups—the pretesting might be fairly costly. Essentially, it could amount to a smaller version of the larger assessment development and administration. By contrast, where testing experts expect fairly homogenous groups or where assessment of all groups can occur within a small area, pretesting can be more informal than the regular assessment and much less expensive. For example, regularly employed assessment personnel can do the actual assessment, thereby eliminating the need for training and preparing teachers; actual assessment sites can be kept to a minimum, so sorting, numbering, and bundling instruments becomes a simple process; existing clerks can input results without much chance of mixing up the instruments.

After the pretesting and coding, the same software to be used to analyze the final assessment is also used to analyze the pretest. Computer time and some materials are costly at this stage, although experts' time is the largest expense.

Administration

Administration of the instrument involves a number of steps before students are involved. Many of these steps are costly but necessary. The planning committee should make sure that the economist is fully aware of all the steps and ingredients needed to complete this step.

How will instruments be sorted, counted, numbered, and labeled? A critical step in the assessment process, and one that is rarely adequately costed, is the complex process of sorting, counting, numbering, labeling, and boxing instruments. Given that most national assessments will not assess all students at all levels, careful labeling of instruments is a necessity, otherwise the necessary weighting and reporting cannot be conducted and the assessment becomes virtually useless. For this process, at least one assessment specialist must spend some time organizing and listing the types of materials that need to go to each assessment site. At a minimum, this requires a careful list of all the assessment sites and some notion of the contents of a standard package. Much of the cost in time of this process is a function of the variety of tests and subtests and the number of assessment sites. Presumably, the person doing this work will be a central education office staff member, although contracted distribution is a possibility as long as instrument security is assured.

Many countries now have sophisticated computer equipment and trained computer specialists on staff and can integrate data processing techniques into this process by putting the required information into a database. The computer can then generate the necessary lists and labels. Data entry will take some time and information must be carefully checked. Furthermore, a computer specialist will have to design the input screens and output. This process requires a combination of clerical and professional time. Reduced errors; easy manipulation of information; and an efficient means of processing incoming, completed instruments are among the possible benefits. A good computer specialist should be able to produce the necessary forms in about two to three days. Data entry time depends on the variety of instruments and the number of assessment sites. Low-level personal computers are sufficient for this task.

Along with the time needed to sort and organize testing materials, packaging materials for bundling instruments and instructions must be included in the budget. In some cases, simple paper wrappers may be adequate. In other cases supervisors must order shrink wrap, sealable boxes, or envelopes. The quality and quantity of these materials depend largely on the number of assessment sites and the need for security, and the type of transportation used to transport instruments to the sites.

Who will print the instruments? What are the specifications? Many factors affect printing costs. Often, answer sheets or instruments require special types of paper or special types of forms, such as bubble sheets (specially designed sheets of paper where answers are marked in printed circles or bubbles, and later scanned for entry into a computer database). These must meet particular specifications and frequently cannot be printed on local stock. Imported paper can be expensive.

In addition, one needs to consider whether students can use test booklets more than once. Sometimes students in subsequent years reused an instrument if security was adequate during previous uses. In this case, budgets must allot for clerical time needed to cull defaced used booklets. Assuming that students do not use test booklets as answer sheets and assuming that answer sheets will not be read by a scanner, they can often be printed on relatively inexpensive paper.

Security will be a major concern at the printing stage, and the agency in charge will need to consider the costs involved in having guards monitor the process. Just watching the doors may not be enough. One country found that duplicate copies of the instrument were being printed on the inside of a printer's T-shirt for later sale. Thus, monitoring of the printing process is imperative and involves at least one extra salary during the entire process.

Examination administrators need to take all these factors into consideration before deciding who will print the instruments. Government printers may appear to be the cheapest, but they may not be the most cost-effective when security, timeliness, and quality are factored into the process.

How will they be distributed and returned? Timely distribution and return of instruments may be a critical factor in their validation. Capturing all test takers at a particular time in their school year is critical in instrument validation. Thus, the normal distribution channels for schools may not be appropriate for assessments. Special arrangements will probably have to be made for distributing and returning instruments. A number of factors can figure into the costing here: contracts with vehicle drivers; use of disparate types of transportation such as boats, motorcycles, or even sea planes; existence and reliability of various mail/delivery/messenger services. In all cases, the choice is not just the cost of the distribution, but its efficiency and security.

Who will administer the assessments? In many cases, the implementing agency can employ local teachers to administer the national assessment. Often they can do this during their regular school hours and at their own or neighboring schools at no budgetary cost to the national assessment effort (although a cost in terms of lost teaching time must be considered). In other cases teachers, educational administrators, or local community leaders might be paid a nominal fee to administer the assessments outside the school setting. Another alternative is that specialists may have to go to assessment sites from central locations. Here, in the section on "Steering Committee," both compensation and transportation costs need to be considered.

How much do security costs add to the overall costs of assessment? This question implies that security costs are a discrete item in the assessment budget, but, this is not the case. Good instrument security affects nearly the entire range of assessment processes. Assessment security is thus not a step in the process, but a modification of the process. Security measures and their associates costs must be incorporated into the assessment plan even though a national assessment is usually not a high stakes test.

Costs will vary depending on (a) the level of security needed, and (b) the existing security situation. Because national assessment results are rarely used to decide a particular student's future, if one instrument is leaked, the entire assessment is not necessarily invalidated. Although, the cost involved in weighting and analysis may well increase during the effort to neutralize some invalid results. Nevertheless, any leakage is costly insofar as it may contribute to inaccurate results, which could hinder the interpretation of the results, and may even result in the adoption of unsuitable policies. Reducing the probability of leakage to a very small percentage is possible with reasonable security measures. Reducing this probability to zero may raise costs substantially and in some countries may be virtually impossible to achieve.

As concerns the existing security situation, some countries have a reasonable tradition of privacy and notion of a common good, while others have only haphazard processes for handling private papers and enforcing security. In the latter cases, any assurance of assessment security requires an entire process of providing security education, building security capacity, and devising security procedures. The assessment planning committee needs to undertake a separate study of security processes where they suspect security standards are far below what they will need to be for the national assessment process to go forward. Such a study will require its own budget.

Analysis

The cost of analysis will depend heavily upon the type of items used and the technology employed for scoring and aggregating. High-tech solutions to analysis may be a costly alternative to hand scoring when technicians and replacement parts are of low quality or in short supply. In weighing alternatives, the assessment planning committee needs to consider sustainability of analysis processes. The economist needs to estimate costs under normal, not optimal conditions.

What type of scoring will be needed for objective items? Many testing specialists assume that objective items are cost-effective when it comes to scoring. This widely held notion is only true where the costs of labor are relatively expensive and those of technology are relatively low. Because one cannot assume this situation in many countries, the method of scoring must be carefully considered. Several options are possible.

Some instruments are adequately hand scored and aggregated at the local level. Assuming an adequate level of training and security, local clerks or teachers can score and record assessments. The nature of hand scoring often limits the types of score obtainable at a local level: subscores of particular instruments are generally not available nor are item analysis possible unless each student's response to each item is coded. Thus, while relatively cheap, aggregation at the local level has limited uses.

The next level involves coding or keying in item responses at a district or regional level and forwarding them to a central location. This keeps labor costs low as labor in smaller cities and rural areas is often cheaper than in the main city. Again, assessment planners must weigh cost savings against possible losses in accuracy, monitoring, and security. If cost-cutting measures jeopardize accuracy, the assessment results are useless.

The process can, of course, be undertaken at a central location, and frequently is. Often central locations process objective tests in more sophisticated ways, such as scanning bubble sheets (or test booklets for very young test takers). Examination coordinators must consider carefully the use of such technology before they validate it as cost-effective. At a minimum, two scanning machines must be available in case one breaks down; only well-trained clerks should feed the instruments through the scanners; and computer specialists must construct the interface between the scanner and the software and monitor it to make sure it is doing the job. In addition, magnetic storage (tape backup machines, removable hard drives, or Bernoulli boxes) must be available and kept in peak running order to hold the assessment results.

The annualized cost of using a scanner was US$500 for the 20,000 students in Jamaica. Costs would increase an additional US$146 if, for example, 5 percent of the Jamaican tests required special handling because of damage or improper marking. Thus the total for scanning instruments was US$646. The cost would have been US$2,917 if key punch operators hand keyed the instruments into a computer at the rate of five minutes per instrument (key punch operators were costed at US$14 per day each). For Jamaica, which had the capacity to use and maintain the technology and where transporting tests to a central location was not a problem, scanning tests was clearly the lower cost option for objective tests.

The section on the "Instrument Content and Construction" noted that scoring costs are a major factor in costing various types of items and instruments. That section discussed the link between the type of items used and the compensation costs for professionals involved.

What kinds of analysis will be performed? In the best of circumstances, clerks can scan results into a computer and pre-existing software can produce a variety of analyses as well as reports. In this scenario, computer specialist or psychometrician time requirements are minimal. More likely, quite a bit of additional expertise is still required before results are obtained. An item analysis, for example, may reveal items that performed in strange ways and thus require the time of a computer specialist and psychometrician.

Is the technology appropriate? The appeal of technology converts many an assessment specialist and foreign expert to "true believers." Computers and their peripherals are getting cheaper by the year and can handle many of the more mundane assessment procedures quickly and efficiently. Yet, more than one assessment process has been the victim of inappropriate or ill-considered technology. Equipment that seems fast and efficient in an optimal setting can prove to be a poor investment in the wrong setting. Several rules of thumb can help minimize disasters.

To begin with, analysts should use the simplest machines that will do the job. The fewer parts, and the more common the spare parts, the more likely that the equipment can be repaired locally and be relatively cheap to replace. In many settings, many computer-related personnel may only need low-power terminals. Data entry site management and item response input require little computing power. Only a central computer need have the power for data manipulation. High-speed laser scanners may be less desirable than lower technology scanners that are cheaper and that a local repairperson could fix.

The authorities should stock up on spare parts and contract with someone to fix ailing equipment. All too often, an expensive machine is left to collect dust for years because a simple part is missing or the ministry does not have a process in place for getting such equipment repaired. Such purchases and activities should be explicitly budgeted for when making the original purchase.

If the assessment agency does not employ the appropriate staff, it should contract with someone to be on call for quick hardware, software, or data entry problems. Quick, efficient advice can speed the scoring process substantially.

Reporting

The implementing agency needs to make available several types of information: raw or converted scores, analysis, technical information on assessment processes, validity and reliability, and implications of results. The assessment planning committee must decide which types of information should be made available to whom. Also, they will need to decide the format of this information. Some of the information may require carefully designed mass media formats. The implementing agency might carefully label and file other information and make it available to a select group of people.

How will information be communicated? In a national assessment examination, the scores of individual students or assessment sites are rarely reported (although a hybrid assessment that combines achievement testing with national assessment testing might be employed, in which case scores of individual schools or children may be required). Thus, reporting involves something in the nature of reporting research findings. A kind of research report format generally provides the type of information needed. Other types of reporting might require accompanying reports with technical information on the instrument, sampling, and content.

Many different kinds of reporting may be required: reports to government officials or funding agencies; reports to the press; and reports to schools, professionals, or regional offices. Each of these types of reports will require a specific type of document and will require a different mix of people to put it together.

Clearly costs will vary depending on the content. Two- or three-page photocopied reports cost less than slick, full-color, bound reports. Printing costs, however, may be only a relatively small part of the overall production costs when production costs involve professionals' time.

How important will layout and explanations be? In addition to reporting actual results, most assessment reports have to expend some effort to educate the audience. For example, if results are being reported for various ethnic groups, explaining whether the differences measured were significant is important. Furthermore, many types of measures are technical and need an explanation, possibly with examples. Coordinators may need to employ graphic artists and copyeditors if presentation and ease of reading are required. If issues surrounding the assessment are controversial, a public relations person might construct particularly careful wording.

Who will be informed? Getting information to the right people can be expensive if the intended audience is local community members who have little understanding of standardized instruments. Getting results widely distributed and understood may be a fundamental goal in the case of building support for a national educational reform, for example. This kind of audience will require both transportation for the primary informant, and much of this person's time as he or she first educates, then explains the results to the audience. In a populous or geographically dispersed country, these costs could be substantial as the economist must consider both travel and delivery time. The discussion on "Steering Committee" covers the various types of costs involved in professionals' time and travel.

The audience is, however, much more likely to be relatively small. The intended audience is also likely to have enough of a background in assessment so that a carefully constructed text can adequately clarify anything new. In this case, development of the materials may be the primary cost. Relatively cheap regular mail can often be used.

Conclusion

On the face of it, national assessments do not appear to be a major expenditure item relative to running an entire educational system. A superficial look at such assessments reveals a professionally printed version of quizzes and examinations teachers give to their students all the time. However, the costs of successful assessments are largely hidden, and budgeting for the proper mix of expenditures is critical to its success. Leaving out a particular item may well mean that the results are useless (see Dougherty 1977 for an overview of misallocation issues in education).

This chapter described a set of assessment steps. Combined with a simple framework for costing components, it serves as a general guideline to the costing process. It is useful to keep in mind that costing an assessment is a process rather than a product. When budgets are constrained, costing an assessment system will involve an iterative process. Although costing specialists may well have the costs in hand, they cannot make budgetary decisions or weigh costs against quality of output. These are decisions for planners, assessment specialists, policymakers, community members, and finance experts to decide jointly. Asking the right questions and developing a system that generates quick estimates of various options is the costing specialist's role. Performing the role successfully is a critical step in a successful national assessment system.

References and Bibliography

Coombs, Philip, and Jacques Hallack. 1987. *Cost Analysis in Education: A Tool for Policy and Planning.* Baltimore, Maryland: The Johns Hopkins University Press.

Dougherty, Christopher. 1977. "Measuring the Cost of Misallocation of Investment in Education." *Journal of Human Resources* 12(4): 446–59.

Ilon, Lynn. 1992. "A Framework for Costing Tests in Third World Settings." PHREE/92/65. Washington, D.C.: World Bank.

Ilon, Lynn, and Abigail Harris. 1992. "Economic Analysis of Testing System for Jamaica." Prepared for the World Bank's project on rationalizing testing in Jamaica.

Jesson, David, David Mayston, and Peter Smith. 1987. "Performance Assessment in the Education Sector: Educational and Economic Perspectives." *Oxford Review of Education* 13(3):249–66.

Levin, Henry. 1983. *Cost-Effectiveness: A Primer.* Beverly Hills, California: Sage Publications.

Troman, Geoff. 1989. "Testing Tensions: The Politics of Educational Assessment." *British Educational Research Journal* 15(3): 279–95.

Appendix A: Ingredient Clusters

People
    Educational specialists (external)
    Educational specialists (staff)
    Teachers
    Steering committee members
    Clerical/administrative
    Other skilled labor
    Unskilled labor

Equipment
    Computers
    Typewriters/personal computers
    Scanner
    Adding machines
    Telephones
    Photocopying machine
    Facsimile
    Overhead projectors
    Printing machines
    Light tables

Supplies
    General office
    Test packaging supplies
    Paper

Piece Work
    Print masters
    Test booklets
    Instruction books
    Answer sheets

Professional Materials
    Computer software
    Books
    Reports
    Sample tests

Communication and Transport

    In-country postage/courier
    In-country calls
    International calls
    In-country faxes
    International faxes
    International postage
    In-country shipping
    Vehicles (days)
    International shipping

Conference
    Distance
    Accommodation
    Meeting rooms
    Meals

Per Diem

    Staff
    Consultant

Travel
    International
    Domestic

Appendix B: Modules

Conceptualizing
  People
  Equipment
  Supplies
  Professional materials
  Communication and transport
  Conferences
  Per diem
  Travel

Data Processing
  People
  Equipment
  Supplies
  Professional materials
  Per diem
  Travel

Informing
  People
  Equipment
  Supplies
  Communication and transport
  Conferences
  Per diem
  Travel

Physical Processing
  People
  Equipment
  Supplies
  Communication and transport

Producing
  People
  Equipment
  Supplies
  Piece work
  Communication and transport

7

The Design of Tests for National Assessment Purposes

John Izard

> Educational planners in most countries have generally focused their work on matters concerned with forecasting numbers of students, teachers, and support staff, and predicting the demand for, and location of, the buildings and equipment required by education systems at any one point of time. The majority of this work has usually provided detailed information about various educational inputs, but has provided little or no information about teaching-learning processes or educational outcomes (Somerset and Ekholm 1990, p. 15).

Educational planners have to take account of what happens in schools and classrooms. National planning officials require high quality information about teaching-learning processes and educational outcomes to make broad policy decisions relating past practice and future intentions, to devise plans and assign resources to meet these intentions, to recommend interventions, and to decide on the most effective and efficient intervention where intentions are not being met. Such educational decisions depend upon valid (and therefore reliable) measures to inform those who make the decisions.

One valid approach to gathering evidence is to observe everything that is taught. In most situations this is not possible, because there is so much information to be recorded. Instead, one has to select a valid sample from the achievements of interest. Special tests can be designed by education ministry staff or an external agency to provide some of this hard evidence. The design of such tests for national assessment purposes is the focus of this chapter.

What Is a Test?

A test is a collection of assessment tasks (items) that are chosen to document learning achievement or to describe the ways in which students are learning. Single, discrete items may not be reliable (or consistent) indicators of achievement or process. However, when a number of similar items or tasks are combined as a test, patterns of success on the test

---

In the discussion of test development in this chapter I have made use of material I prepared for the United Nations Educational, Scientific, and Cultural Organization (UNESCO) and for the International Institute for Educational Planning, UNESCO, as a training booklet entitled module *C1: Overview of Test Construction.*

can be investigated. Such patterns tend to be more dependable indicators because they are based on multiple sources of evidence (the various separate assessment tasks). Clearly, the answer for one item should not depend on the answer to another item or this notion of combining independent pieces of evidence would be lost.

As schools are expected to provide their students with the capacity to complete various tasks successfully, one way to assess each student's learning is to give the students a number of these tasks to do under specified conditions. Several varieties of tests are available, each with its own function and purpose. Some tests provide evidence of factual knowledge, some provide evidence of the extent to which a pupil can generalize skills to other contexts, and some provide information about students' capacity to undertake advanced work.

Conventional pencil and paper test items (which may be posed as questions) are examples of these specially selected tasks. However, other tasks may also be necessary for a comprehensive, valid, and meaningful picture of the learning. For example, in learning science subjects educators generally consider practical skills to be important, thus the assessment of science subjects should include some practical tasks. Similarly, students learning music may be required to give a musical performance to demonstrate what they have learned. In this way test items or tasks are samples of intended achievement. Sometimes performance in an actual real-life context is assessed.

When data from a test are available, the requirements of the various audiences interested in the results differ. This can be illustrated using the matrix of information shown in figure 7-1.

Figure 7-1. Matrix of Student Data on a Twenty-Item Test

Items	Students																	
	1	2	3	4	5	6	7	8	9	10	11	12	13	14	15	16	17	
1	0	1	0	1	1	1	0	1	1	1	1	1	1	1	1	1	1	14
2	0	0	0	0	1	1	1	1	1	1	1	1	1	1	1	1	1	13
3	0	0	1	1	0	1	1	1	1	1	1	1	1	1	1	0	1	13
4	0	0	0	1	1	0	1	1	1	1	1	1	1	1	1	0	0	11
5	1	0	0	0	1	1	1	1	1	1	1	1	0	1	1	1	1	13
6	0	0	0	0	0	0	1	0	1	1	1	1	1	1	1	1	1	10
7	0	0	0	0	0	0	0	0	1	0	1	1	1	1	0	1	1	7
8	0	0	0	1	0	1	1	1	1	1	0	1	1	1	1	1	1	12
9	0	0	0	0	1	0	0	0	1	1	0	0	1	1	1	1	1	8
10	0	1	0	0	0	0	1	0	0	0	0	1	1	1	0	0	1	6
11	0	0	0	0	1	0	0	0	1	0	0	1	1	1	0	1	0	6
12	0	0	0	0	0	0	0	0	0	0	0	1	1	1	1	1	1	6
13	0	0	0	0	0	1	1	0	0	1	1	0	0	0	1	1	1	7
14	0	0	1	0	0	0	1	1	1	1	1	0	1	0	1	1	1	10
15	1	0	1	1	0	0	0	1	1	1	1	1	0	1	1	1	1	12
16	0	0	0	1	0	0	0	1	0	0	1	1	0	1	1	1	1	8
17	0	0	0	0	0	1	0	1	0	1	1	0	1	0	1	1	1	8
18	0	1	1	0	0	1	0	0	0	0	0	0	0	1	0	1	1	6
19	0	0	0	0	0	1	0	1	0	0	1	0	0	0	0	1	0	4
20	0	0	0	0	0	0	0	1	0	1	0	0	0	0	1	1	1	5
	2	3	4	6	6	9	9	12	12	13	13	13	13	15	15	17	17	179

The students and their parents will focus on the total scores at the foot of the columns. High scores will be taken as evidence of high achievement and low scores will be taken as evidence of low achievement. However, in summarizing achievement these scores have lost their meaning in terms of particular strengths and weaknesses. They give no information about which aspects of the curriculum students knew and which they did not understand. Teachers, subject specialists, curriculum planners, and national policy advisors need to focus on the total scores shown to the right of the matrix. These scores show how well the various content areas have been covered. Low scores show substantial gaps in knowledge where the intentions of the curriculum have not been met. High scores show where curriculum intentions have been met (at least for those questions that appeared on the test).

Tests used in national assessments are likely to differ from the usual public examinations. Traditional examinations give every student the same task so that individuals can be compared, for example, by means of the column totals in figure 7-1. As time is limited and the cost of testing large numbers of candidates is high, the number of tasks used has to be relatively small. As the costs of assessment are roughly proportional to the number of cells in the matrix, the number of questions asked in traditional examinations will be limited to contain costs. The resulting matrix will be wide to cater for many students, but not very deep because of the limited number of test items (see figure 7-2).

Figure 7-2. Traditional Examination Data Matrix

Students . . .
Items
.
.
.
.

Information about many important issues cannot be collected because so many students have to be tested. Traditional examination questions are a sample of those assessment tasks that can be given to all students in a convenient format, and they ignore all those assessment tasks that cannot readily be given to all students. By contrast, national assessments, which gather information on a much larger number of topics, will need to limit the number of students to contain costs. The resulting matrix will be narrow, but very deep because of the larger number of test items (see figure 6-3).

Figure 7-3. National Assessment Test Matrix

Students . . .
Items
.
.
.
.
.
.
.
.
.
.
.
.

If the number of questions in a national assessment is large, the testing required may be more than can be expected of typical students. Thus more than one representative sample of students will be needed to collect information on each important issue.

What Features Should National Assessment Tests Have?

National assessment tests should have wide and relevant coverage of the curriculum, should provide information to appropriate audiences in a meaningful format, and should be cost-effective.

Wide and Relevant Coverage

National assessment tests need to be comprehensive in terms of their coverage. They should cover all important aspects of the intended curriculum rather than just a small sample as in the case of traditional examinations. Care is also needed to gather associated information that is important in interpreting the test data. For example, socioeconomic circumstances are known to influence student achievement. In evaluating the contribution of the education system to student learning, investigators must make allowances for such circumstances to obtain a fair measure of the impact of the education system.

By contrast, other variables can be manipulated to produce changes in student achievement, for example, providing in-service training for teachers and improved instructional materials for students can improve achievement. When evidence of changes is reported, it is important to ensure that the effects of variables for which schools can be held accountable are not confused with the effects of variables that schools cannot influence.

Functional Questions

The function of the assessment tasks in a national assessment is to provide meaningful evidence. Pencil and paper test items that only require students to have memorized material are much easier to write, but cannot provide other essential evidence. For example, being able to give the correct answers to number facts such as 6+3=?, 9+5=?, and 7x3=? does not indicate directly whether a student can read a graph or measure the length of a strip of wood. If reading graphs is important, then the assessment tasks should include some tasks involving the reading of graphs. If measuring lengths is important, then length-measuring tasks must be used to decide whether this curriculum objective has been met. Test constructors often draw up a list of topics and types of skills to specify what the test should cover. Such test specifications are essential in national assessments.

The range of complexity of tasks should be at least as wide as the expected range of achievement of the students being assessed if evidence of learning is required about all students. That is, the tests have to include easier tasks as well as more difficult tasks. The easier tasks will allow students to show more of what they have learned. The more difficult tasks will allow the best students to show where they excel.

National assessment tests can be more diverse than national public examinations. National assessment tests can include practical tasks, group work, and more complex performance. For example, in the Australian state of Victoria, open-ended test questions constructed to assess science beliefs were scored in terms of the quality of the scientific thinking shown in the students' responses, whether in sentences or as drawings (Adams, Doig, and Rosier 1991).

A Basis for Useful Inferences

Describing changes in terms of total scores only is counterproductive. The assessment data can only be understood in the context in which they were collected. For example, a score of 59 percent is meaningless without knowing what teaching-learning situations had been provided, how long the educational program had been offered, whether the student had actually been present for all or most of the program, what questions were asked, and what answers were expected.

Numerical or letter grade scores on tests generally relate to relative standing without explicit reference to a particular population. A high score suggests that this person is better than another person, without stating whether the tested group was specially selected or whether the group was representative of all students in the nation. By their nature, national assessments of education are an attempt to describe the current status of the nation with respect to educational development. At basic levels of education, such assessments should refer to the whole of the age group, not just the successes of those currently in school. Reports of national assessments should endeavor to document the proportion of the target group who have met the required levels of proficiency.

Sampling of Content and Process

National planners do not need to know every detail of every individual's school performance. Just as a medical practitioner can take a sample of tissue or body fluids under standard conditions, subject the sample to analyses, and draw inferences about a person's health, a national assessment can take a sample of performance by students under standard conditions, analyze the data, and draw inferences about the health of the education system. If the sample of evidence is not appropriate or representative, the inferences drawn about the current status of learning will be suspect, regardless of how accurately the assessments are made. It is possible to make consistent assessments that are not meaningful in the context of the decisions to be made. For example, the students could be weighed, and the highest scores give to those with the largest mass. This assessment could be very consistent, particularly if the scales were accurate. However, this assessment information is not meaningful when trying to judge whether learning has occurred.

While gathering information about each of the important aspects of the curriculum is possible, asking large numbers of questions for each aspect is generally not possible. The types of questions used for particular aspects of the curriculum should reflect the information needed, as discussed earlier. The number of questions used for each aspect is a function of the precision required. (In general, using more questions gives greater precision, but increases the costs.) As some questions prepared for trial may not be of the quality required for national assessment, test constructors should prepare enough questions for trial so that the most appropriate questions can be selected.

Audiences

The choice of what to assess, the strategies of assessment, and the modes of reporting depend upon the intentions of the curriculum, the importance of different parts of the curriculum, and the audiences needing the information that assessment provides. If education ministry staff are responsible for conducting the assessment, they will be able to marshal resources to see that it happens, but may be distracted by other duties. An external agency will avoid such other duties, but may not transfer essential test development and interpretation skills to the education staff. National assessment audiences may include both those who will be making decisions and those who need to know that such action has been taken.

Those who are taking action will need to know the likely direct and indirect effects of various action options and the costs associated with those options. They will include politicians; high-level advisors; senior administrators; those responsible for implementing the curriculum, assessing the effects of the curriculum, and teacher training (preservice and in-service); and other educational planners. Those taking action need to be able to show that their actions do pay off: politicians have to be able to convince their constituents that the actions taken were wise, and senior administrators need to be able to show that programs have been implemented as intended and to demonstrate the effectiveness of those programs.

The Timing of National Assessments

National assessment tests need to be given more than once so that changes can be identified. For example, to assess the impact of new programs to improve schools, baseline measures of the effectiveness of the teaching provision before the innovation are needed, so that subsequent measures can be used to judge the effectiveness of the innovation.

> It is particularly important for national officials to be sensitive to long-term trends in their education system's capacity to assist all students to make progress towards achieving a high standard of physical, social and cognitive development. In some circumstances these trends will call for intervention in what is seen as an emerging and widespread inability of students to achieve success in a specific part of the curriculum. In other circumstances, the focus will be on the curriculum itself because it may be seen as being in need of revision and restructuring in order to take account of recent research and/or new social and economic conditions (Somerset and Eckholm 1990 p. 18).

Comparability and Validity

Test developers need to take care that the questions used on one national assessment are comparable to those used on another. One way to ensure the comparability of questions is to use the same test with a different (but still representative) sample of students.

On some occasions test constructors may have to choose some different representative tasks because of curriculum changes. These new questions still need to be comparable, even though they may not be the same questions, and this comparability must be demonstrated empirically. Usually this means that both sets of questions are given to another representative sample of students and questions that are apparently similar with respect to content and coverage can be checked to see whether students responded to the questions in a comparable way.

Questions that are comparable will have similar ranges of difficulty, will reflect similar performance by significant subgroups of the population (such as males, females, ethnic minorities, city students and rural students), and will have similar discrimination patterns over the range of achievement. In other words, low achievers will perform similarly on both sets of questions, as will middle level achievers and high achievers.

National or regional examinations are unlikely to help assess changes by comparing data collected at one point in time with data collected after the changes have been implemented. Such examinations fail to collect some of the important information that policymakers need, such as the extent of community resources for education, and generally have different questions on each occasion, making the measurement of change close to impossible. The time constraints and costs of such examinations preclude using more thorough questioning and the use of measures that require a complex task to be carried out under supervision. National examinations cannot show how much teaching skills have improved or the size of improvements resulting from policy changes.

The Costs of Test Development for National Assessments

Writing tasks or items with desirable properties requires a great deal of skill over and above knowledge about the curriculum and about how students learn. A team of item writers can produce a better range of items to consider than an individual. Item writing without the benefit of interaction with colleagues is generally inefficient and tends to be too idiosyncratic, representing only one person's limited view of the topic to be assessed. When that person lacks inspiration the items written may degenerate to a trivial level.

Development of the additional test questions to give comprehensive coverage may cost more initially because the levels of skill needed to write such tests are much higher. Generally teams of item writers are required rather than a limited number of individuals to write all the questions. The pool of experienced teachers with such skills will increase if teachers are encouraged to prepare students for higher quality assessments. Furthermore, item writing skills develop with practice. Such experience of item writing and knowledge about how students think is gained gradually. Many good item writers are experienced classroom teachers who have developed the capacity to construct items that reveal correct or incorrect thought processes.

At the national level, because the information required must relate more to policy issues, national planning, and the resource implications of alternative education plans than to a single individual's ranking, having a good team to devise the key questions for national assessment tests is important. Without an investment in the training of those preparing questions, the expenditure on subsequent data collection may be a waste of valuable resources. Questions on national assessment tests have to be informative and well developed, because planners will be depending on the quality of the information being gathered. Planners also have responsibilities with respect to the questions used in national assessments. They must provide advice on the need to assess both anticipated and unanticipated outcomes of intervention as well as long-term trends.

Which Students Should Take National Assessment Tests?

The students chosen for assessment have to represent all regions and significant population subgroups and all age levels of interest. National assessments that give the same assessment tasks to everyone in the population at once rather than just to a sample waste resources because of the duplication of effort for some tasks, while other tasks are excluded. Representative samples of students will provide an economical way of estimating regional or national performance and allow greater coverage of the curriculum.

Because the students are sampled and not all of them need to answer the same questions, the testing can be limited in time. This has at least two benefits: there is less of an intrusion into the work of the schools involved, and the costs of field trips for those administering the instruments may be lower. Those designing a national assessment can ask a wider range of questions and collect other information that will help interpret the test data, for example, information about the teachers' experience, the availability of family and community resources to support the school, the time students take to travel to school, the extent to which they attend regularly, and their general health can all contribute to understanding the results obtained.

What Purposes Will National Assessment Tests Serve?

Test results are interpreted in many ways. One important way involves comparing each student's score with the scores of a group of students who are supposed to be like that student (norm referenced tests). Such comparisons can tell us how well students scored relative to the reference group, but do not tell us which students are competent in a chosen area or suggest what might be done to improve performance. A second important way of interpreting results involves comparing each student's results with a set of fixed requirements (criterion referenced tests). Such comparisons can tell teachers and administrators the proportion of students in the national assessment sample with acceptable levels of skill and can identify those topics that need extra or different teaching and learning.

Comparing Students

Norm referenced tests provide the results of a reference group on a representative test and test scores are presented in terms of comparisons with the reference group. If the reference group serves as the baseline group and the test is the same one used with the reference group, norm referenced scores can provide evidence of learning improvement or decline for the national assessment sample, although this is in terms of a change in score rather than an indication of what students can now do or not do compared with what they could do before. (A parallel test could be used provided that it had the same test specification and had demonstrated the same psychometric properties.)

If changes in score are reported, for example, a difference in average score, administrators have little evidence about specific strengths and weaknesses. This could result in increased expenditure on the wrong topic, while the real problems are not addressed.

The evidence may also be compromised if teachers know about the actual test ahead of time. They (quite naturally) will emphasize the work assessed in the test and scores may well rise. This rise does not provide evidence of improved performance on the curriculum as a whole by teachers and students. Where the rise is at the expense of studies in other important parts of the curriculum not sampled in this particular test, the effect is to destroy the representative nature of the actual test as a measure of progress in the curriculum.

Use of norm referenced tests also depends on the curriculum remaining static. If curriculum changes are introduced or time allocations are changed, a representative snapshot of the initial curriculum may not be representative of the changed curriculum. Comparisons with the original reference group are then not appropriate.

Norm referenced tests often cover a wide range of complexity. When every student attempts the test, norm referenced tests of relevant skills can be used to provide an order of merit for competitive selection purposes. However, the scores used to determine each candidate's standing provide little information of direct use. Other information is required if one of the objectives is to provide educational planners and curriculum developers with information. Such tests are often prepared with a particular curriculum in mind, or in the case of international studies, cover what the test designers believe that each nation has in common.

Where the test questions are prepared outside the country, it is important for national representatives to check each question against the national curriculum to see whether the curriculum assumed by the test authors matches the actual national curriculum. For example, Australian mathematics syllabuses introduce algebra and geometry in the seventh year of schooling, but some curriculum statements from North America assume that geometry is introduced much later. Furthermore, the balance of items may not match the balance in the national curriculum. If some test items are inappropriate for the national curriculum, then the comparison of scores against the norm referenced group will not be meaningful. Some test agencies will be able to recalculate the tables for meaningful comparison, but this depends on the availability of full data and of staff able to do the recalculation. Few tests provide users with a strategy for making such adjustments for themselves, although some tests prepared using item response modeling (sometimes called item response theory or latent trait theory) do enable qualified and experienced users to estimate new norm tables for a subset of items.

Comparing a Student with a Fixed Requirement

Criterion referenced tests report performance in terms of the skills and knowledge the students of interest have achieved and do not depend explicitly on comparisons with other students. Often a curriculum statement will include all the criteria of importance (rather than rely on a sample as in the case of norm referenced tests). Criterion referenced scores can provide evidence of learning improvement or decline of the student population as an indication of what students can now do or not do compared with what they could do before. This evidence may be reported as proportions of students who have achieved particular skills and is less susceptible to curriculum changes (provided those skills are still required in the changed curriculum).

There is less likelihood of criterion referenced tests being compromised by the actual test becoming known to teachers. If they emphasize the work assessed by each test (rather than particular items being used for a test) they will have covered important objectives of the curriculum. A rise in the proportion of successful students will provide evidence of improved performance on the curriculum as a whole by teachers and students (provided that the rise was not achieved by excluding students on the basis of school performance or by being more selective in enrolling students).

Mastery tests are generally criterion referenced tests with a relatively high score requirement. Students who meet this high score are said to have mastered the topic on the assumption that the mastery test has sufficient items of high quality to ensure that the score decision is well founded with respect to the domain of interest. For example, in mathematics the domain might be addition of pairs of one-digit numbers where the total does not exceed nine. A mastery test of this domain should have a reasonable sample of all possible combinations of one-digit pairs because mastery implies that all can be added successfully even though all are not tested. A more complex example is the regular testing of airline pilots. Failure to reach mastery will result either in further tuition or withdrawal of the permission to fly.

Terminology

The following paragraphs explain some of the terminology used when discussing tests.

OBJECTIVE TEST AND NONOBJECTIVE TEST. The term objective can have several meanings when describing a test. It can mean that the score key for the test needs a minimum of interpretation to score an item as correct or incorrect. In this sense, an objective test is one that requires task responses that can be scored accurately and fairly from the score key without having any knowledge of the test's content. For example, a multiple choice test can be scored by a machine or by a clerical worker without any expertise in the material being tested.

A less common usage relates to the extent of agreement between experts about the correct answer. If there is less argument about the correct answer, the item is regarded as more objective. However, the choice of which items will appear on a test is subjective in that it depends on the personal preferences and experiences of those constructing the test.

STANDARDIZED TEST. The term standardized also has a number of meanings with respect to testing. It can mean that the test has an agreed format for administration and scoring so that the task is as identical as possible for all candidates, and there is little room for deviation in the scoring of candidates' responses.

Another meaning refers to the way in which the scores on a test are presented. For example, if scores are given as a raw score divided by some measure of dispersion like the standard deviation, the resulting score scale is said to be in terms of standardized scores (sometimes called standard scores).

Finally, the term can refer (loosely) to a published test prepared by standard (or conventional) procedures. The use of standardized tests has become somewhat confused, because published tests often present scores interpreted in terms of deviation from the mean or average and have a standard procedure for administering tests and interpreting results.

PRACTICAL TEST. In some senses an essay test is a practical task. The essay item requires a candidate to perform by conveying meaning by writing prose in a particular format. However, the term practical test often goes beyond tasks used in traditional pencil and paper examinations. The term may refer to practical tasks in trade subjects (such as woodwork, metalwork, shipbuilding, and leather craft), in musical and dramatic performance, and in skills such as swimming or gymnastics, or it may refer to the skills required to carry out laboratory or field tasks in science, agriculture, geography, environmental health, or physical education.

What Types of Tasks Should Be Chosen?

The kinds of questions to be used depend upon the age and learning experiences of the students, the achievements to be measured, the extent of the answer required, and the uses to be made of the information collected. The choice of tasks can be influenced by the number of candidates and the time available between the collection of the evidence and presentation of the results.

Tasks Requiring Constructed Responses

Some items require a response to be composed or constructed, whether written, drawn, or spoken. An essay question, for example, "Write three paragraphs tracing the development of national assessments in Asia and identifying the key issues that facilitate such assessments," generally requires the student to compose several written sentences as the response. An oral test may have a similar task, but the candidate responds orally instead of in writing. The task may require production of a diagram, flow chart, or drawing; manipulation of equipment, as in finding the greatest mass using balance scales; or even construction, for example, weaving or building a model.

Some tasks will require students to integrate a number of skills, as in a musical performance, while others will require a practical task, such as measuring the area of a room or making an item of clothing. More extensive tasks such as projects and investigations may require students to prepare a report that identifies the problem and describes the approach to dealing with the problem as well as the results obtained while attempting to solve the problem.

Scoring such prose, oral, drawn, and manipulative responses involves some difficulties. An expert judge is required, because each response requires the judge to determine a score. Judges vary in their expertise; vary in the way they score responses over time because of fatigue, difficulty in making an objective judgment without being influenced by the previous student's response, and so on; and vary in the importance they assign to handwriting, neatness, grammar, and spelling.

One technique to avoid or minimize such problems is to train a team of scorers. Such training often involves a discussion of the key issues that students have to present in their responses. The scorers should then apply what they have learned by scoring the same batch of anonymous real responses to ensure that they can distinguish between high quality, medium quality, and low quality answers and assign marks appropriately. Higher quality answers should get better scores than the medium quality answers, and medium quality answers in turn should get better scores than low quality answers. These results are then compared and discussed. The aim is not for each scorer to get identical results. Rather, the aim is to improve agreement among scorers about the quality of each response. We expect that there should be greater agreement between the scorers where the responses are widely separated in quality. Making more subtle distinctions consistently requires more skill. Members of the scoring team may differ in the importance they place on various aspects of a task, and fairness to all candidates requires consistency of assessment within each aspect. Even when team members agree on the rank ordering of responses, the marks awarded may differ because some team members are lenient while others are stricter. A more subtle difference occurs when some judges see more shades of gray or see fewer such gradations (as in the tendency to award full marks or no marks).

Short answer items may require students to recall knowledge rather than to recognize it. The answers may be something like miniature essays or the oral or drawn equivalent, or may require students to insert a word or phrase. Recognition tasks may require students to identify a key element of a drawing, photograph, diagram, or prose passage, for example, they could be asked to proofread to test spelling or to choose the part of a poster that has a safety message.

Scoring short responses entails some of the same difficulties as scoring more extended responses, but it is generally easier for judges to be consistent, if only because the amount of information to be considered is smaller and likely to be less complex. However, the quality assurance process is still a necessary part of the scoring arrangements for short responses. Tests that have only short responses may neglect the real world's need for extended responses.

Tasks Requiring a Choice

Some items present a task and provide alternative responses. The student's task is to identify the correct response or the best alternative.

Sometimes such tasks require students to match items in one list with items in another list, but these tasks tend to be artificial, and good tasks of this type are difficult to construct. Also, those who succeed in choosing some of the links have their task of choosing the remaining links made easier. Having success on one task influencing success on another separate task is not usually regarded as good practice.

Multiple choice items present some information followed by three or four responses, one of which is correct. The others, called distracters, are unequivocally incorrect, but this should be obvious only to candidates who know that aspect of the work. An extreme case is where students are given only two choices (as in true-false, yes-no, feature absent-feature present).

There are some difficulties with multiple choice items. For example, students can score without knowing any of the answers. Correcting for guessing does not work (those who are lucky in guessing correct answers do not lose their advantage and those who are unlucky in their guessing do not get any compensation) and increases the markers' work. It also provides an opportunity for calculation errors that reduce the accuracy of the scores.

The likelihood of getting high scores without knowing the answer is greater if only two choices are provided. This, combined with the difficulty of constructing pairs of plausible choices and the fact that correction for guessing does not work, makes the use of two-choice items unwise. However, a well-constructed test with an adequate number of items, each with three to five distracters, makes the probability of achieving a high score by random guessing very small. If all the students answer all the items in a test, then applying a correction formula does not alter their rank order. In the educational context, most (if not all) tests should allow enough time for most students to attempt most items to permit gathering an adequate sample of performance.

Is One Type of Question Better than Another?

One important advantage of multiple choice items is that the scoring is consistent from marker to marker, is relatively rapid, and can be done by machine or by clerical staff. By contrast, performance tasks such as essay items require markers skilled in assessing them and in the appropriate topic, take longer, and are less likely to be marked consistently.

However, the critical issue is the skills and knowledge assessed in relation to curricular objectives. Having items of both types in the national assessment (perhaps administered in separate sessions) may be appropriate. It may also be necessary to combine these assessment results with other evidence from assessment of more complex practical tasks, particularly when assessing vocational and technical competence.

The Test Construction Steps

Before deciding to construct a test, one needs to know what information is required, how quickly it is needed, and the likely actions that are to be taken based on the test's results. The crucial question is: "What information do we need about student achievement?" A second important question is: "Can we afford the resources needed to gather this information?" These resources include the costs involved in developing a test specification, constructing and analyzing the test, using teachers for trials, providing the paper on which the test (and answer sheet if appropriate) is to be reproduced, producing copies of the test materials and the instructions for administering them, distributing test packages to schools in the sample and retrieving them, and scoring and analyzing the results.

Content Analysis and Test Blueprint

A content analysis summarizes the intentions of the curriculum in content terms. What content is the curriculum supposed to cover? Does this content have particularly significant sections? Which content areas should a representative national assessment include?

A test blueprint is a specification of what the national assessment should cover rather than a description of what the curriculum covers. A test blueprint should include the fundamental purpose of the test; the aspects of the curriculum the assessment covers; an indication of which students will take the test; the types of tasks that will be assessed and how they will fit in with other evidence to be collected; the uses to which the information collected will be put; and the conditions under which the test will be given, that is, time, place, who will administer the test, who will score the responses, how the scoring accuracy will be checked, whether students will be able to consult books or use calculators while taking the test, and any precautions that will be taken to ensure that the responses are only the work of the student attempting the test. A comparison of the test blueprint with the curriculum should show that the test is a representative sample of the curriculum's content.

Test blueprints may also include other dimensions. For example, they may indicate the desired balance between factual recall questions and questions that require interpretation or application, or between different item formats (constructed responses versus recognition responses). Test blueprints with several dimensions, such as content and category of skill, place additional constraints on the assessment tasks used to gather evidence of achievement. The number of questions in a cell of the test specification matrix has to reflect the relative importance on both dimensions. For example, a mathematics test with 30 percent computation questions (category of skill) and 20 percent decimal fraction questions (content) requires 6 percent of the questions to be computation with decimal fractions (figure 7-4).

Figure 7-4. Mathematics Test Blueprint Example

CONTENT

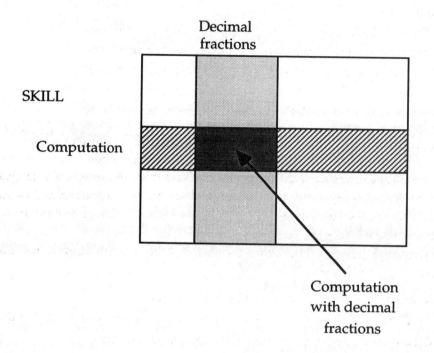

Item Writing

Item writing is the preparation of assessment tasks that will reveal the knowledge and skill of students. Tasks that confuse, that do not engage the students, or that offend them obscure the assessment by either failing to gather the appropriate information or by distracting students from the intended task. Sound assessment tasks will be those that students want to tackle, that are clear about what is required of the students, and that provide information about the students' intellectual capabilities.

Items are needed for each important aspect of the national assessment as reflected in the test specification. Some item writers fall into the trap of measuring what is easy to measure rather than what is important to measure. This enables item writers to meet superficial question quotas, but at the expense of validity.

Item Review by Checking Intended Against Actual

Writing assessment tasks for use in tests requires skill. Sometimes the item seems clear to the person who wrote it, but may not be clear to others. Before trials, a review panel should review assessment tasks and address such questions as those posed below:

- Is the task in each item clear? Will the person attempting an item be likely to know what is expected?
- Are the items expressed in the simplest possible language?
- Is each item a fair item for assessment at this level of education?

- Is the wording appropriate to the level of education for which the item will be used?
- Does the item give unintended clues to the correct answer?
- Is the format reasonably consistent so that students know what is required from item to item?
- Is there a single clearly correct (or best) answer for each item?
- Is the type of item appropriate for the information required?
- Do the items contain any statements that might give offense?
- Do any items reflect bias on racial or other grounds?
- Are the items representative of the behaviors to be assessed?
- Are there enough representative items to provide an adequate sample of the behaviors to be assessed?

This review should ensure that the test avoids tasks that are expressed in language too complex for the idea being tested, redundant words, multiple negatives, and implausible distracters. The review should also identify items with no correct or best answer and items with multiple correct answers.

Those preparing and administering the test will require answers to questions like those below:

- How much time will students have to do the test?
- What time will be set aside to give instructions to those students taking the test?
- Will the final number of items be too large for a single test?
- How will different test versions be assigned to children in the same classroom?
- Will the students be told how the items are to be scored?
- Will the students be told the relative importance of each item?
- Will the students be given advice on how to do their best on the test?
- What test administration information will be given to those who are giving the trial test to students?
- Will the students be told that the results will be returned to them?
- Are the tests to be treated as secure tests (no copies left in the test location)?
- Do students need advice on how to record their responses? If examples are to be used for this purpose, what variations should there be and how many examples will be needed?
- Will the answers be recorded on a separate answer sheet or in a test booklet?
- What information should be requested in addition to the actual responses to the items? (This might include students' names, schools, year levels, sex, age, and so on.)
- Has the layout of the test and answer sheet been arranged for efficient scoring of responses?
- For multiple choice questions have the distracters been arranged in some logical order?

- Have the items been placed in order from easiest to most difficult to encourage candidates to continue through the test? Has the layout of items avoided patterns in the correct answers?

Item Scoring Arrangements

For multiple choice tests, clerical staff or computers can use score keys to score the tests. In the case of constructed responses, test organizers need to decide ahead of time what preparation the scorers need. Should they practice with a sample of papers? Should a second person review each paper without knowledge of the other assessment? If large differences occur in the marking, what should the next step be?

Item Review Using Responses by Students

Following a review of the proposed items, the items should be subjected to empirical trial with students similar to those who will take the actual test to ensure that students understand both the general instructions and individual items.

Empirical trials can identify instances of confused meaning, alternative explanations not already considered by the test constructors, and for multiple choice questions, options that are popular among those lacking knowledge and incorrect options chosen for some reason by able students.

This trial allows the gathering of information about each item: whether it distinguishes knowledgeable students from those lacking knowledge; whether it is of an appropriate difficulty (how many students attempted it and what percentage responded correctly); and in the case of multiple choice items, whether the various options performed as expected. The item trials also provide an opportunity to collect information about how an item performs relative to other items in the same test and to judge the consistency of the whole test.

The observed patterns of success by achievement level help identify questions that distinguish between those who are knowledgeable and those who are not as judged by success on the rest of the test. Questions with patterns like those shown in figure 7-5 and 7-6 are performing as expected. Each group A is more successful than other groups, each group B is more successful than all but group A, and so on. Figures 7-6 and 7-7 show items that are not performing as expected. In figure 7-7 the different achievement groups have similar success rates, and in figure 7-8 the most able groups are the least successful and vice versa.

Several approaches to more sophisticated test analysis are available. Approaches that focus on performance on particular questions are the most useful for national assessments. Implications for the focus of the curriculum and for development of teachers are easier to interpret when each type of task required by the curriculum is considered in turn.

Many test development agencies have used the item response modeling (also known as item response theory or latent trait theory) approach to test analysis (Izard 1992). This approach seeks to separate the qualities of the test questions from the attributes of those answering the questions, and to present both questions and students on the same continuum. Proficiency levels along that continuum can be chosen arbitrarily. The questions that correspond in difficulty to that student achievement range can be used to describe the typical capabilities of students at that level in terms of the skill represented by the assessment tasks. For an example of the practical implementation of such an approach to assessing basic skills in reading, writing, and mathematics see Masters and others (1990).

Figure 7-5. Patterns of Success on Test Item W by Achievement Level

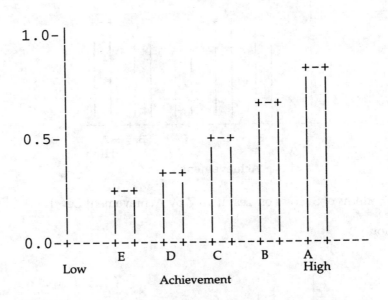

Figure 7-6. Patterns of Success on Test Item X by Achievement Level

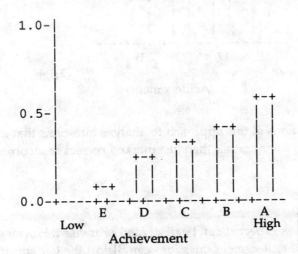

Figure 7-7. Patterns of Success on Test Item Y by Achievement Level

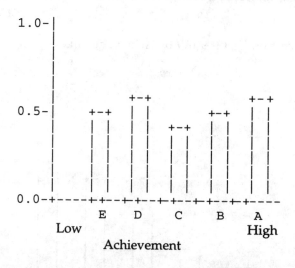

Figure 7-8. Patterns of Success on Test Item Z by Achievement Level

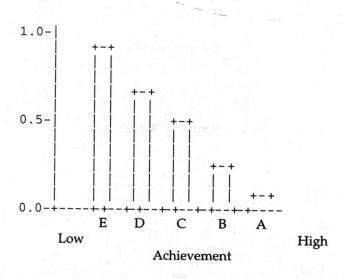

Test analysts use variations of this approach to analyze questions that are marked on a scale (such as 0, 1, 2, and so on) rather than just marked correct or incorrect (see Wright and Masters 1982).

Amending the Test

Items that do not perform as expected can be discarded or revised. However, discarding questions in the absence of replacement questions can distort the test specification. If the original specification represents the best sampling of content, skills, and item formats in the judgment of those preparing and reviewing the test, then omitting some areas will result in a less than adequate test. To avoid this possibility, test constructors may prepare three or four times as many questions as they think they will eventually need.

Assembling the Final Test

After trial, tasks may be rearranged to take account of their difficulty. Tests usually give the easiest questions first, although minor changes may have to be made for layout reasons. Some questions may have minor changes to wording, while others are replaced. The item review procedures described above are repeated.

A Change of Perspective and Developing Expertise

In traditional examinations relatively few simplified tasks are given to a substantial number of students, and scoring is relatively simple and economic. Tasks that most students can complete do not contribute to selecting the best candidate to continue schooling or to enter employment, and therefore selection testing usually ignores such tasks. National assessments address different issues; the selection of individuals is irrelevant. Tasks chosen for national assessments must reflect what is required of the education system. The total score is less important than documenting which aspects are in accord with expectations, which have been partly achieved, and which need additional resources and changed strategies to reach expectations.

Although some teachers and educational administrators will find adjusting to this different perspective difficult, such a change in focus is an essential first step in developing a test specification for a national assessment. A second step is to recognize that assessing improvement in an education system requires comparable measures on at least two different occasions. Such measures can describe the knowledge and skills of one age cohort (not just those at particular schools) and a similar group at a later time. Expert advice on sampling students will be needed to ensure that each sample is representative (see, for example, Ross 1993).

Many teachers have some skills in preparing assessment tasks, but receive little feedback on which tasks are valid and useful. Those preparing questions for national examinations may receive some feedback on the quality of the assessment tasks they have prepared, but only if the examining authority conducts the appropriate analyses. Without such quality feedback the skill level remains low. Expertise in developing non-pencil and paper assessment tasks is an even more scarce resource.

Developing test construction skills requires an expertise sharing approach so that the test construction skills of the trainer are transferred to those involved in national assessment. The team writing the questions has to be aware of students' responses to those questions and must discuss the subsequent analysis of trial data. Test preparers must develop the expertise to understand what was intended and what actually happened in practice. As the team gains experience in developing and administering tests and interpreting the responses, they should require less help from external trainers and can spend more time developing novice test constructors.

Those preparing assessment tasks for national assessment purposes require information about the actual performance of the questions under trial in a succinct and readily understandable format. Experts in test analysis usually require postgraduate studies and supervised practical experience. Some countries arrange for key assessment staff to be attached to testing agencies to gain this practical expertise. Established testing agencies adopt a similar process to maintain and enhance the skills of their own staff and encourage active participation in professional meetings relating to assessment, for example, the annual conferences of the International Association for Educational Assessment, and in educational research.

A View of Testing for National Assessments

This chapter asserted that assessment of student learning provides information on which to base decisions about education. This information should help policymakers and others to evaluate teaching programs, make statements about student competence, or make policy decisions about the development of teaching expertise. Clearly, the quality of the information gathered is critical for making sensible policy decisions.

To improve the quality of the information, the tasks chosen should not be limited to the usual pencil and paper tasks used in national examinations. The use of carefully selected, relatively small samples of students provides an opportunity to gather a wider range of evidence than is usual in selection testing. Remember that information about what has been achieved is required as well as about what needs to be achieved.

The procedures for test construction described in this chapter have been developed over many years. Some of the advice has come from research and some has been derived from the practical experiences of many research and development staff working at various agencies around the world. Improving the quality of the information gathered is not an easy task, and reading a book about the procedures will not suffice. Improving one's skills as a test constructor will require working as a test constructor in concert with others and analyzing results with the help of those experienced in developing tests and interpreting test data.

References

Adams, R. J., B. A. Doig, and M. J. Rosier. 1991. *Science Learning in Victorian Schools: 1990*. ACER Research Monograph No. 41. Hawthorn, Victoria: Australian Council for Educational Research.

Izard, J. 1992. *Assessing Learning Achievement*. Educational Studies and Documents No. 60. Paris, France: United Nations Educational, Scientific, and Cultural Organization.

Masters, G. N., J. Lokan, B. Doig, S. T. Khoo, J. Lindsey, L. Robinson, and S. Zammit. 1990. *Profiles of Learning: The Basic Skills Testing Program in New South Wales, 1989*. Hawthorn, Victoria: Australian Council for Educational Research.

Ross, K. N. 1993. *Sample Design for International Studies of Educational Achievement*. International Institute for Educational Planning Annual Training Programme Module on Monitoring and Evaluating Educational Outcomes. Paris, France: UNESCO.

Somerset, A., and M. Ekholm. 1990. "Different Information Requirements for Different Levels of Decision-Making." In K. N. Ross and L. Mahlck, eds., *Planning the Quality of Education: The Collection and Use of Data for Informed Decision-Making*. Paris, France: UNESCO; Oxford, U.K.: Pergamon.

Wright, B. D., and G. N. Masters. 1982. *Rating Scale Analysis*. Chicago, Illinois: Mesa Press.

Part III: Cases

8

National Assessment in Chile

Erika Himmel

In Chile, assessing the performance of the education system became necessary once the system had reached the stage of providing equal access to education, but people had begun to question the equity of the service offered. In addition to providing education for everyone, all children in the system must receive an equal education in terms of quality. The authorities can determine whether or not this is the case by means of national assessment programs.

The aim of this chapter is to analyze the *Programa Nacional de Medición de la Calidad de la Educación Basica Chilena* (National Program for Quality Assessment of Basic Chilean Education), known as SIMCE, and to discuss its historical and political background and its achievements and shortcomings. Before turning to the SIMCE, however, one must first understand the *Programa de Evaluación del Rendimiento Escolar* (School Performance Assessment Program) (PER), introduced during the period 1981–84, because without this program implementing the SIMCE would have been much more difficult.

General Features of the Chilean Education System

Chile's formal education system has some 3.2 million students enrolled at the preschool, elementary, secondary, and tertiary levels in some 10,000 schools with about 100,000 teachers. Annual state expenditures on education currently run at around US$900 million. Determining private expenditures on education is difficult, but estimates indicate that they come to some US$160 million per year for 200,000 students. About 58 percent of students in preschool and elementary school attend public schools, while another 32 percent go to schools subsidized by the state but privately managed. Thus the state pays for the education of 90 percent of children.

Coverage in primary education is 95 percent and in secondary education is 75 percent. All schools, public and private, have been exposed to the PER and the SIMCE. Curricula for primary and secondary education are the same across the country by law and are governed by a large number of administrative regulations. Only a small proportion of schools, most of them private, have been exempted from the national curriculum.

Historical Background

SIMCE was implemented in 1988. Before describing it, some background on policy developments and the introduction of PER will be provided.

Decentralization Policy

Chile began designing a decentralization policy in the 1970s, which started in 1981 with the division of the country into thirteen administrative regions. Prior to decentralization the Ministry of Education managed most schools, which placed a heavy burden on the ministry. Even the most insignificant problems, such as temporary replacement of a teacher, had to be taken care of at the central level.

A relatively influential group of professionals and academics drew attention to this problem, and also pointed to the general inefficiency of the education system and the poor quality of the education provided despite the considerable expenditure on education. The group argued that the central bureaucracy was but a means of perpetuating inefficiency. Some members of the group even suggested that management of the education system should be based on the law of the market. Parents could be given a subsidy in the form of a voucher that they could exchange for education for their children at whatever school best met their needs and interests (see Friedman 1979).

Under decentralization the Ministry of Education would maintain its supervisory and regulatory functions. As originally conceived, decentralization incorporated the following measures:

- Creating regional education secretariats that operated as local education authorities;
- Transferring a high percentage of the public schools to the authority of municipalities (a process that was supposed to be completed by 1985);
- Providing the municipalities with state subsidies based on average monthly student attendance and not with a fixed yearly amount as had been done in the past;
- Creating a national system of school supervision whose functions were mainly technical and pedagogical;
- Reducing the number of central administrative staff;
- Reformulating curricula and making them more flexible so that they could be adjusted to reflect local conditions;
- Promoting the foundation of privately managed schools subsidized by the state.

The deadlines for implementing these actions were not met because of the recession of 1982, and decentralization was not completed until 1988, by which time economic conditions had improved.

The Origins of the PER

In 1978 the Ministry of Education asked the Pontificia Universidad Católica de Chile to design and implement an information system for education. The university appointed an interdisciplinary team of academics to perform this work, but given the vagueness of the request the work took longer than expected, and finally turned out to be a proposal to study the major variables that affected student achievement. By the time the study had been completed the leadership of the Ministry of Education had changed and the minister's new advisors suggested that what was needed was a system to assess the quality of education. The results could be given to parents so that they could exercise their right to demand better education for their children. This would shift the use of information from the managers of education to the consumers.

This change in emphasis demanded a reformulation of the study. The final result was a technical and financial feasibility study for implementing the PER. The study gave the Ministry of Education a number of options to chose from, and suggested that initially the PER be applied to grades 4 and 8. The Ministry of Education and the university signed an agreement whereby the university was responsible for implementing the entire assessment program.

Variables Affecting Student Achievement

From its inception, one of the PER's major concerns was to try and understand the factors that determined the achievement of the minimum learning objectives, because the authorities considered that understanding these factors was vital for designing programs. The PER was constantly amended based on two years of pilot studies, three years of implementation, a review of both foreign and Chilean literature on the subject, and various research projects conducted by the university team (Himmel, Majluf, and Maltes 1980; Himmel and others 1982; Himmel and others 1984; Himmel Maltes and Larraín 1985; PER 1980). Table 8-1 summarizes the explanatory variables of student achievement that the team identified.

The variables that affect school performance can be measured at five different levels—students and their homes, teachers and the classroom, principals and the school, the local community, and the national environment—and can be classified according to whether or not they can be changed in the short term.

The variables that can be changed in the short term are those that depend on the decisions of those involved in the education process, especially teachers and principals. Variables that are more difficult to change are those that fall in the category of structural social conditions that cannot be altered in the short term, such as students' socioeconomic backgrounds. At the time the university team conducted the studies the hierarchical linear models that permit isolating the impact of the different levels of variables (Burstein 1980; Raudenbush 1988) had not yet been developed. Thus the team estimated the variables' impact on school performance by means of multiple linear models using variable aggregation by school.

The concept of the alterability of the variables played a fundamental role in the design of both the PER and the SIMCE in connection with dividing schools according to the socioeconomic level of the population they served. The team considered this an important variable, because its research had revealed that school performance was strongly correlated with socioeconomic differences. The socioeconomic criteria on which the schools were divided have remained basically the same since the PER and the SIMCE were originally developed. The team hypothesized that differences between schools at the same socioeconomic level basically depended on variables that the schools could control (Himmel, Majluf, and Maltes 1980; Himmel and others 1982). This hypothesis was central to the final report and the data dissemination strategy.

Table 8-1. Explanatory Variables of Student Achievement

Level	Alterable variables of student achievement (modifiable in the short term)	Structural variables (non modifiable in the short term)
Level I Student and home variables	Student learning abilities; willingness to learn. Parent interest and participation in their children's education; educational expectations for their children.	Student background, school history; socioeconomic level.
Level II Teacher and classroom variables	Teacher abilities; willingness to teach; teachers' expectations on students' capabilities. Teaching process and methodologies; classroom climate.	Teachers' background; socioeconomic level; training; professional development; teaching experience.
Level III Principal and school variables	Principal abilities; administrative, educational and social leadership. Principal expectations on teachers' professional work and students' learning. School educational orientations and objectives; administrative and discipline regulations for teachers and students. Promotion of parents' participation in school activities.	Principal background; socioeconomic level, training, professional development; experience. Availability of resources, infrastructure, and instructional materials.
Level IV Local environment variables		Socioeconomic group being served by school; availability of complementary educational resources in the community.
Level V Institutional variables	Structure and organization of the educational system, educational policies; financing policies.	

The objective of the PER was to assess the achievement of learning objectives at both the student and class level, and results were aggregated at the school, municipality, regional, and national levels for comparison purposes. For a more precise estimation of the performance models, the team used quantitative (correlational) and qualitative (ethnographic) methodologies. The latter were useful for estimating the weights of the process variables.

An Interdisciplinary Approach to Educational Assessment

The interdisciplinary team in charge of carrying out the feasibility study and implementing the PER consisted of professors at the Universidad Católica, most of whom had postgraduate degrees from U.S. universities. Of this group, three were engineers, three were psychologists, three were educators, and one was a sociologist. The engineers were responsible for management, logistics, and informatics, while the psychologists and educators prepared the various measurement instruments and liaised with national educational officials and regional education administration organizations.

This was the first attempt at an interdisciplinary effort in education in Chile. The team's work was considered successful (Himmel, Maltes, and Larraín 1985; Majluf 1988) for the following main reasons:

- The problem, as defined, had both educational and management components. The PER's central feature was technical-educational and accounted for some 10 percent of the program's budget. The remaining 90 percent was allocated to logistical and management costs, including printing and distributing tests, defining operational procedures, managing the regional network, processing the information collected, and printing and distributing the final reports to schools and other users.
- The group's structure was relatively loose. The team set up a coordinating committee and one of the group members acted as general manager.
- The group's members shared operational decisionmaking and responsibilities despite differences in their areas of competence.
- The approach used was scientific. Thus educational research played a central role in the PER's design.
- The team believed it had been assigned a task that was a professional and academic challenge, and one that was likely to have a positive impact on the quality of education in Chile.

Objectives and Characteristics of the PER

The overall objective of the PER was to help improve the quality of education by decentralizing responsibilities. The team expected all those involved in the education process to assume a more active role, especially teachers, school principals, and parents. The underlying assumption was that the data on student achievement of the basic learning objectives might stimulate teachers and principals to use their potential to the full, especially given the reduced constraints once the education system was decentralized. At the same time, the PER would provide policymakers at the higher levels with more objective and reliable data on which to base their decisions.

The PER's specific objectives were as follows:

- To provide explicit information about learning targets, the achievement of which the Ministry of Education regarded as an essential minimum for primary education.

- To supply parents, teachers, and education authorities with information about educational achievements in line with the needs of each group.

- To provide the ministry with the information it needed to perform its new regulatory and supervisory functions. This information would identify those schools that needed more technical and financial assistance; allow the monitoring of schools and local councils; and permit the realignment of the central planning function in regard to the development of curricula, the in-service training of teachers, and the preparation of textbooks and other teaching materials.

The achievement of educational objectives were assessed in grades 4 and 8, grade 4 because this is the end of a subcycle of general basic education where a single teacher teaches all the subjects to a class, and grade 8 because this is the last year of compulsory education. All students were tested in Spanish reading and writing and in arithmetic, as these are considered the basics. For the rest of the assessment—natural and social sciences and personal development—the testing followed a matrix design (see table 8-2).

Table 8-2. Description of the Test Battery

Content	Type of test	Design
Cognitive Domain		
• Spanish	Multiple choice	Full
• Writing	Essay	Full
• Mathematics	Multiple choice	Full
• Natural sciences	Multiple choice	Matrix
• Social sciences	Multiple choice	Matrix
Affective Domain		
• Self-concept	Likert type scale	Matrix
• Attitudes toward school and learning	Likert type scale	Matrix
• Peer and social relations	Likert type scale	Matrix
• Vocational orientation (grade 8 only)	Likert type scale	Matrix
• Values acquisition (grade 8 only)	Likert type scale	Matrix

All the multiple choice tests were progressive, that is, they covered the educational objectives of an entire cycle. Thus, grade 4 tests covered objectives from grades 1 through 4, and grade 8 tests covered objectives from grades 5 through 8. The tests were constructed to conform to strict international standards and included the following stages: preliminary and final selection of learning objectives, item writing and editing, assembly of trial versions, item analysis, selection of final items, assembly of final versions, and estimation of reliability.

The team decided to administer the tests to virtually the entire grade 4 and grade 8 population under the assumption that policymakers would get a better feel for such results than from a sample of the population. Thus, only schools with fewer than five pupils in grade 4 or grade 8 or those in remote locations were excluded. Each year 400,000 students took the test, which represents almost 90 percent of all grade 4 and 8 students.

In line with the team's research, the schools were divided into homogenous groups based on the socioeconomic level of the population they served so as to separate the impact of school variables from the impact of structural variables. These groups of schools were called socioeconomic structures. The team conducted a thorough analysis to ascertain whether to provide data on the students' average socioeconomic indicators by school along with the test results as done in California (Alkin 1981). They concluded, however, that the structures solution was preferable and easier for the users to understand when provided with clear definitions of each socioeconomic structure.

Before the first PER was administered, the concept was explained to local authorities, principals, teachers, and parents by means of presentations and written materials that included examples of the types of questions that students would be asked. Further pre sentations later explained how to interpret the results.

The tests were given at the end of the school year under controlled conditions. An administrative network of 640 people was organized to supervise the process and 12,000 examiners were trained. The tests were protected by strict security measures so that questions would not leak out ahead of time. The results were reported during the first months of the next school year. Different audiences received the results at different levels of aggregation, for example, by class for teachers and by school and grade for principals.

The reports of the results included two major benchmarks besides the results of the class or school: the results obtained by schools within the same socioeconomic structure and those achieved by the country's lowest 5 percent and highest 5 percent of schools. Total results by learning objective were presented graphically, and after the first year the reports also supplied comparative information. The Ministry of Education received ad hoc reports on schools that urgently required technical and financial support, and teachers of the grades assessed received pedagogical orientation manuals covering the learning objectives in which students were the weakest. Finally, based on the PER's finding the team submitted a set of suggestions to the ministry for purposes of school certification, inspection, and supervision.

During subsequent PERs the team introduced a number of innovations that they always tested empirically before applying, particularly when they contradicted the views of the educational establishment. For example, teacher surveys showed that teachers believed that answer sheets could not be used with fourth graders. The team tried out answer sheets on a sample of fourth graders from low socioeconomic backgrounds and found that the differences between the answers of those children that used answer sheets and those that answered directly on the test booklet were insignificant.

The End of the PER

Even though during the three years the PER was administered it was unable to show a substantial improvement in educational achievement, it did point to significant improvements for certain objectives for which initial results were very low, and for which teachers and schools had undertaken remedial actions, for example, word problem solving in arithmetic, which for both grades showed a 10 percent improvement.

An interesting point is that during the period the PER was administered there were six ministers of education, with the consequent changes at the higher levels of ministry staff. At the beginning of 1984, the year in which the agreement with the Pontificia Universidad Católica ended, the sixth minister announced that the PER would be discontinued despite efforts by supporters of the PER at the ministry to change his mind. The reasons for abandoning the PER were never discussed with the team and remain unclear.

One possible reason for terminating the PER was its costs, which amounts to US$5 per student, that is approximately US$2 million per year, which during a recession is a substantial sum. A follow-up study (Himmel and others 1985) revealed that senior ministry officials during that time did not support the program and thought that its costs were excessive.

Another possibility is the existence of almost constant conflict within the ministry among those in favor and those against having the Universidad Católica manage the PER. The political context is probably also relevant. At the time the dominant view was that put forward by a group of economists who favored a social market economy approach, which contrasted with the view of teachers, who supported the *estado docente* (teaching in the hands of the state) approach. Furthermore, during this period the process of administrative decentralization had virtually ground to a standstill.

The team managed to implement the assessment program during the terms of the six different ministers of education, with the concomitant difficulties of explaining its rationale to each new set of officials. Even though the PER was officially discontinued as of 1984, the team gave the same arithmetic and Spanish tests administered in 1984 to a sample of grade 4 students from schools in low socioeconomic structures in 1985 and found a drop in the percentage of objectives achieved from 50 to 40 percent. The team also carried out a follow-up study of the actions taken during the implementation of the PER. This study showed that schools had taken action to improve student learning, including analyzing curricula to establish learning hierarchies, reviewing the evaluation methods teachers used, and introducing new administrative practices.

Factors that Led to the Development of the SIMCE

The decentralization process was completed in 1988 with the transfer of public schools to the municipalities' jurisdiction. The number of personnel in the central administration was also reduced, and a new minister of education was appointed who came from an academic environment and showed interest in the PER. The economy had improved and the political situation suggested that the forthcoming plebiscite would go against the authoritarian government then in power and lead to general elections in 1989. While the government did not concede that it was likely to lose power, it passed a series of laws to ensure that the reforms it had implemented would continue. The government also wanted to demonstrate that it had improved education to justify the budget increases it had granted the education sector that, among other things, had increased the supply of textbooks in state-subsidized primary schools.

During 1986 the Ministry of Education had tried to develop an assessment system similar to the PER, but had failed because of its lack of resources and technical skills. Thus the last data available on student performance dated back to 1984. Education supervisors continued to rely on the results from the 1984 PER, together with statistical data the schools provided on attendance and on repetition, promotion, and dropout rates, and on their own observations during their rare school visits. While the supervision system had some 1,000 supervisors, which averages out to ten schools per supervisor, most of them felt overwhelmed by their administrative duties and other responsibilities. This group was extremely interested in the PER and welcomed any suggestion for reinstating it or for introducing similar innovations.

While a number of staff within the ministry believed that they were sufficiently qualified to develop a program to assess school performance if provided with adequate financial resources, the minister and his advisors were aware that the problem was not one of resources, but one of technical expertise and experience. To gain political support for a national assessment program and reduce its costs, this latter group suggested taking the following steps to reinstate the PER and make it acceptable:

- Change the name of the program to avoid association with the PER. This new system to assess education quality would now be called the *Programa Nacional de Medición de la Calidad de la Educación Basica Chilena.*

- Sign a new three-year agreement with the Universidad Católica. The university would be responsible for the bulk of project execution, but the project team would comprise both university professionals and Ministry of Education staff who would be trained by the academic staff during the project period. In the fourth year project execution would be transferred in its entirety to the ministry and the university staff would provide advisory services only.

- Assess all children in Spanish and arithmetic.

- Assess a 10 percent student sample in natural sciences, history, and geography.

- Assess personal development in addition to academic subjects, assess attitudes of students, parents, and teachers to education, plus some indicators of school efficiency, such as repetition, promotion, and dropout rates.

- Apply the assessment alternately to students in grades 4 and 8.

- Entrust the administration of the test and the appointment of examiners to the ministry. The SIMCE was implemented in mid-1988.

The SIMCE has gained in importance since the democratic government came into power, because education was a priority sector in the government's platform and it has used assessment results to implement programs intended to improve the equity of the education provided.

The Aims of the SIMCE

The aims of the SIMCE are to help the Ministry of Education regulate and supervise the education system, help the regional and provincial authorities with their supervision responsibilities, evaluate the quality of every school, enable comparisons among schools, explain performance differences, assess the results of pedagogic programs, and guide teacher in-service training activities and resource allocation. As noted earlier, the aims of the PER and the SIMCE are basically the same.

Implementation of the SIMCE

While the SIMCE created a type of joint venture between the Ministry of Education and the Pontificia Universidad Católica, the representatives of the two organizations each had some specific functions. The responsibilities of the ministry's representatives included preparing a test to assess the development of the affective domain and surveys to examine students', teachers', and parents' perceptions about the education system; designing the indicators of educational efficiency; organizing a network to administer the assessment instruments and appointing examiners; and disseminating the results according to a strategy prepared by the university's representatives. The responsibilities of the university's team members were to construct the Spanish, arithmetic, natural sciences, history, and geography tests; design all the administrative procedures, including preparing a complete register of schools, printing tests and supporting materials, design the final reports, and ensure quality control of each of these activities; create the computer know-how to process the SIMCE, including designing databases for schools, maintaining computerized control over materials, arranging for data entry and scoring of results, generating and printing reports, and ensuring the appropriate validation procedures were applied; design the SIMCE's dissemination strategy; train the ministry's staff in constructing tests and in administrative and computer procedures; and oversee accounting and financial management.

Organizational Structure

The university representatives submitted a proposal for an organizational structure to execute the project. This proposal was modified somewhat during the project's three stages to accommodate its evolving nature. The three stages were the implementation stage conducted by the university, the transfer of the SIMCE to the ministry, and the management of the SIMCE by the ministry alone. The project reached the final stage in 1993.

Operating a project such as the SIMCE requires having an orderly sequence of tasks, each of which is carried out to meet its deadline. As a process that is repeated every year, the achievement of its objectives depends both on the coordination of its various elements—human and financial resources, equipment, and so on—and on the integration of experience acquired. Coordination of the different elements of the project requires that procedures be defined. The project's tasks and procedures are divided into three basic operational areas: technical, informatics, and administration and logistics.

Technical Area

This area covers all the technical procedures needed to prepare the assessment instruments and analyze the results. It therefore includes developing and improving the assessment procedure. The task of preparing the assessment instruments is divided according to school subjects and test content: Spanish, arithmetic, natural sciences, history, geography, personal development, and perceptions of the education system.

The main responsibilities of those working in this area are as follows:

- Selecting the learning objectives from the curricula;

- Selecting and training item designers and preparing guidelines for the elaboration of items and criteria for their evaluation;
- Setting up committees to evaluate items in accordance with the guidelines and organizing their work;
- Assembling experimental versions of the various tests;
- Selecting the samples of students that will take the trial versions of the tests;
- Analyzing the results of the trial versions of the test instruments;
- Assembling the final versions of tests and estimating their reliability;
- Preparing documents for dissemination, including brochures for teachers and manuals for guiding testing;
- Designing a plan for national dissemination of the results.

Informatics

This area covers all the computer procedures of the assessment, much of it involving the processing of test results in both their trial and final versions. The rest of the work consists of supporting the administrative and logistical tasks. The informatics work must be closely coordinated with the work of the other two areas.

Some of the main activities of the informatics staff are the following:

- Preparing a database for schools, including student numbers and socioeconomic characteristics and their exact geographical location (the Ministry of Education does not as yet have a database that the SIMCE could use);
- Validating the data resulting from scanning and key punching;
- Providing information to support the administrative function, such as the socioeconomic levels of schools and the data needed to select school samples;
- Creating material in support of test logistics, such as labels to identify materials, control lists, and the actual materials;
- Scoring the results;
- Analyzing the results;
- Processing the results for dissemination;
- Producing reports for the different audiences.

Until 1991 three engineers performed the informatics function for the SIMCE. The ministry only managed to put together its own team in 1991, but still did not have the necessary hardware, which it acquired in 1992.

Logistical and Administrative Area

This area covers all the administrative procedures required for smooth operation of the SIMCE, including defining and coordinating financial and material resources so that the other two areas can function and coordinating the activities of the different areas. This task has become more complex since activities devolved to the ministry because of the number of different departments involved.

The major duties of the logistical and administrative staff are as follows:

- Planning activities for all the stages and groups involved in the SIMCE;
- Appointing staff for specific jobs, such as teachers to write test items, committees to evaluate the items, and packers to get the materials ready for shipment;
- Ensuring security for the tests;
- Designing materials and supervising their packing and transportation;
- Contracting for printing, scanning, key punching, and transportation of materials;
- Defining and acquiring support materials required for both trial and final testing.

Staffing

The university assigned five engineers, two education evaluation specialists, one psychologist, and one sociologist to the project's first stage. Most of these staff spent half their time on the project, and most had been involved in the PER. The university also hired two engineers, two education evaluation specialists, and one psychologist from outside the university to work on the project.

The Ministry of Education assigned five teachers with some evaluation experience, three engineers and a secretary to work with the university team. The ministry also hired two secretaries, one store keeper, and one assistant to work on the project.

Later during the implementation additional staff were hired as necessary, and duties were shifted as called for, especially once the university's role was reduced and the ministry began to take over full responsibility for the SIMCE.

The First SIMCE

The first SIMCE will now be described. This took place during 1988.

Measurement Instruments

During its first year of operations, the SIMCE began its activities in the middle of the semester. This prevented the running of trial versions of the assessment instruments. This led to the use of items from the PER for the assessment of academic subjects. For the assessment of self-image and self-esteem the ministry adopted an instrument that a ministry team had validated some years before, and constructed a survey for students, parents, and teachers to collect their opinions of the education system.

Like the PER, all the tests to assess whether or not learning objectives in the cognitive field had been met were progressive. All students took the Spanish and arithmetic tests, which consisted of forty-five questions each. The natural sciences, history, and geography tests were in a matrix design, and each student answered the equivalent of half a test, or sixteen questions for each subject. The reliability of all the tests was equal to or greater than 0.90.

In the writing test students had to describe a sequence of events presented in one of two alternative sets of pictures. All students took the same self-image and self-esteem tests, which consisted of pictures of situations for which the examiner presented a context, and the students had to check the pictures with which they identified. Table 8-3 de-

Table 8-3. Instrument Used in SIMCE, 1988

Content	Type of test	Design	Respondents
Cognitive Domain			
• Spanish	Multiple choice	Full	All grade 4 students
• Writing	Essay	Full	All grade 4 students
• Mathematics	Multiple choice	Full	All grade 4 students
• Natural sciences	Multiple choice	Matrix	10% of grade 4 students
• History and geography	Multiple choice	Matrix	10% of grade 4 students
Affective Domain			
• Self-concept	Multiple choice	Full	All grade 4 students
• Questionnaire	Likert type scale	Full	All grade 4 students
Teachers' questionnaire	Likert type scale	Full	5 teachers per school
Parents' questionnaire	Likert type scale	Full	All grade 4 students' parents

scribed the instruments used in the SIMCE in 1988. The data needed to determine efficiency indicators were obtained at the local administrative level.

Promotion of the SIMCE

As three years had passed since the last assessment exercise, the PER, the authorities launched an intensive promotion campaign before actual testing began. The aim of this campaign was to develop a positive attitude toward the SIMCE among the public, to assure people that the information that would be derived would be credible, and to explain what the results would reveal and how they could improve the education system.

Depending on the audience, the information was presented by means of technical brochures or of videotapes and posters. All the information was designed to present a consistent appearance so that the SIMCE had its own identity. In addition, a television program broadcast across the country explained the SIMCE's purpose. Some of the material was used to train the examiners, for whom a manual was also prepared. The examiners were teachers, but teachers were not allowed to participate in the application of SIMCE tests in their own schools.

Implementation of the SIMCE

The materials for applying the SIMCE were distributed around the country two weeks before the test date. The tests were given during two consecutive days in November, the end of the school year. Almost the entire grade 4 student population took the test, a total of 230,000 pupils in 5,100 schools. All students took the Spanish, writing, mathematics, and self-image tests and the survey assessing perceptions of the education system. Students in 10 percent of the schools took the natural sciences, history, and geography tests.

A total of 8,200 examiners were hired and trained to administer the SIMCE. Returning all the tests to Santiago took fifteen days.

Scoring

After a careful review of all the materials returned from the schools, key punchers entered the information from the answer sheets into computers, while the writing test was scored manually. Thirty-four teachers of Spanish performed the latter task, which was done in three stages. In the first stage thirty teachers did the initial scoring. In the second stage four teachers reviewed the work done in the first stage to ensure that the scoring followed the guidelines and corrected any errors in the marking. The final stage consisted of a review to sort out any discrepancies between the first and second stages. As for the rest of the marking, this was done through a computerized process for which a validation procedure was available.

Report Preparation and Dissemination

Prior to preparing the reports the SIMCE team classified the schools according to the socioeconomic level of the population served and their administrative status (municipal, subsidized private, completely private). The actual reports, which were distributed in April, presented information by classroom and gave the average percentage of correct answers for all the questions that assessed the same learning objective and the average number of correct answers for the entire test. Subsequently, the results were aggregated by school, location, region, and nationally. Each classroom and school was ranked by percentile in comparison with both other schools in the same socioeconomic structure and nationally.

To supplement the reports and help users interpret the results, SIMCE staff prepared a manual and a videotape and trained supervisors to explain the results. The manual explained the reports and how the schools could use them. It also included suggestions for teachers on how to improve their students' achievements of the most important learning objectives. The aim of the videotape was to explain the responsibilities of the various parts of the education system for the results, that is, principals, teachers, parents, and the community.

Use of the Results

The 1988 results were very similar to those yielded by the PER in 1984. The main users of the information from the first SIMCE were the school supervisors, who also reported back to the ministry on how individual schools were using the results. According to them, 35 percent of teachers were using the results effectively (Horn, Laurence, and Vélez 1992). The supervisors identified those schools that were trying to overcome low performance on the assessment, as well as those that simply ignored the results. One factor that might have led to relatively low use of the results was the incorporation of percentiles together with the percentages, which according to the supervisors caused some confusion among principals and teachers.

The reports on the self-image test and the survey on perceptions about the education system received little attention after their distribution, probably because interpreting the results at the aggregated level was difficult. The results of the parents survey were not used, and the ministry decided that this section would be eliminated the following year.

Subsequent Assessments

While preparations for administering the assessment to grade 4 students were being made in 1988, trial tests were also being prepared for grade 8 students for administering in 1989. That year 195,000 eighth graders took the SIMCE tests.

Over the years the system for selecting learning objectives for assessment has changed slightly, but not for the basics such as reading comprehension, spelling, writing, arithmetic, and understanding of basic scientific concepts. The personal development instruments and survey have also changed little despite proposals to introduce different instruments.

The sampling procedures used for pretesting were also changed from a proportional allocation sample to an optimum allocation sample. This did not allow direct comparison between 1981 and 1990 nor between 1989 or 1991 programs. However, it improved the reliability of the cognitive proficiency tests.

The authorities also revised the procedure for disseminating results. They decided that promoting the SIMCE with slides and videotapes was no longer necessary, but organized a contest for grade 8 students to design a poster promoting the test, which generated a good deal of interest among students and teachers.

Other improvements were designed to simplify the administrative procedures and reduce costs without sacrificing quality. Specifically, the ministry redesigned supporting materials and improved the methods for distributing and collecting materials. Data entry of the results was also improved by using scanning in place of key punching, which reduced the time for data entry from two months to fifteen days.

Because of the difficulties teachers had had in interpreting the percentile ranks, average percentages of correct answers were reported for schools and compared with averages for structures and nationally. The reports to parents were issued once again, but in a simpler form that only reported global results on students' performance in Spanish and arithmetic.

In 1991 the SIMCE was transferred entirely to the Ministry of Education according to the agreement between the ministry and the university, with the university team retained only to provide advisory services. This advisory service turned out to be particularly important for processing because the computer specialists that the university staff had trained had left the ministry and new staff had to be hired and trained. Other staff also left, and the workshops and seminars that had been organized to train staff during the initial three years of the SIMCE's development and implementation continued until 1993.

Chile's Experience with the SIMCE

Several aspects of the SIMCE experience can be considered as successes, namely:

- In each of the five years since the program started it has become more effective and efficient. One example of this improvement is that results are now delivered to the schools much more quickly than in the beginning and arrive during the first month of the school year.

- Both the public and the government agree that the program should be maintained. Moreover, the authorities are currently conducting a technical and economic feasibility study for implementing the SIMCE at the secondary level.
- The strategy used to delegate implementation of the program to an external institution and gradually transfer it to the ministry resulted in the formation of an interdisciplinary team at the ministry with the necessary skills to continue the program.
- The simplification of the reports has resulted in better understanding by the different audiences.
- The use of the results by teachers, schools, and government policymakers has been gradually increasing. One outcome has been the implementation of a financial support program (to improve infrastructure and educational resources) and a pedagogic program (including teacher training) for 1,200 schools in the lower socioeconomic levels, whose SIMCE results have been extremely poor. The ministry has also used SIMCE results in the review of curricula.
- School supervisors now have basic information that is regularly up-dated about the schools they supervise.
- The authors of instructional materials seem to be emphasizing the objectives measured by the SIMCE when preparing or revising materials, particularly those objectives with which students have had problems.
- The authorities have tried to maintain the SIMCE's cost at US$5 per student, which is acceptable by international standards.

While one cannot really speak of failures given the short length of time the SIMCE has been in operation, it has encountered the following problems, which might be overcome with time:

- While the use of the results has increased, many users still expect remedial actions to be initiated by central authorities.
- Measurement of the affective domain has not been successful and should, perhaps, be abandoned.
- As the schools have come to understand the correlation between students' performance and their socioeconomic status, they have realized that their relative performance will be much better if they report that their students come from extremely poor homes. The schools' reports about the increased numbers of deprived students do not match actual economic conditions, which have improved. Thus the schools should not be classified anew each year according to their socioeconomic structure.
- The authorities have not taken any measures to ensure the comparability of tests in successive years, making a comparison of changes in schools' performance from year to year difficult.
- The current system of testing fourth graders one year and eighth graders the next does not allow successive assessment of the same cohorts, which would permit better evaluation of changes taken as a result of remedial actions.

- The system of testing all students rather than just a sample should be questioned given that changes in education take place slowly. Perhaps all students should be tested in some years and samples in others.
- No research has been initiated within the context of the SIMCE to examine its results. This is a serious limitation for its future development.
- The expectation that the SIMCE would stimulate more parents to participate in their children's education has not come about except in some private schools. In the rest of the schools parent participation is still minimal.

All in all, the SIMCE program can be considered a success.

Essentials for Developing a National Assessment System

The first important essential before a country can develop a national assessment system is that the political will to implement a program of this nature must be present, along with a consensus about the need for it. If the political will is absent, the funding for such is program is likely to be reduced over time and reallocated to competing educational priorities. If the consensus is lacking, any initiative is doomed to failure, as occurred with the PER.

Next, before an assessment is implemented the authorities must carry out a political, technical, and economic feasibility study that suggests a number of viable options. While the experiences of other countries are valuable in this context, each country has its own characteristics that prevent the direct transfer of national assessment methods from one country to another, whose political, cultural, and social climate may be quite different.

Another requirement is an interdisciplinary team of experienced professionals who are qualified to develop and manage an assessment program. Putting together such a team takes time. Given the complexity of educational administration systems in many countries, one way to get such a team going and the work started could be to start the project with a team from outside the ministry of education and gradually transfer it to the ministry.

In addition to those areas discussed in this chapter—technical, informatics, administrative and logistical, and dissemination of results—a research effort is needed to update, renew, and develop the program to prevent its stagnation.

An issue that some countries must take into account is the use of a number of different languages across the country. This complicates the national assessment process.

The plan for disseminating the results must be determined ahead of time. Not only must the authorities distribute the results on a timely basis and explain how the various recipients use them, but the results should be kept at a low level of statistical sophistication to ensure that audiences understand and use them.

Finally, the program's impact must be evaluated to ascertain whether the changes expected as a result of the assessment are actually taking place.

References

Alkin, M. 1981. *The Feasibility of Measuring Educational Attainment in Chilean Schools. PER.* Report No. 8. Santiago: Pontificia Universidad Católica de Chile.

Burstein, L. 1980. "The Analysis of Multilevel Data in Educational Research and Evaluation." *Review of Research in Education* 8:158–233.

Freidman, M. 1979. *Free to Choose: A Personal Statement.* New York: Harcourt, Brace and Janovich.

Himmel, E., N. Majluf, and S. Maltes. 1980. *Efecto de Variables Macroestructurales y del Colego sobre el Rendimiento en las Pruebas de Seleccíon Universitaria.* Report No. 10. Santiago: Pontificia Universidad Católica de Chile.

Himmel, E., N. Majluf, S. Maltes, and P. Gazmuri. 1984. *Efectos de Política Educacional sobre el Rendimiento Escolar en Chile: Proyecto del Fondo Nacional de Ciencia y Technología.* Report No. 139/84. Final Report. Santiago: Pontificia Universidad Católica de Chile.

Himmel, E., N. Majluf, S. Maltes, and J. Guiterrez. 1982. *Análisis de los Efectos de Variables Socioeconómicas y del Colegio sobre el Rendimiento Escolar.* Proyecto DIUC No. 42/81, Final Report. Santiago: Pontificia Universidad Católica de Chile.

Himmel, E., S. Maltes, and H. Larraín. 1985. "Universidad y Desrrollo: Una Experiencia Interdisciplinaria." *Revista Universitaria* 16:20–23.

Horn, R., W. Laurence, and E. Vélez. 1992. *Sistemas de Evaluacíon en América Latina: Reseña Temática y Experiencias Receintes.* Bulletin No. 27 of the Main Education Project, pp. 67–31. Santiago: UNESCO.

Majluf, N. 1988. "The National Assessment of Education in Chile." In G. K. Rand, ed., *Operational Research '87.* pp. 66–81. The Netherlands: Elsevier Science Publishers-B.V.

Programma de Evaluacíon del Redimiento (PER). 1980. *Folleto Técnico.* Santiago: Pontificia Universidad Católica de Chile.

Raudenbush, S. W. 1988. "Educational Applications of Hierarchical Linear Models: A Review." *Journal of Educational Statistics* 13:85–116.

9

National Assessment in England and Wales

Thomas Kellaghan

This chapter discusses the national assessment system introduced in the United Kingdom following the Education Reform Act of 1988. Since its introduction, the system has been continually reviewed and modified, so that even at this stage one cannot say what form it will finally take. However, it is worth considering for several reasons, especially its comprehensiveness, its innovative approach to assessment, and the implementation problems that have arisen. Of particular interest is an evaluation of the system's adequacy for monitoring national achievement. The chapter will be confined to what has happened in England and Wales. Curricula and assessment systems differ somewhat in Northern Ireland, and even more so in Scotland.

Before considering the system in England and Wales, we should review their history of national assessment. As far back as 1948, the authorities carried out a survey of silent reading comprehension to obtain data to ascertain whether backwardness and illiteracy had increased during the war. Some information for comparison purposes was available from samples of children from 1938. Following that, surveys of nine-, eleven-, and fifteen-year olds were carried out irregularly up to 1977. In general, the surveys provided evidence of an improvement in reading standards up to the 1960s, which may or may not have represented a return to prewar standards. By the 1970s, there was a strong feeling among academics, politicians, and the public that standards were declining, or were at best at a standstill, a position frequently attributed to progressive education. Noncomparability of samples over time, however, made detecting any trends that might have existed difficult (see Kellaghan and Madaus 1982).

In 1975, partly as a response to the criticism about standards in schools, the authorities set up a more elaborate system of assessment (Foxman, Hutchinson, and Bloomfield 1991). The system was run by the Assessment of Performance Unit (APU), which was located in the Department of Education and Science. Three main areas of student development were targeted for assessment: language (including foreign language), mathematics, and science. Eleven, thirteen-, and fifteen-year olds participated in surveys that the APU hoped would throw light on the role of students' circumstances in their learning. This aspiration, however, was never fully realized.

As well as extending the range of subjects to be assessed beyond reading, the APU also set out to develop assessment procedures that would be related as closely as possible to good classroom practice. While still relying mainly on pencil and paper tests, subsamples of students taking mathematics and science tests also took practical tests. A further somewhat larger subsample responded to an attitude inventory in which students were invited to express positive or negative opinions about the subject. The APU found that some of the materials used in the surveys, particularly ones involving practical and oral assessments, favorably influenced practice in teaching.

Altogether the APU carried out some forty-three surveys between 1978 and 1988. Monitoring change over time always remained on the APU's agenda, even though it had not been mentioned in the unit's terms of reference; however, technical problems in detecting change and the small size of changes that were found resulted in a downgrading of the monitoring function. Some of the problems encountered in monitoring, and they are ones that any system encounters, were changes over time in the areas of achievement that were assessed (for example, extending them to practical skills), changes in modes of assessment (for example, moving from relatively closed and structured questions to a more open framework in language assessment), the aging of instruments (whereby, for example, words used in a vocabulary test had gone out of vogue), and changes in curricula over time. Such changes, while they are to be expected in any system that responds to developments in curricula and assessment, create serious problems in the measurement of changes in achievement.

The National Curriculum

The current system of national assessment was introduced in the context of a national curriculum. Prior to the Education Reform Act of 1988, schools at the primary level determined their own curricula, while at the secondary level curricula were largely defined by the independent examination boards for whose examinations schools chose to enter their students (at about ages sixteen and eighteen). The act changed this situation by requiring all schools to follow the same broad and balanced curriculum during the period of compulsory education, for students aged five to sixteen years.

Government proposed that the national curriculum would comprise three core subjects, English, mathematics, and science, that would be required in all grades together with seven foundation subjects: a modern foreign language (not in primary school), technology, history, geography, art, music, and physical education. The authorities envisaged that in primary school most curriculum time would be devoted to the core subjects. Attainment targets would be set for each of these subjects, which would provide standards against which pupils' progress and performance would be assessed. The extent to which pupils were meeting these targets would be assessed in nationally prescribed tests that all pupils would take at ages seven, eleven, fourteen, and sixteen (Department of Education and Science, Welsh Office, 1987).

National targets or objectives for attainment were set by government in the three core curriculum areas at ten levels to cover the attainments of students between the ages of five and sixteen. The targets state what students should normally be expected to know, understand, and be able to do around the ages of seven, eleven, fourteen, and sixteen (see Department of Education and Science 1991). Targets for each subject were divided into a series of major domains, usually about five for each subject, that set out the knowledge, skills, and understandings that pupils are expected to develop in each area. It was envisaged that the targets would be sufficiently specific to enable pupils, teachers, parents, and others to have a clear idea of what was expected of pupils and to provide a sound basis for assessment (Department of Education and Science, Welsh Office, 1987). Targets were designed in such a way that the typical student could be expected to move up one level about every two years. Age seven was associated with attainment target levels one, two, and three, and age eleven with attainment target levels three, four, and five. A review of the operation of the national curriculum recommended that the number of attainment targets should be reduced (Dearing 1994).

The Assessment Program

The aim of the assessment program, introduced in conjunction with the national curriculum, was to meet a number of specific needs. First, it would ensure that the curriculum was being implemented. Second, it would have a formative role in improving learning. Third, it would provide parents with information on children's performance. Fourth, the aggregation of individual students' results would provide achievement data for individual schools, which would be made available in school reports. Fifth, the aggregation of school-level data within each local education authority would permit comparisons among local education authorities. Thus, for example, results were subsequently published for each authority indicating the percentage of seven-year olds performing at level two or above and at level three or above. Finally, the authorities would be able to compile national statistics indicating levels of attainment by subject, profile component, and attainment target.

The task of advising on assessment procedures for the new curriculum was given to the Task Group on Assessment and Testing (Department of Education and Science 1988), which was set up in June 1987. The group recommended the use of standard assessment tasks (SATs), which would specify "externally provided tasks and procedures designed to produce performance data on a national scale" (paragraph 45). The tasks were designed to obtain information on pupils' performance on a cluster of attainment targets. A major feature of the tasks was that they were integrated into everyday classroom practice: during the course of the special activity that was a standard assessment task, teachers would observe and question children and record their level of performance. Performance would be graded on a system involving the ten levels of attainment from ages seven to sixteen.

The task group provided only a general framework for assessment. It was left to other bodies to define the profile components that would constitute a cluster of attainment targets and to describe the methods of assessment in detail. However, the task group did recommend that the methods of assessment should exploit a wide range of modes of presentation (that is, the method of delivery of questions should include oral, written, pictorial, video, computer, and practical demonstration), modes of operation (that is, the expected method of working should include mental only, written, practical, and oral), and modes of response (for example, choosing an option in a multiple choice question, writing a short prescribed response, open-ended writing, oral, performing an observed practical procedure, producing a practical outcome or product, or computer input).

A body called the Schools Examination and Assessment Council, now superseded by the School Curriculum and Assessment Authority, was given overall responsibility for implementing the national assessment program. Research or development agencies constructed the tests, and pupils' own teachers carried out the testing and were expected to assess pupils informally in the subject areas of the standard attainment task and to record the result before administering the more formal tests. Following testing, teachers from a group of schools brought examples of children's work to a moderation meeting, at which they compared the spread of results on tests with the spread on their own assessments. While the original intent was to give equal weight to teachers' assessments and to test results, in practice, in the early stages of the program, where a difference existed between the teacher's assessment and the pupil's score on the SAT, the SAT score took precedence. Teachers' assessments of practical skills, which were not formally tested in the SAT, were, however, accepted.

The national assessment system was remarkable for at least two reasons. First, the plan was to test all pupils at the relevant age grades: about half a million seven-year olds were assessed in 1991. Second, the assessment procedures represented a complete dissociation from the types of standardized tests that earlier surveys had used and also went well beyond the performance tests that the APU had introduced. Tests were designed to be embedded in teaching, with questions arising naturally from this situation, and pupils may not have been aware that they were being tested. The design of tests as pieces of classroom activity was a major innovation.

The authorities believed that embedding tests in classroom practice would have several advantages, and they would serve as models of good learning of which assessment would be an integral part (Black 1992). First, the approach avoided the use of formal tests, recognizing that they involve a strange occasion for pupils, especially young ones, and depend on a pupil's ability to understand what the strange situation requires. Furthermore, because most formal tests depend on reading or writing skills or both, children who were weak in these areas would not demonstrate their achievements adequately. Second, embedding the SATs in teaching avoided the situation in which external tests exerted pressure on teaching methods, forcing teachers to drill pupils to perform well in a way that could damage good teaching. Third, the SAT system of testing was designed to allow teachers to devote time to developing pupils' higher-order thinking skills, which are difficult to measure in traditional standardized tests, which tend to emphasize isolated and disconnected pieces of knowledge. Fourth, because teachers knew their pupils well they were considered to be in a better position to assess their pupils' work than an external test. Fifth, the hope was that the SAT testing procedure would develop teachers' assessment abilities and engender a new positive relationship between teaching and assessment. Finally, the authorities considered that giving teachers the responsibility for assessment enhanced their professional status. This aspiration, however, was eroded at an early stage by lowering the value of teachers' assessments as noted earlier.

The logic of the SAT system does indeed point to many possible benefits in the use of assessment in the classroom. In particular, the system promised to be useful for diagnostic purposes (that is, to identify learning difficulties so that appropriate remedial help and guidance could be provided), and for formative purposes to guide the appropriate next steps in learning. It might also promote a more systematic approach to the summative evaluation of the achievements of individual students. However, a major purpose of the system was also to provide information that could be used to assess and report on some aspects of the work of a school, a local education authority, or some other discrete part of the education service (Department of Education and Science 1988), and whether a single system of assessment could adequately serve this purpose as well as the other purposes envisaged is doubtful.

Implementation of the Assessment Program

The first major assessment of the achievements of pupils took place in 1991 with seven-year olds. This was preceded by pilot testing in 1990 and by in-service training for the teachers who would be carrying out the assessments. In-service training, for which local education authorities were responsible, was based on a cascade model: the authorities trained a number of trainers who then went on to train others. In general, teachers appeared to have viewed the in-service provision as inadequate. In particular, it paid insufficient attention to management problems in the administration of the SATs.

Given the nature and complexity of this new and unique form of national assessment, it is hardly surprising that many problems came to light when it was administered (Madaus and Kellaghan 1993). The findings of several studies raise problems about the quality of the SAT data (British Educational Research Association Policy Task Group on Assessment 1991; Broadfoot and others n.d.; Gipps and others 1991; National Union of Teachers and School of Education, University of Leeds 1993). The assessment did not yield comparable, reliable, and robust data largely because of a lack of standardization in the administration of the SATs, problems in making judgments about pupils' performance, and wide variations between schools in support for the assessment and in the amount of changes in school and classroom practices and routines occasioned by them. For example, one local education authority provided ten hours of auxiliary teacher help to each school regardless of size, which the larger schools saw as unfair. In some schools the assessments were administered by the children's teacher in the classroom; in others the teacher administered them in a less familiar setting such as a resource room, the library, the principal's office, or behind a screened-off area in the classroom. Some settings were cozy and quiet, others large and noisy. Schools also differed in whether a principal, part-time teacher, special needs teacher, or some other adult administered the assessment. In some classrooms a parent who had volunteered to help was present, and the number of adults present varied from one to three. Schools followed different strategies in preparing children for the experience and in the actual administration. For example, one teacher prepared children by having them practice talking into a tape. For others, preparation involved giving children practice in using worksheets.

There were other departures from a standardized administration related to teachers' perceptions of the SATs. All schools in the Gipps and others' (1991) evaluation felt that the SATs should not be presented to children as tests. Therefore teachers disguised the assessments as "group work," "experiments," "games," "different but fun." We can only guess how variations in the methods teachers employed to make the SATs less stressful or how parents' knowledge of what the SATs were about and concern about their children's performance affected performance.

Several teachers admitted to not sticking to the "letter of the law" during administration. For example, they permitted some bilingual children to give oral rather than written responses. When, as part of the SAT exercises, teachers were required to form groups to work on a problem, the groups varied in how they were composed and how they interacted. For example, some children were assigned to particular groups to give them a better chance. Some teachers administered tests individually to timid or quiet children or retested children who seemed flustered (Gipps and others 1991).

Other variations in administration arose because teachers felt that the requirement that they should avoid giving children direct help or that they should ask children questions that led to a correct response was an unnatural way of working. Thus, some children made disproportionate demands on teachers' time and attention during the individual administrations while some were given several opportunities to respond. Hints, nudges, and leading questions were observed, particularly where teachers were anxious that a child achieve. Reassurances were given pupils about tasks in general or about specific things with which they were having difficulty (Broadfoot and others n.d.)

Ambiguity in instructions to teachers about the judgments they had to make about performance must also have contributed to a lack of comparability of results across individuals and schools. For example, Sapsed (1991) found disagreement among teachers regarding the evidence required to decide that a pupil had reached a particular level of attainment.

The quality of the moderation by visiting principals also raised problems. This can be seen in the case of an exercise that required children to add and subtract numbers up to ten without any obvious counting or computation. One girl, whose teacher felt that her knowledge and understanding of mathematics were very good, nonetheless worked slowly and carefully. The moderator, however, insisted that she give her answer by the count of three. Broadfoot and others (n.d.) pertinently ask what was being assessed: mathematical ability, reaction times, speaking style or confidence?

Another serious problem from the point of view of standardization arose from teachers' exploration of pupils' performance at the three levels relevant to seven-year olds. While the test designers anticipated that levels one to three of the ten levels encompassed by the national curriculum would cover the range of performance of seven-year olds, investigators found that a small percentage of pupils could probably have reached a higher level (Burstall 1992). While level four test materials were included in the test in the following year, clearly no comparable data on level four performance is available for 1991.

A more serious problem arose from differences between teachers in the levels at which they tested pupils. The instructions specified that the level at which children were to be tested should first be the level of performance that had already been recorded for each child as part of the teacher's own informal assessment. If pupils succeeded at that entry level, they should then have been tested at the next level up (unless entered at level three). If the pupils did not succeed, they should have been tested at the next level down (unless entered at level one). However, a substantial minority of teachers failed to follow these instructions. Some started all children at level one, while others did not move to an adjacent level following testing at the entry level (Burstall 1992). Clearly, if procedures differ in this way from teacher to teacher, meaningful comparisons between schools or over time will not be possible.

Conclusion

Implementation problems can hardly be regarded as unexpected for a new systemwide program involving so many teachers in schools across the country. However, from the point of view of using the results for national assessment, we have to ask whether the experience indicates that the process was sufficiently standardized in schools to allow meaningful aggregation of data and comparisons across schools and over time. The answer to this would seem to be that the serious lack of standardization that was a feature of the administration of the SATs must call into question the comparability of individual pupil scores or aggregate school scores.

A review initiated by the Secretary of State for Education in 1993, largely in response to the problems that teachers were experiencing in implementing the reforms of the 1988 act, addressed many of the problems that had arisen in the design and implementation of the curriculum and its assessment (Dearing 1994). The review body proposed that the program of assessment should be modified. Among its recommendations were that only the core subjects of English, mathematics, and science should be assessed nationally for the next three years at key stages one, two, and three (with the exception that science would not be assessed at key stage one). The review body also proposed to reduce greatly the time required for testing and the number of statements of attainment on which teachers would be required to make judgments. While the original system was envisaged as one that would provide wide-ranging, process-based, criterion referenced assessment, the proposed modifications signal a return to more streamlined and conventional tests. However, teacher assessments and test results will be reported separately and given equal status in future. Finally, the review body recognized the failure of the attempt to produce an assessment system that would equally well serve a variety of functions, and stated that the purpose of national tests was primarily to provide summative information on performance. Diagnostic or formative elements should be considered subsidiary.

At least two lessons can be drawn from the experience of national assessment in England and Wales in recent years. First, the use of complex assessment tasks, however worthy the objective of integrating assessment with teaching may be, leads inevitably to problems in standardizing administration and procedure, which in turn leads to problems of comparability, both between schools and over time. The move to more conventional tests is an attempt to deal with this problem. A second lesson that emerges is that it is extremely difficult, perhaps even impossible, to devise assessment tasks that will serve a multiplicity of purposes equally well, particularly when high stakes are attached to performance, as is the case when test results are made public. This view now seems to be recognized in the decision to accord priority to the summative function in national assessment in the future.

References

Black, P. 1992. "The Shifting Scenery of the National Curriculum." Presidential address to the Education Section of the British Association, University of Southampton, August.

British Educational Research Association Policy Task Group on Assessment. 1991. *A Comparison of the Proposals for National Assessment in England and Wales, Scotland and Northern Ireland.* Unpublished paper.

Broadfoot, P., D. Abbott, P. Croll, M. Osborn, and A. Pollard. n.d. *Look Back in Anger? Findings of the PACE Project Concerning Primary Teachers' Experiences of SATs.* Bristol, U.K.: University of Bristol. Unpublished paper.

Burstall, C. 1992. "Recent British Experience of National Assessment." Paper presented at the American Educational Research Association Annual Meeting, San Francisco, April 20–24.

Dearing, R. (chair). 1994. *The National Curriculum and Its Assessment. Final Report.* London: School Curriculum and Assessment Authority.

Department of Education and Science, Welsh Office. 1987. *The National Curriculum 5–16. A Consultation Document.* London.

Department of Education and Science. 1988. National Curriculum Task Group on Assessment and Testing. *A report.* London.

———. 1991. *Testing 7 Year Olds in 1991: Results of the National Curriculum Assessments in England.* London.

Foxman, D., D. Hutchinson, and B. Bloomfield. 1991. *The APU Experience 1977–1990.* London: School Examination and Assessment Council.

Gipps, C., B. McCallum, S. McAllister, and M. Brown. 1991. "National Assessment at Seven: Some Emerging Themes." Paper presented at the British Educational Research Association Annual Conference.

Kellaghan, T., and G. F. Madaus. 1982. "Educational Standards in Great Britain and Ireland." In G. R. Austin and H. Garber, eds., *The Rise and Fall of National Test Scores.* New York: Academic Press.

Madaus, G. F., and T. Kellaghan. 1993. "British Experience with Authentic Testing." *Phi Delta Kappan* 74:458–69.

National Union of Teachers and School of Education, University of Leeds. 1993. *Testing and Assessing 6 and 7 Year Olds. The Evaluation of the 1992 Key Stage 1 National Curriculum Assessment.* London and Leeds.

Sapsed, S. 1991. "Key Stage One SATs in Schools." *British Journal of Curriculum and Assessment* 1(3):8–9, 12.

10

National Assessment in Thailand

Kowit Pravalpruk

Education in Thailand is based on an examination system. Children's futures are largely determined by examination results. No matter how well children perform during their school careers, what counts as a valid index of their ability are test scores. As a result, students study hard for examinations.

Currently, the most important examination is the university entrance examination, which determines the career options of students who have reached this level. The assumption is that the three-year higher secondary education system is to prepare students for this examination. Because the university entrance examination covers only cognitive learning outcomes, it conflicts with the learning outcomes specified in the secondary school curriculum, which also emphasizes values, moral conduct, and practical ability. The effect of the entrance examination is to reduce actual learning outcomes to only pen and paper knowledge of one component of a larger set of desirable outcomes.

The Ministry of University Affairs administers the university entrance examination annually. Every student who would like to attend one of the limited enrollment government universities has to sit for this examination. Students have six options in applying to these universities and their test scores are ranked with those who select the same college or program. Students are accepted if their ranking falls within the predetermined quota for each college. The examination is very competitive and its result will determine the students' future. Those who fail the examination can enroll in the two open universities and other private universities, but these are considered second best options.

The Ministry of Education has been trying to lessen the effects of the university entrance examination on what is taught in schools by introducing its own national assessment program, but these efforts have had only a limited effect on improving the situation. This chapter describes the development of this national assessment system and the issues that affect its impact.

Thailand's Education System

The Ministry of Education determines all curricula and standards for all schools in Thailand and sets the appropriate rules and regulations. The ministry's Department of Curriculum and Instruction Development is the implementing agency for these areas, and its responsibilities include monitoring student achievement.

School administration is divided among three ministries and among various departments in the Ministry of Education. The Ministry of Education administers almost all primary and secondary education, the Ministry of the Interior is responsible for primary education in municipal areas and Bangkok, and the Ministry of University Affairs is responsible for some demonstration schools at the primary and secondary levels and for higher education, although the Ministry of Education is responsible for polytechnic institutes, teacher colleges, agricultural colleges, physical education colleges, and colleges of business and trade.

With the expansion of basic education from six to nine years, the Ministry of the Interior is beginning to offer secondary education in some municipal schools. The Ministry of Education's Office of the National Primary Education Commission, which administers nearly all primary schools in Thailand, has recently begun to offer lower secondary education in some primary schools. In general, however, the responsibility for secondary education remains with the Department of General Education in the Ministry of Education. The Office of the Private Education Commission of the Ministry of Education administers all private schools at the primary, secondary, and higher education levels.

In 1992, Thailand had 1,349,725 preprimary students, 6,906,280 primary school students, 1,682,882 lower secondary students, and 904,098 upper secondary students in 36,952 schools with 524,647 teachers. Specific types of schools and learning centers were available for out-of-school children, which are not included in these statistics. Table 10-1 presents the numbers of schools, teachers, and students according to the agency responsible for them.

Table 10-1. Numbers of Schools, Teachers, and Students by Responsible Agencies

Agency	No. of schools	No. of teachers	No. of students
Primary level			
Office of the National Primary Ed. Commission	31,427	340,902	6,703,854
Bangkok M.A.	427	12,744	243,679
Ministry of the Interior	473	11,877	253,137
Border Patrol	167	981	18,817
Secondary level			
Department of General Education	1,959	102,210	1,906,816
Both levels			
Department of General Education	41	1,431	20,658
Teachers Education (Demonstration)	23	n.a.	8,664
Fine Arts	11	854	6,536
Private	2,612	54,425	1,254,117
Ministry of University Affairs	13	1,058	16,843

Source: Author's Data.

The administration of education in Thailand is highly centralized. Everything is decided at the ministry level and instructions are passed down to offices and schools for implementation. The government has attempted to introduce policies to decentralize education, but the system remains basically unchanged.

The National Assessment Program

A new higher secondary school curriculum according to the 6:3:3 scheme was implemented in 1981. According to this new curriculum, teachers were responsible for evaluating the outcomes of student learning in their courses. The national examination at the end of secondary education was abolished. The Ministry of Education was concerned about the quality and standards of education and worried that the standards of education might be lower than had been revealed by the national examination. It appointed a committee to recommend measures to maintain high standards. The committee decided that Thailand should introduce an external examination that did not count for school leaving or for a pass or fail in school learning, but that assessed the quality of school leavers against what was specified in the curriculum. The result was the creation of the national assessment program and the establishment of the Office of Educational Assessment and Testing Services in the Department of Curriculum and Instruction Development.

The aims of the national assessment program were twofold. The first was to report on national standards of education. The assessment had to ascertain the level of achievement of students in the whole country, the thirteen educational regions, the seventy-two provinces, and Bangkok. The expectation was that this exercise would have an effect on school administration. The results for each school, aggregated for the whole country and by region and province, would be sent to all schools so that they could compare their performance and try to improve quality accordingly. The committee hoped that data from the national assessment program would be used for educational planning at all levels.

The second aim of the assessment was to set the scope of the evaluation so as to make the schools realize that learning outcomes should not be only those emphasized by the university entrance examination. As the new curriculum emphasized affective learning outcomes, such as attitudes toward work, moral values, and social participation, the paper and pencil type of examination tested only part of what was learned. The national assessment program had to cover these affective learning outcomes and practical skills to make schools realize that desirable outcomes were more than cognitive development in specific content areas. The committee expected the assessment to serve as a check on the entrance examination's narrow focus on one component of education.

The Office of Educational Assessment and Testing Services

As noted earlier, Thailand's education system is highly centralized. Everything is decided at the ministry level. About a century ago, when education along Western lines was introduced to the general public, the examination was part of this system. Schools were built in the provinces and outside the Royal Palace in Bangkok. At a very early stage of schooling in Thai history, the examination was used as the curriculum. Quality was specified in areas of the examination and a central body conducted the examination.

School leaving and certification were based on results in this examination. Scholars in various disciplines set the questions and marked the responses. The examination was time-consuming because all the answers were in essay form, which takes a lot of time to read.

The Ministry of Education's Test Bureau conducted the year end examinations, and the subject matter specialists who set and marked the papers served as the examination board. The first national examination was in 1882, and in 1941 the responsibility for the examination was transferred to the Office of Education Assessment and Testing Services. Subject matter specialists were still responsible for setting the questions and marking the paper according to rules and regulations set down by the Ministry of Education. The office was responsible only for the administrative and support aspects of the examination. Around 1960 the concept of multiple choice was introduced into the schools, and the national examination began to include some multiple choice items. By the 1970s most of the questions were multiple choice, with only some short written responses forming a small part of the examination. By 1980 the Office of Educational Assessment and Testing Services was capable of conducting modern examinations with standardized test practices, including machine scoring.

Responsibility for the national assessment program was given to the office in 1981. The office was under the administration of the Ministry of Education. It has the status of a division, with a director reporting directly to the director general of the department. There was no board, but only department committees and various working committees that carried out all the tasks. Currently, the office has ninety-three staff members as shown in figure 10-1, of which sixty are professional staff. In terms of educational qualifications three of them have doctorates, twenty-one have masters degrees (eleven in educational measurement), and the rest have at least a bachelors degree with a short training course in educational measurement. Eight of the professional staff were educated abroad. The office invites personnel from other departments and from universities to serve on subject committees to help develop test items and to carry out on-site evaluation.

The First National Assessment

The first group of students to complete the higher secondary school curriculum introduced in 1981 graduated in March 1984. The first national assessment was therefore conducted in December 1983. The assessment consisted of multiple choice paper and pencil assessments, that covered five subjects: Thai language, social studies, physical education, sciences, and mathematics. The Ministry of Education required all twelfth graders to sit for the assessment, which was administered like the year end national examination, only without the same consequences. The assessment took two days. Every student did the same exercise at the same time throughout the country.

Work began in September 1983 with the appointment of various committees. Each subject had its own committee made up of twelve to eighteen members. Each subject assessment was designed to take one-and-a-half hours. The number of items for each subject would depend on their difficulty and the amount of time the students would need to work out the answers. The committees set the number of items at ninety for Thai, ninety for social studies, sixty for physical education (one hour), sixty for science, and sixty for mathematics.

Figure 10-1. Staffing of the Office of Educational Assessment and Testing Services

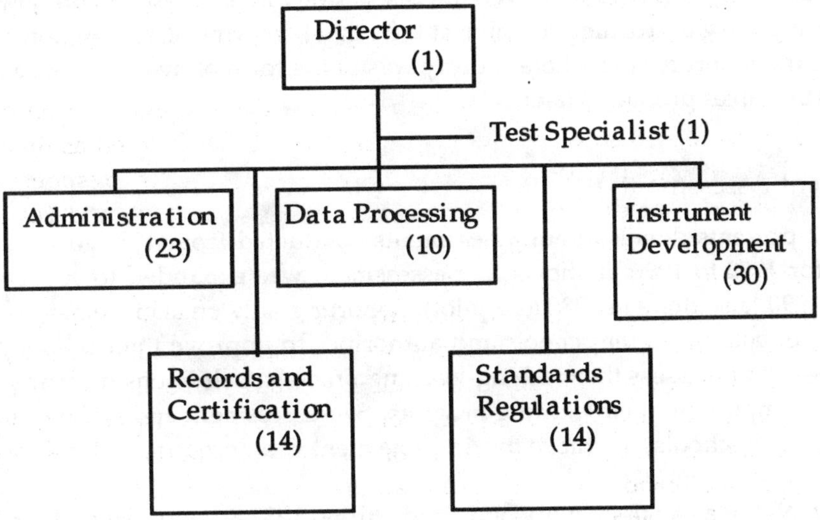

```
                        ┌─────────────┐
                        │  Director   │
                        │    (1)      │
                        └──────┬──────┘
                               │
                               ├──────── Test Specialist (1)
                               │
        ┌──────────────┬───────┼───────────────┐
  ┌───────────┐  ┌───────────┐         ┌──────────────┐
  │Administra-│  │Data Pro-  │         │ Instrument   │
  │tion       │  │cessing    │         │ Development  │
  │(23)       │  │(10)       │         │ (30)         │
  └─────┬─────┘  └─────┬─────┘         └──────────────┘
        │              │
  ┌───────────┐  ┌───────────┐
  │Records and│  │ Standards │
  │Certifica- │  │Regulations│
  │tion       │  │  (14)     │
  │(14)       │  │           │
  └───────────┘  └───────────┘
```

From August 1983 to September 1983 the committees worked on test design and item development. They decided to use the standardized achievement approach because most committee members were trained in this method and because the public seemed to understand this method better. Each committee then constructed a table of specifications to indicate the content area for both cognitive and affective learning outcomes for each exercise. The items were selected either from an item bank or newly developed following the bank's style and pattern. Items testing recall of facts or methods were specifically excluded.

The committees were also responsible for validating test items. For each item members would evaluate whether the item was appropriate for the paper and whether it measured the specified ability according to the table of specifications. For each subject, abilities to be measured were specified, for example, the Thai language assessment measured four abilities: reading comprehension, usage, critical thinking, and the creative use of language. For each ability specific tasks were also stated. Committee members had to agree whether each item was measuring a specific ability and task.

The committees sent the finished assessment papers to the administrative section to be typed and printed, which was done under tight security. Packages of exercises, instructions, answer sheets, and supplies were delivered to the schools at the beginning of December 1983 and stored in locked cabinets until the morning of the assessment, which was conducted on December 13–14, 1983. Test administration was much the same in all schools and all provinces.

Answer sheets were sent back to the office, reviewed, and made ready for machine scoring. T-scores were used to report student profiles. Means and standard deviations were reported for each individual school, province, and region. Student scores and school mean scores, together with provincial and regional statistics, were sent back to the schools. Each school received only its own report and not the results for other schools. They were advised to compare their performance with provincial and regional means, not with other schools. These printouts were sent to schools in March 1984 and the final report was finished in July 1984. It was presented at the annual meeting of provincial administrators in August 1984 for general discussion and suggestions on how to use the report for planning academic programs at the school, provincial, and regional levels. For the public the report for the whole country was in the form of mean percentage scores as shown in the tables presented later.

Subsequent Assessments

Table 10-2 presents details about assessments conducted from 1983 to 1991 and those planned for 1992 to 1996. It shows that assessment was expanded to cover school processes in 1990 (also done in 1988 as a pilot). Reporting only on achievement from 1983 to 1986 had not convinced the schools and authorities to improve their school practices. It was necessary to reassess the teaching-learning process itself to ensure that schools paid attention to improving their learning program. Self-assessment and self-monitoring were to be used in all schools to achieve this improvement in a decentralized fashion.

Table 10-2. National Assessments Conducted During 1983–91 and Planned for 1992–96

Academic year	Number of students who took the tests: achievement			Number of students assessed: processes		
(May to March)	Grade 6	Grade 9	Grade 12	Grade 6	Grade 9	Grade 12
1983	n.a.	n.a.	147,834	n.a.	n.a.	n.a.
1984	n.a.	53,071	49,437	n.a.	n.a.	n.a.
1985	253,955	n.a.	174,124	n.a.	n.a.	n.a.
1986	n.a.	43,991	172,277	n.a.	n.a.	n.a.
1987	n.a.	n.a.	164,837	n.a.	n.a.	n.a.
1988	106,927	100,570	144,229	n.a.	n.a.	n.a.
1989	n.a.	n.a.	n.a.	n.a.	n.a.	n.a.
1990	113,306	131,422	46,377	283	143	126
1991	n.a.	n.a.	n.a.	n.a.	n.a.	n.a.
1992	√	n.a.	n.a.	√	n.a.	n.a.
1993	n.a.	√	√	n.a.	n.a.	n.a.
1994	√	n.a.	n.a.	√	n.a.	n.a.
1995	n.a.	√	√	n.a.	√	√
1996	√	n.a.	√	√	n.a.	n.a.

√ plan to conduct assessment.
n.a. Not applicable.
Source: Author's Data.

The assessment procedure used after the first year was much the same as for the first assessment, as was item development. Only two aspects were changed. First, in some years the assessment was conducted on a sample of students in grades 6 and 9. Second, subject areas and competencies measured changed somewhat. As concerns reporting, the percentages of students whose level of performance was satisfactory was added for later assessments. Tables 10-3, 10-4, and 10-5 present the results for various years.

Table 10-3. Results of Average Grade 6 Assessments, 1985, 1988, and 1990
(percentage mark derived from raw scores)

Area of assessment	1985	1988	1990
Thai language	47.67	53.29	59.00
Social studies			
Cognitive	n.a.	60.72	62.26
Affective	n.a.	80.99	80.50
Physical education	n.a.	68.63	n.a.
Career education			
Cognitive	49.03	55.43	47.66
Affective 1	n.a.	75.09	67.27
Affective 2	n.a.	n.a.	80.85
Science	55.91	54.64	61.43
Mathematics	43.57	50.32	58.86
Problem solving	n.a.	48.29	56.13
Values	67.03	77.06	72.24

n.a. Not applicable.
Source: Office of Educational Assessment and Testing Services.

Table 10-4. Results of Grade 9 Assessment
(average percentage mark derived from raw scores)

Areas of assessment	1984	1986	1988	1990
Thai language	41.36	36.58	61.68	64.34
Social studies				
Cognitive	44.92	45.37	56.06	60.22
Affective	76.46	76.32	76.02	82.07
Physical education				
Cognitive	58.64	54.90	61.27	n.a.
Affective	72.86	68.68	n.a.	n.a.
Career education				
Cognitive	50.96	47.82	58.54	59.85
Affective	73.03	60.78	75.02	71.70
Sciences	45.72	40.71	64.42	53.06
Mathematics	n.a.	n.a.	40.79	39.98
Problem solving	n.a.	n.a.	48.73	51.28
Values	51.08	n.a.	67.45	72.24

n.a. Not applicable.
Source: Office of Educational Assessment and Testing Services.

Table 10-5. Results of Grade 12 Assessment
(average percentage mark derived from raw scores)

Areas of assessment	1983	1984	1985	1986	1987	1988	1990
Thai language	51.99	46.72	45.40	49.40	48.99	62.10	63.64
Social studies							
Cognitive	50.28	43.44	48.12	43.04	51.36	62.65	59.84
Affective		78.04	77.46	77.41	79.40	76.49	80.52
Physical education							
Cognitive	52.35	63.78	60.20	56.41	54.60	64.97	n.a.
Affective	n.a.	74.43	70.78	68.17	62.27	n.a.	n.a.
Career education							
Cognitive	n.a.	53.98	52.10	46.20	58.03	56.53	58.39
Affective	n.a.	74.66	70.32	68.17	74.94	74.65	70.68
Sciences	44.00	n.a.	36.13	n.a.	n.a.	49.33	55.44
Mathematics	47.98	40.40	n.a.	42.53	44.34	n.a.	n.a.
English	n.a.	29.46	n.a.	26.92	39.43	n.a.	n.a.
Problem solving	n.a.	n.a.	n.a.	n.a.	n.a.	48.85	53.71
Values	n.a.	51.32	n.a.	n.a.	88.58	80.08	71.49

n.a. Not applicable.
Source: Office of Educational Assessment and Testing Services.

The process assessment implemented in 1990 was designed to cover three aspects of curriculum implementation: preparation, administration, and classroom instruction. For each aspect key indicators of successful implementation were identified and manuals developed.

The preparation aspect had six items—public relations, cooperation with other education agencies, preparation of personnel, administrative systems, school database, and procurement of materials—with eleven indicators. For each indicator, a rating of five to one was used to represent the stage of operation, from five representing fully integrated into daily activities to one representing just initiating. Evaluators, who were trained education supervisors, were advised to look for concrete evidences of implementation. Examples of key indicators were parents' seminars for public relations, teachers' seminars for preparation of personals, and information about students' aptitudes and interests for the database.

For curriculum administration there were four items with seventeen key indicators. The four items were overall planning, academic planning, implementation of the plan, and evaluation and follow-up. Key indicators were identified around three categories of activities: self-diagnosis, innovation, and involvement of all school personnel.

For classroom instruction there were five items with fifteen key indicators. The evaluation of teaching-learning activities was developed according to the process skills, which were the main focus of the curriculum.

Before implementing the process assessment all educational supervisors were appropriately trained. A team of three supervisors would conduct a school visit and assess the school's activities according to the assessment form, which might involve interviews with key staff. After each visit three supervisors would discuss their assessment and come to an agreement.

Lessons Learned from the National Assessment Program

As noted earlier, the purpose of Thailand's national assessment program was to look at the quality and standards of education and to make teachers realize that learning should not focus entirely on cognitive learning outcomes. The authorities expected that the assessment would affect school practice in such a way that more effective learning activities would take place in classrooms.

Observers noted that teachers were trying to include assessments of affective learning outcomes in their own evaluations. However, the classroom evaluation still used children's behavior to reach conclusions about their values and attitudes. The national assessment examinations helped teachers realize the importance of affective learning outcomes to some extent.

Concerning the impact on educational planning, especially school academic planning, some schools and provinces have been using data from the national assessment program to help them in planning. Some schools even used outcomes from the national assessment examination for student promotion and transfer purposes and to select students for scholarship programs.

The most important impact of the national assessment program was reflected in curriculum development. The result of the assessment clearly showed that achievement in both science and mathematics, especially in the application of knowledge, were unsatisfactory. They also indicated that the level of achievement in some subjects had been declining, especially in the area of thinking skills. From these qualitative indicators the Department of Curriculum and Instructional Development decided to revise the curriculum in 1989 to emphasize more process skills.

The most important factor contributing to the success or failure of the assessment was support from administrators at all levels in using its results for educational planning. If school principals saw that the assessment achievement profile was useful in selecting areas for further development, they would fully support the exercise. Otherwise they would ignore it. Some actually misused the results when they stated that low scores were a result of poor teachers.

The history of testing in Thailand suggests that the university entrance examination has had a powerful effect on what actually gets taught at the lower education levels. Efforts to expand what is important in learning has now taken place in Thailand, however, primarily through the Department of Curriculum and Instruction Development's national assessment program. While some progress has occurred in getting schools to pay more attention to values, moral conduct, and practical ability, tests alone cannot achieve this. Ultimately principals and teachers need to take the initiative to improve the quality of education they provide to their students. This represents a significant challenge, given the centralized nature of education decisionmaking in Thailand.

11

The Colombian Education Assessment System

Carlos Rojas

The Colombian education system consists of preschool, basic education, middle education, and higher education. The constitution states that "The State, the society and the family are responsible for education and that education will be obligatory between the ages of five and fifteen and will include, at a minimum preschool and nine years of basic education."

Preschool refers to the education provided to children under six years of age and is basically an urban phenomenon. Fewer than 10 percent of those enrolled in preschool are from rural areas. Private institutions play a significant role in the provision of preschool education. According to the latest statistics, nearly 60 percent of preschool students (approximately 300,000 children) attend private institutions. (Unless otherwise indicated, the statistics presented in this chapter are drawn from those compiled by the Ministry of Education in 1987.)

Basic education begins after six years of age and includes five years of primary education and the first four secondary grades, for a total of nine years of compulsory education. It is in primary education that public education has its greatest participation. Approximately 4.2 million children are enrolled in primary schools, of whom 86 percent attend public schools, while the remaining 14 percent go to private schools. Students attend approximately 34,000 public schools and 3,500 private institutions around the country.

Almost 36 percent of primary school students are from rural areas, while 64 percent live in cities. Despite significant efforts to improve the system's internal efficiency, high dropout, repetition, and absenteeism rates still prevail. Only 18 percent of the children in rural areas complete their basic primary education. In urban areas the figure is close to 62 percent.

As mentioned before, one of the main problems Colombia's Ministry of Education faces concerns the system's inefficiency. As table 11-1 shows, despite significant gains in the rate of retention of pupils, only 18.3 percent of the 1978–83 cohort of rural children who entered school completed the basic cycle.

The number of years spent in school paints an even darker picture for the rural areas, as on the average the cohorts completed less than two years of schooling, compared to almost four years in the urban areas. Unfortunately, statistics for more recent years are unavailable. However, the indications are that recent policies, such as the universalization of the basic cycle and the Escuela Nueva (new school) program expansion, have im-

Table 11-1. Internal Efficiency of the Primary Education System, Selected Cohorts

Cohort	Retention %		Mean number of years of schooling	
	Urban	Rural	Urban	Rural
1961–66	41.3	3.2	—	—
1969–73	53.2	11.0	3.1	1.6
1978–83	62.4	18.3	3.8	1.7

— Not available.

Source: Ministry of Education statistics (1987).

proved the system's internal efficiency significantly. Nevertheless, the illiteracy rate remains high despite several campaigns by different governments. According to the last census, Colombia has almost 33 million people, of whom almost 12.2 percent are illiterate.

The middle education cycle (grades 6–11) offers students different options, such as academic courses, science, arts, industry, commerce, agriculture, and teacher-training. Of secondary students, 60 percent attend public schools and 40 percent attend private schools. According to the National Department of Planning, 2.6 million students were enrolled in secondary school in 1990. This number represents less than 50 percent of the age group.

After finishing secondary school, students can continue their education in postsecondary institutions that offer intermediate technical training or apply to a university for a four-or five-year higher education program. Almost 60 percent of the students in higher education are enrolled in private institutions. In Colombia, as in most Latin American countries, enrollment at this level has expanded rapidly. At present, Colombia has nearly 240 institutions of higher education, of which 30 percent are public and 70 percent are private. These institutions enroll approximately 435,000 students, or 13.7 percent of the age group.

A History of Education Assessment in Colombia

In Colombia the use of education tests has been closely related to the student selection needs of the universities, especially the public universities. (This section is a summary of the most relevant issues presented in Caro 1990). In 1912 Colombia's largest public university, the National University, introduced entrance examinations by national decree, and these soon spread to other public universities under the supervision of the Ministry of Education.

During the following decades the authorities modified and adjusted the examinations somewhat. Perhaps the most relevant change concerns the introduction of questions on subject areas considered fundamental for any university program. Despite the differentprograms the higher education system offered, the authorities found that most students were selecting programs leading to the most traditional careers, such as law, medicine, or accounting, and tended not to enroll in science, mathematics, and engineering programs. As a result, the authorities created the Professional Orientation Service in 1959, which designed and administered entrance examinations to students requesting admission to institutions affiliated with the National Association of Universities. Critics of this service argue that what was conceived of as a means of guiding students in their selection of a program was progressively transformed into a massive testing service aimed exclusively at selecting high school graduates for university entrance.

During the 1960s the testing service offered examinations to evaluate such areas as verbal and mathematics aptitude, abstract reasoning, spatial relationships, social sciences, philosophy, physics, biology, and chemistry. In 1967, within the framework of what was then called the Basic Plan for Higher Education, the government created a national testing service that would help lower the high rate of dropouts and would permit the most able students to enter the tertiary cycle.

In 1968 the government created the Colombian Institute for the Enhancement of Higher Education (ICFES), which incorporated the National Testing Service (NTS) as one of its divisions. The main task of the NTS is to design and administer the national examinations given to all students who finish high school and want to apply to university. In 1980 the ICFES was reorganized by decree and the national examinations became obligatory for all students in the last year of secondary school. As a result the NTS became a special administrative unit within the ICFES with two main branches: the research and test design division and the test administration division.

The decree described the new functions of the NTS as follows:

- To establish the criteria for the design, development, administration, and interpretation of its tests;

- To organize, coordinate, and direct the development of the national examinations required for university entrance and of equivalency tests for high school and other levels;

- To coordinate the research needed to improve the quality of the instruments, their use, and the interpretation of the results;

- To organize and coordinate follow-up studies on the academic performance of students at the primary and secondary levels at the Ministry of Education's request;

- To report to the Ministry of Education on the academic quality of Colombian schools based on the results of the national examinations.

Since its creation twenty-six years ago the NTS has accumulated a great deal of experience in designing, administering, and analyzing tests. However, most of its critics argue that it has become an institution where testing is the final objective rather than a means of analyzing the problems the education system faces.

As for reporting the results of the national examinations, the NTS provides each student with a personal report and periodically publishes a series of descriptive statistics describing the school population by academic track, sex, type of high school attended, and the careers and universities students prefer. It also produces a report that analyzes school performance. It reports on schools' achievement by type of school (public, private, single sex, coeducational); academic shift (day, night); academic track (arts, science, commercial, industrial, agricultural); geographic region, and municipality.

In terms of cost, the amount payed by each student taking the exam does not cover the NTS' costs, hence the system is subsidized by the government. During 1990 alone, the NTS had a deficit close to U$425,000.

The National Education Assessment System

Educators in Colombia have been aware of the lack of information about the quality of the education system. The NTS has concentrated on the entrance examinations, neglecting research on quality.

The idea of having a national assessment system to monitor the quality of education was reinforced in 1986 by a law the government enacted to reorganize the Ministry of Education. The law established a division within the ministry responsible for evaluating the quality of education and for the following functions:

- The assessment of the quality of the service provided;
- The establishment of a test bank;
- The definition of criteria for evaluating institutions, plans, and education programs.

To accomplish these functions the ministry, with support from the World Bank, decided to establish a national education assessment system that would allow the central, regional, and local authorities to enhance the policy decisionmaking process. The following paragraphs summarize its characteristics, objectives, structure, and implementation strategies. (This section is based on Ministry of Education 1992.)

Characteristics

According to the evaluation division created within the Ministry of Education the assessment process should be committed to solving the problem of low educational quality. Given the seriousness of the situation, its activities should concentrate mainly on improving the quality of education.

The goals of the assessment system are to promote national awareness of the urgent need to implement periodic assessment as a primary means of generating activities that lead to positive change. The system also aims at creating a new culture of assessment so that the process can be used as an avenue for change. To reach these goals key figures in the schools need to be convinced of the necessity to make assessment a fundamental process in the achievement of quality in education. Assessment activities also need to be relevant to curricular objectives, which will correct the general belief that assessment methods do not provide any information useful for promoting change. Finally, the intended goals of the assessment were to be clearly specified and the education community be made aware of how the results were planned to be used.

The national education assessment system will focus not only on students' academic performance, but also on their nonacademic achievement. The academic dimension is defined in terms of the extent to which students' performance reaches or exceeds the accepted minimum for various areas of the curriculum. The nonacademic dimension of the quality of education is intended to measure areas not included in the measurement of parts of the curriculum, but which are necessary to the process by which individuals adjust to the social, cultural, and political environment of their country. Creativity, self-esteem, and democratic values are some of the noncognitive dimensions that the system will measure.

In addition, the system will pay special attention to determining factors or variables that may affect the quality of education. If an assessment system is to have a real impact on education, it should be able to measure such factors and take their relationship to academic achievement into account. This will facilitate the search for the best ways to improve quality. Examples of such factors include the school setting, specific conditions related to the classroom and the teachers, and the characteristics of the students and their families.

Objectives

The objective of the assessment system is to monitor the quality of education in Colombia and to determine what factors are associated with quality of education, so as to contribute to the design of policies and plans in the education sector. Specifically the system seeks to gather information on the quality of education in Columbia by testing performance in academic and nonacademic subjects, to examine the effect of various factors within the school and the general environment on the quality levels observed, to carry out research on the data collected to explain the findings, and to ensure that the findings have been interpreted correctly and that they are useful in seeking solutions to the problems of quality in education.

Structure

Located within the Ministry of Education, the assessment system has three closely related units: assessment, research, and dissemination. The team working on the assessment component is directly involved with test design for cognitive and noncognitive areas as well as with questionnaires to determine the factors affecting achievement. It is also involved with the sampling process, the organization of data collection procedure and data analysis. This is the primary data collection and processing unit, although its findings are subsequently reprocessed and reinterpreted.

The research team re-examines the data produced by the assessment unit, processes the unrefined data obtained from students, and promotes the execution of several projects aimed at interpreting the findings. In other words, the research team complements the activities of the assessment unit by designing new assessment instruments and introducing new data collection and processing techniques.

The dissemination unit is responsible for designing and implementing various methods for communicating assessment results. This implies selecting different alternatives and methodologies depending on the audience (for example, central and regional authorities, researchers, the education community, and the general public will). This unit also pays attention to how the information is used by encouraging accurate interpretation of the results, modifying users' expectations, and supporting the policy design process.

Implementation

The first phase of the assessment system was put into operation in 1991. This consisted of designing and implementing tests of cognitive performance in mathematics and Spanish for a representative sample of students in grades 3 and 5 in public and private schools in both rural and urban areas in thirteen states. In carrying out this task, those involved worked closely with the ICFES's National Testing Service to design and analyze fifth grade tests. The SER Research Institute and the Ministry of Education developed testing instruments for the third grade. The SER Institute was also responsible for designing the instruments to determine the characteristics of the schools, the teachers, and the students and was also in charge of administering the instruments and analyzing the data collected.

In accordance with educational policy, the system will shortly expand the scope of the assessment to include grades 7 and 9 to establish points of reference at uniform two-year intervals.

During the first years of implementation the system will concentrate on assessing mathematics, Spanish, and personal development. Natural and social sciences will be included as the system matures and expands (table 11-2).

Thirteen states in which 60 percent of the population live have been included during the first assessment, during the following years the Ministry of Evaluation is expecting to expand its geographic coverage to the entire country.

The assessment system will reach total coverage in elementary and secondary schools (grades 3, 5, 7, and 9) for mathematics, Spanish, natural and social sciences, and two non-academic areas by the end of 1995.

Table 11-2. Expansion of the Coverage of the National Assessment System

Year	Grade	Calendar	Area	No. of states
1991	3, 5	A	Mathematics, Spanish, FNCP-1[a]	13
1992	3, 5	B	Mathematics, Spanish, FNCP-1	13
	7, 9	A	Mathematics, Spanish, FNCS-1[b]	22
1993	7, 9	B	Mathematics, Spanish, FNCS-1	4
	3, 5	A	Natural and Social Science, FNCP-2	29
1994	3, 5	B	Natural and Social Science, FNCP-2	4
	7, 9	A	Natural and Social Science, FNCP-2	.
1995	7, 9	B	Natural and Social Science, FNCP-2	.

Notes: Colombia has two school calendars. Calendar A runs from January to November and calendar B runs from September to June.

. to be decided.

a. First noncognitive area for primary education.

b. First noncognitive area for secondary education.

Source: Author's Data.

In the first phase of implementation, tests on cognitive achievements in mathematics and Spanish were given to a national sample of third and fifth graders along with instruments dealing with personal and social development. Complementary activities for this first phase included the following:

- Determining a representative sample for the thirteen states, which included the city of Bogotá, taking into account the characteristics of each area (urban or rural) and the type of school (public or private);
- Designing four instruments to assess cognitive performance in mathematics and Spanish for third and fifth graders;
- Designing instruments to collect information from schools, teachers, and students;
- Processing and analyzing the data obtained using these instruments.

The sample included both urban and rural elementary schools. Approximately 650 students were selected from grade 3 and 500 from grade 5 in each department selected.

GRADE 3 MATHEMATICS. The team in charge of the design of this instrument considered it important to assess the use of algorithms and problem solving skills. The instrument included items dealing with addition, multiplication, ordering, additive ordering and multiplication. The items can be arranged into three levels according to degree of cognitive complexity: direct resolution, data transformation, and data combination.

Problem solving was assessed based on the most difficult problem solved for each topic. The process used to solve the problem was evaluated and graded.

GRADE 3 SPANISH. The third grade Spanish test is consistent with the curriculum. Its emphasis was on extracting meaning from written material rather than on the rules of writing. The following indicators were used: comprehension of the material being read and adequate command of the language in terms of syntax and semantics. The entire test consisted of twenty-nine questions classified into three difficulty levels.

GRADE 5 MATHEMATICS. The level of cognitive achievement in a range of skills, including numeric systems, measurement, geometry, use of probabilities, and mathematical representations, were assessed. The fifth grade mathematics test consisted of thirty-seven questions divided into five levels of cognitive achievement.

GRADE 5 SPANISH. The level of competence in communication was measured. The instrument contained thirty-five questions, thirty of which were multiple choice and five were open-ended. Students were classified based on four levels of achievement.

FACTORS RELATED TO ACHIEVEMENT. Several studies (Avalos and Haddad 1981; Fuller 1987; Lockheed and Verspoor 1991; Schiefelbein and Farrel 1982; Velez and Rojas 1988) have identified variables that seem to have a direct impact on student's achievement. The Colombian NAS designed questionnaires to collect data on student's gender, teachers, and school administrators. The measure included indicators related to student's gender; age; place of residence; education experience, including any repetition; work history; frequency of homework; time devoted to homework; time spent watching television; attitudes toward the school, subjects and teachers; education and work expectations; family size; quality of dwelling; facilities available at home; and so on.

Teachers' information gathered included: gender, age, residence, formal education, specializations, in-service training, other employment, pedagogical experience, and so on.

For institutions the following information was gathered: sector (rural or urban); type of institution (public or private); academic shifts (morning, afternoon, evening); infrastructure; teaching aids; number of teachers; textbook availability; presence of a library; length of school day; and so on.

DATA COLLECTION AND ANALYSIS. Each state selected to be part of the assessment process had a coordinator who was in charge of teams that conducted the field work. The regional and local teams were trained to conduct the evaluation and interview the teachers. The teams administered the tests to the students without their teachers being present. Scoring and coding were done at the central level.

For each of the areas evaluated, mean achievement scores were calculated by state, sector (urban or rural), and type of institution (public or private). Analysis revealed that urban schools performed better than rural schools and private schools performed better than public schools. Profiles of schools, school administrators, and teachers in the departments with the highest and lowest achievement levels were also obtained.

After calculating the students' achievements by sector and type of institution, a second level of analysis was performed to identify the relationship between the students' average performance and the characteristics of the institution, teachers, and principal using linear regression models. For public schools the following variables showed a significant effect on achievement: the emphasis given by teachers to specific areas, teachers' education, living conditions of students, textbook:student ratio, effort the student had to make to get to the school (distance), number of siblings, time spent watching television, and student's gender (girls performed better than boys in Spanish and worse in mathematics). For private schools the following variables were identified as having a significant impact on achievement: teachers, education, effort the student had to make to get to school, the student's age, and the number of siblings.

The analysis also found that teachers' education is an important factor in student achievement, however, the number of in-service training courses teachers took did not seem to play a role.

DISSEMINATION OF RESULTS. The results of the assessment have been presented to the public by means of special publications as well as through the mass media (television, radio, and newspapers). The Ministry of Education organized workshops at the central and state levels to discuss the results and the implications for future actions. The evaluation division of the ministry recently organized a national seminar to present the findings of the evaluation to deans from faculties of education, researchers, teachers, principals, supervisors, and representatives from teacher training institutions. The participants discussed the actions that should be taken to improve the quality of the education provided. At the state level more than thirty seminars have been delivered for local authorities, school superintendents, and teachers.

Lessons Learned

The most important factors affecting the design and implementation of the national assessment system have been the creation within the Ministry of Education of the evaluation division and the political will, commitment, and direct involvement of the minister and vice minister of education and other key senior officials.

Despite only two years of experience, the education establishment learnt some valuable lessons from implementing the first national assessment. Perhaps the most important is that the Ministry of Education, aware of its limitations in terms of human resources and capabilities, decided to contract with the National Testing Service to design the instruments to evaluate mathematics and Spanish. The NTS' solid experience played a significant role in producing tests that were both valid and reliable.

Similarly, the involvement of a private institution, the SER Research Institute, with broad experience in work of this nature, guaranteed smooth and timely pilot testing and data collection, coding, cleaning, and analysis. This collaboration between the public and private sector also proved that a national assessment system can be implemented by institutions outside the Ministry of Education. In addition, the collaboration gave the system a sense of independence from the government, thereby increasing its credibility among the general public as well as among key stakeholders.

As far as the scope of the system is concerned, the decision to implement the system progressively rather than to assess the whole country right away permitted adjustments to be made much more readily in response to problems that arose.

Making final statements about the accomplishments and failures of the system is not yet possible, but the indications suggest that the system has been moving in the right direction.

References

Avalos, B., and W. Haddad. 1981. *A Review of Teacher Effectiveness Research in Africa, India, Latin America, Middle East, Malaysia, Philippines and Thailand: Synthesis of Results*. Ottawa, Canada: International Development Research Center.

Caro, Blanca Lilia. 1990. *El Servicio Nacional de Pruebas en Colombia*. IFT-196. Bogotá, Colombia: Insituto SER de Investigación.

Lockheed, M., and A. Verspoor. 1991. *Improving Primary Education in Developing Countries*. Oxford, U.K.: Oxford University Press.

Ministry of Education. 1987. *Estadísticas de la Educación 1982–1986*. Oficina Sectorial de Planeación Educativa. Bogotá, Colombia.

Ministry of Education. 1992. *Sistema Nacional de Evaluación de la Calidad de la Educación. Primera Fase: Estructura, Avances y Resultados*. Bogotá, Colombia.

Schiefelbein, E., and J. Farrel. 1982. *Eight Years of Their Lives*. Ottawa, Canada: International Development Research Center.

Velez, E., and C. Rojas. 1988. *Bachilleres Colombianos: Aspiraciones y Logros*. Bogotá, Colombia: Instituto SER de Investigación.

12

The Grade 3 and 5 Assessment in Egypt

David Carroll

Following the 1993 National Conference for the Development of Primary Education Curricula, which recommended dividing primary education into two stages, grades 1–3 and grades 4–5, with an evaluation at the end of each stage, Egypt is progressively introducing a new regime of formal testing. The new national tests, in mathematics and Arabic at grades 3 and 5 and in science and social studies at grade 5, will partially replace promotion testing. The emphasis at grade 3 is on basic skills and at grade 5 on the use of these skills in everyday activities.

Political and Educational Factors in the Development of the Grade 3 and 5 Assessment

In accordance with the Jomtien "Education for All" declaration, Egypt has been working both to increase access to and to raise quality of basic education. Policymakers have identified relatively high rates of dropout in primary education as a problem to be addressed. According to official Ministry of Education figures (1994 and other documents), about 75 percent of children actually complete a five-year course of primary education, but because of grade repetition, the average child takes more than six years, with the typical dropout having an average of four and a half years of schooling. In the absence of formal promotion testing before grade 4, repetition is concentrated in grades 4 and 5. Figures presented to the Nine-Country Education for All Meetings show that grade repetition approaches 20 percent at the end of each of these grades (Ministry of Education 1993, table 4, p. 13).

Because most primary-level students (77 percent) are in two- or three-shift schools, the primary schools are not easily able to absorb this level of repeaters. Thus grade repetition is delaying the achievement of the ministry's long-term goal of offering every child a full school day.

Many also believe that much of the grade repetition may be unnecessary, or at least be based on inadequate or inappropriate testing. The same publication (Ministry of Education 1993, p. 18) identifies four main weaknesses in the current decentralized system of promotion testing:

- Teachers are not clear about the objectives or procedures of assessment because of weak central control over content and the lack of sufficiently detailed specifications,
- Test item quality varies because teachers are not trained in test writing,
- Weak students are not given sufficiently focused help because testing is not linked to guidelines for remedial action,
- Standards vary because of the lack of any national or regional norms to which performance can be related.

Furthermore, grade repetition may not meet the needs of the repeater, because no specific remedial provision is made. Hence, current policy is to rationalize and minimize grade repetition and emphasize the development of remedial teaching.

Development of a census-based standard assessment at grades 3 and 5 that reflects curriculum objectives accurately and uses consistently high quality tests is seen as an essential element in achieving this. While setting a rigorous standard in this way may not reduce grade repetition in the short term, it allows teachers and students to prioritize their work more effectively, and should therefore raise standards in the medium term as well as rationalize decisions about repetition. To minimize the number of students repeating a grade, from 1994–95 on the assessment will be linked to a summer remedial program, and pre-session make-up tests.

Aims of the Grade 3 and 5 Assessment

The basic aim of the assessment is to provide decisionmakers at the local level—including parents and administrators who take decisions about grade repetition—with better information about pupils' achievement in the basic skills of reading, writing, and arithmetic at grade 3 and grade 5, and also their understanding of the basic concepts of science and social studies at grade 5. The 1993 National Conference for the Development of Primary Education Curricula identified these subjects as the foundation on which future learning is built, and their early acquisition is therefore vital. The first assessment takes place at grade 3 to identify those at risk in grade 4 and enable them to receive preemptive remedial attention. The second assessment takes place at the transition from primary to preparatory school, and provides an opportunity for remedial attention at that stage.

The present localized examination system is not an adequate measure for this purpose because: (a) standards are not monitored and the only external intervention consists of the publication of nonmandatory examination specifications, (b) the examinations do not focus on priority skills, and (c) question writers have not been adequately trained.

As promotion tests are set and administered at the school level, they cannot provide the necessary monitoring information when concern prevails about standards. Judgments about adequacy of performance, made using tests of uneven technical quality constructed by teachers and not related to external criteria, are often not well founded.

The primary goal of the assessment is to set an acceptable standard that all schools will meet in due course to ensure that students receive an adequate basic education, and to help restore parents' and students' faith in the benefits of that education. The assessment is census-based rather than sample-based because its goal is to help raise individual achievement. By focusing on basic skills, it defines success in terms that offer tangible future benefits or improved prospects to encourage children to stay in school.

To help teachers and students meet the standard, those who fail at the first attempt in May will be able to attend remedial programs during the summer and sit the tests again in September before being obliged to repeat the grade.

The assessment has obvious potential as a source of information for decision support, either centrally or locally. However, a possibility of conflict arises between the use of assessment information in this way and the primary goals of this assessment, that is, individual monitoring, diagnosis, and remediation. As has been seen elsewhere, for example, in England and Wales, a fear that the new assessment will be used to evaluate the performance of teachers or schools can lead to its introduction being resisted. The use of achievement data provided by the grade 3 and 5 assessment as an element in both ministerial policy analysis and the new inspectorate system currently being established is therefore a secondary goal. The assessment is structured to facilitate analysis of performance on specific topics and comparison of mean scores between groups using different forms of the tests, but this takes second place to the establishment of a national standard.

Implementing Organizations

Educational administration in Egypt is based on the principle of centralized planning and decentralized implementation. The most comprehensive, although not the most recent, description of this in English is in the 1986 submission to the International Conference on Education in Geneva (National Centre for Educational Research 1986, pp. 7–27). The central Ministry of Education is responsible for policy, planning implementation, and follow-up. For administrative purposes the country is divided into governorates. The governor has vice-regal powers within the governorate and "assumes supervision of . . . general policy and has full power over the services and utilities, including those of education." Each governorate has a directorate of education divided into subdirectorates or zones. This division is reflected in the division of the education budget into a central budget and a governorates' budget. The center has limited control over the setting of the governorates' budget. Its control over disbursement is limited to monitoring and advising governorates.

In some areas, the division of responsibility is clear. The Ministry of Education exercises control over the curriculum and the production and distribution of instructional materials. School buildings and maintenance and teacher selection and in-service training are under the effective control of the directorates of education. In the case of examinations, there is a hybrid system. The Ministry of Education administers the general secondary school leaving certificate, but the general certificate at the end of basic education (grade 8) is set, administered, and graded at the governorate level. Responsibility for the general certificate examination at the end of grade 5 is currently with the subdirectorates. Annual and semi-annual promotion tests are organized locally. This system makes automatic allowance for local diversity and meets administrative needs: promotion and transfer to preparatory school are basically local concerns, transfer to secondary school depends on the facilities available within the directorates of education, and admission to university is competed for on a national level. However, the system delegates responsibility for test quality and maintenance of standards in basic education to the local level, where the available expertise is weakest, and makes no provision for national monitoring of standards.

The existing examination system, however, had to be the starting point for establishing a system for the grade 3 and 5 assessment for three main reasons:

- Finance is perhaps the most important reason. Using established promotion testing systems rather than setting up a new, parallel administration is not simply a matter of cost. New, centrally administered examinations at grades 3 and 5 would clash with existing examinations and lines of authority.

- Placing control not only of the information generated, but also of the allocation of work, primarily in local hands, is seen as a means of reducing local resistance.

- Administration would, in any case, have to be contracted out, because no central agency has the facilities to administer census-based testing to a cohort of about 1.3 million students. No independent local survey or research agencies exist that could take on a task of this scale, so the present examination system is the only means available to administer such examinations.

Therefore, responsibility for the assessment was divided between the Ministry of Education, directorates of education, and the National Center for Examinations and Educational Evaluation (NCEEE). The NCEEE is responsible for test specifications and items and the directorates of education for printing, administration, and grading. Test assembly is a shared responsibility.

Structure, Staffing, and Governance of the NCEEE

The NCEEE was founded by presidential decree in 1990. Analogous to a university it is an institution whose aim is to conduct the studies and scientific research needed for setting up examination systems to achieve curriculum goals and evaluating them. The NCEEE's specific goals are

- To establish criteria for measuring and assessing students' knowledge, skills, and cognitive abilities and to establish new examination and grading systems;

- To establish general certificate examination systems at all preuniversity levels relevant to curricula, teaching methods, and instructional materials;

- To monitor and evaluate the quality of examinations at all educational levels and ensure their efficiency in assessing students' abilities and skills;

- To conduct research on the development and improvement of assessment and assessment instruments at all educational levels;

- To organize training programs on setting, grading, and administering examinations and assessing supervisors' and teachers' technical and professional levels;

- To exchange views with, make recommendations to, and otherwise serve universities, higher and technical institutes, Ministry of Education directorates, and all bodies concerned with educational matters in Egypt and overseas.

The minister of education chairs the NCEEE's board. The center's director is equivalent in status to a university vice president. The center has four technical departments: Examinations and Evaluation Development, Examinations and Evaluation Research, Training and Dissemination, and Operations and Information. Each department director is equivalent in status to a university dean. All NCEEE specialist staff are qualified at the postgraduate level, and many are working toward relevant higher degrees. The Department of Examinations and Evaluation Development consists of subject specialists who have been, or are being, trained in testing. At the time of writing, six departmental staff had been trained as examinations officers at the Scottish Examination Board, and during 1995 two staff members will receive training in the development of remedial assessment. This group is responsible for test development for the assessment.

Thus the primary role of the NCEEE is to strengthen the system, not simply to administer examinations. It provides specialist technical expertise not otherwise available to the Ministry of Education and a measure of technical continuity not found in a system where test paper construction is normally undertaken by subject specialists, who may well have no specialist expertise in test development. It is also responsible for improving existing procedures for test development and quality control.

Plans for Implementing the First Assessment

A new curriculum on which future tests will be based was introduced in September 1994 in the first three grades of primary school, and thereafter will be introduced at the rate of one grade per year (grade 4 in September 1995, grade 5 in September 1996, and so on). Full operation of the assessment system requires items to be pretested on the grade for which they are intended, but fairness demands that none of the students taking the test should have seen any of the items before. Therefore the items used in the regular assessment will have to be tried out in the year before they will be used. For items based on the new curriculum, the first year in which this can take place will be 1994–95 for grade 3 and 1996–97 for grade 5, so the first assessment with pretested items for the new curriculum can only take place in 1996 for grade 3 and 1998 for grade 5. The first implementation of the assessment, planned for 1994, and again in 1995, will therefore be, at least partially, trials of procedures for subsequent years. (These assessments took place too late for inclusion in this chapter.)

Because tests in successive years and the May and September examinations in a single year have no common content, the NCEEE is developing the use of Rasch one-parameter Item Response Theory (IRT). When the new curriculum is in place, items will be field tested at least one year before being used, calibrated on a common scale, and banked. This will enable all tests used for the assessment to be assembled from items of known difficulty.

In summary, the plan for the first administration was as follows:

- The NCEEE produces a national test specification in consultation with the Ministry of Education and the governorates.
- The NCEEE writes, reviews, and field tests a pool of items from which the tests will be drawn. These are item-analyzed using "classical" techniques to assure the quality and informativeness of the items. Items selected for use in future years will be calibrated using Rasch one-parameter Item Response Theory to allow tests of known difficulty to be constructed from the pool and allow statistical equating of standards across different forms of the test.

- Each directorate of education's test is assembled jointly by NCEEE and directorate staff from pretested items. In the first and second years, each test must contain sufficient common items for equating forms using either common-item equating or equating of percentiles. In the future, if use of precalibrated items is established, directorates may be able to use any test that can be assembled from the item pool.

- The NCEEE prepares camera-ready copy for each form of the test and supplies it to the directorate.

- Each directorate prints, administers, and grades the test in its area and sends the results to the NCEEE.

- The NCEEE provides the directorate with an analysis of the test results. In the longer term, this will be a valuable source of management information in addition to the impact of the tests in the classroom. In the first two years at least, the NCEEE will seek to establish procedures for future use. Two trial analyses are proposed:

  - An analysis of a sample of tests from one or two directorates to provide feedback about performance on significant items
  - An equating of standards between two or more directorates using both equating of percentiles and common-item equating in the first instance to compare the two methods.

Planning for Future Assessments

The first round of assessment did not follow the above plan presented earlier. In effect, the directorates did not cooperate in mounting the assessment. As a result, the old pattern of promotion testing continued for 1994. The directorates gave two reasons for not cooperating in the assessment. First, they noted that as administration of the assessment is their responsibility, they are free to choose on what day to administer it. Because the directorates hold their tests on different days, each needs a different test, and using common items as proposed by the NCEEE for security reasons is impossible. Second, because at this level test content, within the parameters of the advisory specification distributed by the ministry, is the directorates' responsibility, they claim that they need not use NCEEE test items. If a test containing NCEEE items is administered, the NCEEE should pay for it.

Thus the directorates did not object to the assessment on technical or policy grounds, but because the plan infringed on their acknowledged responsibility for implementation. This was enough. The NCEEE produced items and tried them out, but they were not used.

Considerable debate has taken place about how to get the assessment back on track. It seems unlikely that the underlying concern was any inconvenience the changes might have caused. Adjusting examination schedules would not have been so difficult, and the grade 3 and 5 examinations are not particularly high stakes tests, so the security risks in noncontiguous governorates would, in any case, be small.

The consensus view is that the directorates' lack of cooperation was the result of sensitivity about central intervention in local affairs. At present, central monitoring of implementation depends primarily on reports from the directorates. The Ministry of Education is required to respect the jurisdictions and authorities of the local councils. The ministry can therefore point out problems, but must leave action to the local authorities. The grade 3 and 5 assessment in its original form would have given the ministry an independent measure of achievement in any directorate, subdirectorate, or school, and hence much greater awareness of possible problem areas. The directorates probably wished to forestall this increase in accountability.

If this is the case, then to respond directly to the objections, for example, by producing vastly more test items or finding financing for printing, would probably not lead to the tests being successfully administered. As each problem was solved, other problems would materialize. Therefore plans for the 1994–95 round of testing have been restructured in an attempt to gain the directorates' cooperation. This involves increasing consultation, improving specification design and dissemination, offering training and other services to directorates, and increasing the emphasis on developing remedial work.

Increased Consultation

The problem of securing local participation is being addressed through the Council of Directors of Education, which meets regularly, and which all directorate directors are invited to attend. The NCEEE is using this council to canvass local opinion, persuade directors to accept intervention in local testing, and build up relationships with individual directorates by offering them specialist help.

Improved Specification Design and Dissemination

Until 1994, not much importance was attached to test specifications. They were normally not available in the schools more than a month or two before the examinations, they gave few details about assessment objectives, and they were frequently little more than a list of item types and marks awarded. They were advisory rather than mandatory.

Such specifications were not an effective means of controlling test content and difficulty. From the 1995–96 academic year, the NCEEE specifications will become mandatory, and the NCEEE is developing improved specifications that will include a detailed description of the assessment's objectives, the skills and content to be mastered and how they are to be assessed, and specimen items. The new specifications will give better guidance to test developers, teachers, and students, and also be a much better basis for evaluating the content validity of the assessment instruments. This will help to achieve greater uniformity and higher quality even without other interventions.

Training and Other Services

Since its inception, the NCEEE has had a department for training and public relations. As a result of the problems with the grade 3 and 5 assessment, the center has increased its emphasis on the technical services it offers to directorates, with the aim of establishing both its technical credibility and its value as a collaborator. Hence the importance of this department has increased, as has awareness of the potential for outreach by the Research department. Services planned or currently being offered to directorates include

- Statistical services for score processing, item analysis, and so on;
- Training for governorate staff in item writing and review;

- Training to inspectors and teachers and publicity for students and parents to help them prepare for the assessment.

The scale of these activities will be developed over a period of years.

Emphasis on Development of Remedial Work

Remedial work is not a common feature in Egyptian schools. Tests and examinations are not normally treated diagnostically and few remedial resources are available. Student self-evaluation guides produced by the NCEEE and books provided by the private sector both provide examination practice, but do not aim to help students solve common difficulties they face or give diagnostic assessments. Remedial courses for grade 3 and 5 students began in summer 1995, and the NCEEE has begun to develop placement and exit tests for these courses.

This will be a substantial project. It requires developing question types, grading schemes, and interpretation and feedback systems that are quite different from those used in examinations. At the time of writing, these plans are not sufficiently developed to be discussed in detail.

Compromises Made and Their Likely Effects

The original form of Egypt's grade 3 and 5 assessment made important compromises with the existing system, notably, in dividing responsibility for test assembly between the NCEEE and educational directorates and in decentralizing administration and grading. The proposed system would have achieved significant improvements in test quality for small per capita increases in cost. In the event, however, the compromises were insufficient to secure local cooperation, apparently because the proposed system was still seen as a threat to local autonomy.

Therefore a major rethinking of goals took place. The strategy outlined earlier was developed to maximize progress toward the original primary goal of the assessment. This strategy is a drastic compromise. It sacrifices much of the consistency of standards and high quality of test material that could have been achieved by the use of centrally produced precalibrated items and the possibility of making comparisons between governorates or schools in different governorates using tests of known difficulty. It will, however, lead to benefits. The development of more rigorous examination specifications and monitoring of implementation will lead to some convergence of standards and provide a tool for improving the quality of question writing. The emphasis on remedial work over the summer break will provide a means for reducing grade repetition without relaxing standards. The new channels for consultation and the emphasis on offering training and other services to directorates of education will both strengthen local capacity and build a basis of trust and increased local self-confidence.

However, in itself this is unlikely to be enough to achieve the original aims. The extent to which success in achieving these aims depends on good relations with the directorates is now much better understood, but, if after two or three years' efforts it is still impossible to predict when the directorates will accept national norms, the Ministry of Education may have no option but to move toward sample-based assessment.

Lessons for Planning an Assessment System

One of the most interesting features of the problems of the assessment at grades 3 and 5 is the light it throws on the limits of ministerial power in Egypt. The Ministry of Education has sole responsibility for some areas, but the governates are responsible for others in which the minister may not intervene, except to exhort. In addition, however, there are gray areas where the minister is responsible for policy, but because implementation is localized, ministerial ability to control policy is limited in practice by the discretion allowed to local authorities and the amount and quality of the information available.

Local administrations have considerable leeway in the executive measures they take to implement ministerial policy. Central monitoring of implementation is weak, and the ministry's focus on giving guidance in the form of directives rather than on following up on their implementation is therefore not surprising. The formal system thus defines responsibilities that the minister may lack the necessary leverage to implement in practice. In cases such as this, where local authorities' accountability is divided, the accountability to the governor is actually stronger. A system of this kind releases local administrations from the dead hand of centralism, but unless adequate accountability systems are established, the price is a degree of dependence on the competence and goodwill of the local authorities.

Promotion testing is such a case. The Ministry of Education sets policy through the production and dissemination of examination specifications by the NCEEE, and the directorates implement these in the form of examinations. The NCEEE can review promotion examination papers after the examination, but does not have the authority to force changes. Therefore, the ministry can, in effect, only influence promotion examinations rather than control them, and requires the support of the directorates.

The first form of the grades 3 and 5 assessment fell foul of this informal local autonomy. It was a central initiative to solve a well-known problem and was implemented by ministerial decrees. It was not beyond the minister's power, because the minister was clearly setting policy in an area for which the minister of education has responsibility by law. The directorates resisted not because the assessment was an unsuitable means to achieve their objectives, but because they saw it as having a hidden agenda to increase central control. The main lesson of the Egyptian grade 3 and 5 assessment so far is that if accountability is given up, whether through decentralization or for other reasons, it can be extremely hard to take back.

References

Ministry of Education. 1993. *Education for All in Egypt*. Cairo.

Ministry of Education. 1994. *Growth in Gross Primary Enrollment Ratios from 1986–87 to 1992–93*. Cairo: Ministry of Education, Education Planning and Information Division, and Education Planning Project, Research Triangle Institute. (Prepared for the joint ministry, UNESCO, and UNDP seminar to review progress at mid-decade.)

National Centre for Educational Research. 1986. *Development of Education in the Arab Republic of Egypt, 84/85-85/86*. Cairo.

Part IV: Lessons

13

Lessons Learned

Vincent Greaney and Carlos Rojas

This brief summary reviews lessons learned from five case studies, four of them from developing countries (Chile, Colombia, Egypt, and Thailand), and one from England and Wales. The cases underline that no single way to approach the design and development of a national assessment exists. In each instance the country's authorities have tailored the assessment according to their needs, goals, availability of human resources, and local experience.

Functions of a National Assessment

The case studies show that national assessments can serve a variety of functions. These include monitoring pupil achievement levels, setting achievement standards, providing feedback to various audiences, and pressuring schools to attain government objectives.

In Egypt, the assessment was designed to set standards for the schools to reach; to provide information on achievement in such areas as reading, writing, arithmetic, science, and social studies; and to gather data on grade repetition. The main purpose of Thailand's assessment was to determine national education standards and to highlight important learning outcomes apart from those measured by university entrance examinations.

Government ambitions to implement a newly developed national curriculum prompted the replacement of an existing system of national assessment with a new form in England and Wales. Teacher and school accountability were major objectives of the new assessment program. The national assessment also aimed to provide parents with information about the performance of children and schools.

Two Latin American countries, Chile and Colombia, used national assessment to assess the quality of education. Chile used it to guide teacher in-service training activities and, in a rather novel way, to provide an objective measure to help allocate scarce resources. In Colombia, national assessment achievement data and additional information gathered at the same time helped identify factors related to pupil achievement.

Political Support

While technical issues tend to dominate discussions of national assessment, the cases clearly demonstrate the importance of political support. National assessments in Chile,

Colombia, and Thailand seem to have benefited from a clear political commitment from their ministries of education. This commitment was reflected in the allocation of the necessary economic and human resources to support the implementation of the national assessment.

In England and Wales political enthusiasm was also apparent, although it was not shared by others outside the government. Despite the strong opposition of teachers, the government persisted in pursuing its goal of using national assessment to hold schools and teachers accountable for students' achievement levels. While the case study does not document this, as opposition mounted, the government was forced to change the scope, frequency, and format of the assessment.

Egypt's experience indicates that political support is needed at more than one level of government. Although the national education authorities favored the introduction of a national assessment, lower levels of government viewed it as a threat to local autonomy and succeeded in delaying its implementation.

Implementation Agency

The case studies suggest that the implementing agency for national assessment can be located either inside or outside the ministry of education. Each of the five countries required the assistance of the ministry of education to varying degrees. Government educational institutions played major roles at virtually all stages in Egypt and Thailand. Colombia engaged the services of a reputable outside organization to design instruments, analyze results, and publish and disseminate the results. External agencies were more heavily involved in Chile and in England and Wales than in other countries.

Strong arguments can be made both for and against the ministry of education conducting the assessment. When the agency is located within the ministry, getting schools and other government agencies to support the assessment is generally easier. Furthermore, the level of expertise found in most ministries of education is arguably as great as that found in private and other national institutions. On the negative side, experience in some developing and industrial countries suggests that there may be a justifiably high degree of skepticism about a ministry of education monitoring the effectiveness of its own educational delivery system. Public confidence and trust may be enhanced by having the national assessment carried out by an external, objective, nongovernmental body.

The Chilean case presented an interesting example of an alliance between the government and nongovernmental sectors. Here the ministry, recognizing its lack of technical expertise, contracted the services of a university to carry out the assessment. Over time the university's expertise was transferred to the ministry by seconding ministry staff to work with the university department that was the implementing agency. In this way professional training was provided and the ability of ministry officials to run the national assessment was improved.

Prior to comparing governmental and nongovernmental cost estimates for conducting national assessment, care should be taken to take into account the opportunity costs of using government staff. Government staff such as school inspectors, curriculum personnel, printers, and drivers may have to be released from other responsibilities to work on the assessment.

Professional Expertise

Each of the countries reviewed expended considerable resources on the national assessment. Thailand's assessment unit had a staff of ninety-three professionals. Egypt's center had four separate departments each with its own relatively large staff. Normally technical experts in areas such as sampling, test development, data analysis, and reporting are required. This expertise need not be used exclusively for national assessment, however. The experts can also be used to carry out the kinds of policy-related educational studies that are so lacking in most developing countries. For example, Colombia linked its assessment data with nonachievement data in an effort to identify the correlates of achievement.

Administration

The security and integrity of the data collection procedures are essential if the data are to be used for policymaking. In each instance discussed the authorities seem to have taken care to ensure that assessment instruments were administered according to established procedures. To minimize the risk of assistance from the class teacher, and notwithstanding the additional expense incurred, people other than staff of the targeted schools participated as external moderators or invigilators in most of the national assessments reviewed. In England and Wales, by contrast, much of the assessment was designed to be built into the daily class routine so as to provide teachers with feedback to enable them to address their pupils' learning needs. Lack of standardization and concern about the objectivity of the internal school-based assessment prompted much debate about the validity of the assessment's conclusions. In addition, teachers complained about the inordinate amount of time needed to conduct the internal school-based assessment. While their complaints initially had little effect, over time the internal aspect of the assessment was de-emphasized in favor of external assessment.

Sample or Population?

Most designers of a national assessment favor the use of a sample approach. Governments are generally interested in monitoring the achievement of a targeted age or grade level. They can achieve this efficiently by using carefully selected small samples of students and test items. Sampling, however, is not an essential feature of national assessment. Indeed, three of the five cases described in this book used a population approach. In each of the three cases—Chile, Egypt, and England and Wales—the assessment served a somewhat unusual function because it was designed to have a direct impact on schools and teachers. England and Wales, as we have seen, sought to make schools and teachers accountable, while Chile used the results to help identify schools in need of additional government support, objectives that could not have been attained had a sampling approach been used. Chile supplemented its design by selecting samples of students in some subject areas.

Scope of Assessment

Developing countries contemplating a national assessment should recognize that, in general, the countries focused on a small number of subject areas and on a specific age or grade level. Despite the availability of technical resources, most limited their efforts to assessing mathematics and language competence. With increased experience, Chile, Colombia, and Thailand have tackled areas such as science or social studies. The design of the assessment for England and Wales included testing a range of subject areas at three different levels. These experiences suggest that initial efforts at national assessment in developing countries should be modest in terms of subject areas and grades to be assessed.

Support

At least two of the five case countries adopted modern public relations approaches to develop public awareness of and support for the assessment. These approaches involved preparing and distributing a variety of audiovisual aids, including videos, brochures, and posters explaining the forthcoming national assessment. In addition, national and regional workshops were organized with different audiences to explain the purpose and procedures.

Uses

Information from a national assessment can be used effectively to address policy concerns of the ministry of education or of its political overlords. In England and Wales the results were used to rank order schools. While researchers and others have criticized this use of results, it did help the government meet its objective of giving the public, and parents in particular, information by which to judge school effectiveness. In Chile, the national assessment has enabled the central government to identify schools with relatively low mean achievement scores. It has made special resources available to enable these schools to improve morale and achievement levels.

Conclusion

What additional lessons can we derive from these varied experiences with national assessment?

- Perhaps the main lesson is that a clear and narrow purpose is critical for carrying out a national assessment. Providing information to policymakers is one purpose, providing information to parents another, and instilling accountability is a third purpose.
- A steering committee representing different sectors and community interests should be established from the outset.
- Separate committees should be formed for each subject area assessed.

- Qualified, competent professionals should be entrusted with technical issues such as sampling, test development, and data analysis.

- Despite their limitations, multiple choice tests are an efficient test format for national assessments. Other formats that effectively assess desired learning outcomes should be considered if time and finances permit.

- A national assessment must have clear political commitment and support from key stakeholders if it is to have an impact on the education system. Otherwise it may amount to little more than a periodic academic exercise whose results may be of interest to just a few people within the ministry of education.

- Support for the national assessment must be forthcoming from key regional, provincial, and local levels of the administrative system.

- Teachers should be represented in the formulation and implementation phases of national assessments, otherwise they may feel threatened by the process.

From the initial design stages, funds should be set aside for the dissemination of the results of the assessment. To increase the likelihood that the results will have an impact on policymaking and ultimately teacher practice and student learning, a carefully designed set of activities should be undertaken to inform a broad public through briefings for policymakers including politicians, teacher trainers, textbook authors and publishers, through press releases, reader-friendly reports, presentations at teacher conferences, and radio and television discussions. It may not always be possible to commit a ministry of education to budgetary provisions for dissemination, especially where ministries have a tradition of treating their own studies and reports as confidential documents. Ministries of education may be particularly reluctant to release information that may reflect badly on aspects of the education system, for example, falling achievement scores, over which they are assumed to have some control.

It is evident from the cases reviewed in this book that approaches to national assessment vary considerable from country to country. Despite the variety of approaches used, many have addressed common problems especially in the areas of funding, staffing, test development, sampling, administration, analysis, reporting, and dissemination. Countries undertaking assessments can benefit from the experiences of others, by exchanging reports, holding regular regional meetings, and exchanging consultants. Africa provides a useful example of such cooperation. In the area of public examinations countries in East and Southern Africa have a long tradition of holding annual meetings of examination officers, exchanging some staff, and providing short-term training courses. A similar arrangement would help establish an opportunity for sharing of experiences, could be used for training in technical areas, and help develop a sense of shared purpose and collegiality among professionals some of whom may feel isolated within their own educational systems. Modern technology in the form of World-Wide Web could also be used as an information sharing device.

Carefully designed national assessments that meet the key information needs of critical audiences can contribute to educational policymaking, curriculum and textbook reform, and pre- and in-service teacher education programs. Ultimately, the effectiveness of national assessments should be judged in terms of their contribution to improving classroom instruction and, in particular, to raising the quality of student learning.

Distributors of World Bank Publications

Prices and credit terms vary from country to country. Consult your local distributor before placing an order.

ALBANIA
Adrion Ltd
Perlat Rexhepi Str.
Pall. 9, Shk. 1, Ap. 4
Tirana
Tel: (42) 274 19; 221 72
Fax: (42) 274 19

ARGENTINA
Oficina del Libro Internacional
Av. Cordoba 1877
1120 Buenos Aires
Tel: (1) 815-8156
Fax: (1) 815-8354

AUSTRALIA, FIJI, PAPUA NEW GUINEA, SOLOMON ISLANDS, VANUATU, AND WESTERN SAMOA
D.A Information Services
648 Whitehorse Road
Mitcham 3132
Victoria
Tel: (61) 3 9210 7777
Fax: (61) 3 9210 7788
URL: http://www.dadirect.com.au

AUSTRIA
Gerold and Co.
Graben 31
A-1011 Wien
Tel: (1) 533-50-14-0
Fax: (1) 512-47-31-29

BANGLADESH
Micro Industries Development Assistance Society (MIDAS)
House 5, Road 16
Dhanmondi R/Area
Dhaka 1209
Tel: (2) 326427
Fax: (2) 811188

BELGIUM
Jean De Lannoy
Av. du Roi 202
1060 Brussels
Tel: (2) 538-5169
Fax: (2) 538-0841

BRAZIL
Publicações Tecnicas Internacionais Ltda.
Rua Peixoto Gomide, 209
01409 Sao Paulo, SP.
Tel: (11) 259-6644
Fax: (11) 258-6990

CANADA
Renouf Publishing Co. Ltd.
1294 Algoma Road
Ottawa, Ontario K1B 3W8
Tel: 613-741-4333
Fax: 613-741-5439

CHINA
China Financial & Economic Publishing House
8, Da Fo Si Dong Jie
Beijing
Tel: (1) 333 8257
Fax: (1) 401-7365

COLOMBIA
Infoenlace Ltda.
Apartado Aereo 34270
Bogotá D.E.
Tel: (1) 285-2798
Fax: (1) 285-2798

COTE D'IVOIRE
Centre d'Edition et de Diffusion Africaines (CEDA)
04 B.P. 541
Abidjan 04 Plateau
Tel: 225-24 6510
Fax: 225-25-0567

CYPRUS
Center of Applied Research
Cyprus College
6, Diogenes Street, Engomi
P.O. Box 2006
Nicosia
Tel: 244-1730
Fax: 246-2051

CZECH REPUBLIC
National Information Center
prodejna, Konviktská 5
CS – 113 57 Prague 1
Tel: (2) 2422-9433
Fax: (2) 2422-1484
URL: http://www.nis.cz/

DENMARK
SamfundsLitteratur
Rosenoerns Allé 11
DK-1970 Frederiksberg C
Tel: (31) 351942
Fax: (31) 357822

EGYPT, ARAB REPUBLIC OF
Al Ahram
Al Galaa Street
Cairo
Tel: (2) 578-6083
Fax: (2) 578-6833

The Middle East Observer
41, Sherif Street
Cairo
Tel: (2) 393-9732
Fax: (2) 393-9732

FINLAND
Akateeminen Kirjakauppa
PO Box 23
FIN-00371 Helsinki
Tel: (0) 12141
Fax: (0) 121-4441
URL: http://booknet.cultnet.fi/aka/

FRANCE
World Bank Publications
66, avenue d'Iéna
75116 Paris
Tel: (1) 40-69-30-56/57
Fax: (1) 40-69-30-68

GERMANY
UNO-Verlag
Poppelsdorfer Allee 55
53115 Bonn
Tel: (228) 212940
Fax: (228) 217492

GREECE
Papasotiriou S.A.
35, Stournara Str.
106 82 Athens
Tel: (1) 364-1826
Fax: (1) 364-8254

HONG KONG, MACAO
Asia 2000 Ltd.
Sales & Circulation Department
Seabird House, unit 1101-02
22-28 Wyndham Street, Central
Hong Kong
Tel: 852 2530-1409
Fax: 852 2526-1107
URL: http://www.sales@asia2000.com.hk

HUNGARY
Foundation for Market Economy
Dombovari Ut 17-19
H-1117 Budapest
Tel: 36 1 204 2951 or 36 1 204 2948
Fax: 36 1 204 2953

INDIA
Allied Publishers Ltd.
751 Mount Road
Madras - 600 002
Tel: (44) 852-3938
Fax: (44) 852-0649

INDONESIA
Pt. Indira Limited
Jalan Borobudur 20
P.O. Box 181
Jakarta 10320
Tel: (21) 390-4290
Fax: (21) 421-4289

IRAN
Kowkab Publishers
P.O. Box 19575-511
Tehran
Tel: (21) 258-3723
Fax: 98 (21) 258-3723

IRELAND
Government Supplies Agency
Oifig an tSoláthair
4-5 Harcourt Road
Dublin 2
Tel: (1) 461-3111
Fax: (1) 475-2670

ISRAEL
Yozmot Literature Ltd.
P.O. Box 56055
Tel Aviv 61560
Tel: (3) 5285-397
Fax: (3) 5285-397

R.O.Y. International
PO Box 13056
Tel Aviv 61130
Tel: (3) 5461423
Fax: (3) 5461442

Palestinian Authority/Middle East
Index Information Services
P.O.B. 19502 Jerusalem
Tel: (2) 271219

ITALY
Licosa Commissionaria Sansoni SPA
Via Duca Di Calabria, 1/1
Casella Postale 552
50125 Firenze
Tel: (55) 645-415
Fax: (55) 641-257

JAMAICA
Ian Randle Publishers Ltd.
206 Old Hope Road
Kingston 6
Tel: 809-927-2085
Fax: 809-977-0243

JAPAN
Eastern Book Service
Hongo 3-Chome,
Bunkyo-ku 113
Tokyo
Tel: (03) 3818-0861
Fax: (03) 3818-0864
URL: http://www.bekkoame.or.jp/~svt-ebs

KENYA
Africa Book Service (E.A.) Ltd.
Quaran House, Mfangano Street
P.O. Box 45245
Nairobi
Tel: (2) 23641
Fax: (2) 330272

KOREA, REPUBLIC OF
Daejon Trading Co. Ltd.
P.O. Box 34
Yeoeida
Seoul
Tel: (2) 785 1631/4
Fax: (2) 784-0315

MALAYSIA
University of Malaya Cooperative Bookshop, Limited
P.O. Box 1127
Jalan Pantai Baru
59700 Kuala Lumpur
Tel: (3) 756-5000
Fax: (3) 755-4424

MEXICO
INFOTEC
Apartado Postal 22-860
14060 Tlalpan,
Mexico D.F.
Tel: (5) 606-0011
Fax: (5) 606-0386

NETHERLANDS
De Lindeboom/InOr-Publikaties
P.O. Box 202
7480 AE Haaksbergen
Tel: (53) 574-0004
Fax: (53) 572-9296

NEW ZEALAND
EBSCO NZ Ltd.
Private Mail Bag 99914
New Market
Auckland
Tel: (9) 524-8119
Fax: (9) 524-8067

NIGERIA
University Press Limited
Three Crowns Building Jericho
Private Mail Bag 5095
Ibadan
Tel: (22) 41-1356
Fax: (22) 41-2056

NORWAY
Narvesen Information Center
Book Department
P.O. Box 6125 Etterstad
N-0602 Oslo 6
Tel: (22) 57-3300
Fax: (22) 68-1901

PAKISTAN
Mirza Book Agency
65, Shahrah-e-Quaid-e-Azam
P.O. Box No. 729
Lahore 54000
Tel: (42) 7353601
Fax: (42) 7585283

Oxford University Press
5 Bangalore Town
Sharae Faisal
PO Box 13033
Karachi-75350
Tel: (21) 446307
Fax: (21) 454-7640
URL: http://www.oup.com

PERU
Editorial Desarrollo SA
Apartado 3824
Lima 1
Tel: (14) 285380
Fax: (14) 286628

PHILIPPINES
International Booksource Center Inc.
Suite 720, Cityland 10
Condominium Tower 2
H.V dela Costa, corner
Valero St.
Makati, Metro Manila
Tel: (2) 817-9676
Fax: (2) 817-1741

POLAND
International Publishing Service
Ul. Piekna 31/37
00-577 Warzawa
Tel: (2) 628-6089
Fax: (2) 621-7255

PORTUGAL
Livraria Portugal
Rua Do Carmo 70-74
1200 Lisbon
Tel: (1) 347-4982
Fax: (1) 347-0264

ROMANIA
Compani De Librarii Bucuresti S.A.
Str. Lipscani no. 26, sector 3
Bucharest
Tel: (1) 613 9645
Fax: (1) 312 4000

RUSSIAN FEDERATION
Isdatelstvo <Ves Mir>
9a, Kolpachniy Pereulok
Moscow 101831
Tel: (95) 917 87 49
Fax: (95) 917 92 59

SAUDI ARABIA, QATAR
Jarir Book Store
P.O. Box 3196
Riyadh 11471
Tel: (1) 477-3140
Fax: (1) 477-2940

SINGAPORE, TAIWAN, MYANMAR, BRUNEI
Asahgate Publishing Asia Pacific Pte. Ltd.
41 Kallang Pudding Road #04-03
Golden Wheel Building
Singapore 349316
Tel: (65) 741-5166
Fax: (65) 742-9356
e-mail: ashgate@asianconnect.com

SLOVAK REPUBLIC
Slovart G.T.G. Ltd.
Krupinska 4
PO Box 152
852 99 Bratislava 5
Tel: (7) 839472
Fax: (7) 839485

SOUTH AFRICA, BOTSWANA
For single titles:
Oxford University Press Southern Africa
P.O. Box 1141
Cape Town 8000
Tel: (21) 45-7266
Fax: (21) 45-7265

For subscription orders:
International Subscription Service
P.O. Box 41095
Craighall
Johannesburg 2024
Tel: (11) 880-1448
Fax: (11) 880-6248

SPAIN
Mundi-Prensa Libros, S.A.
Castello 37
28001 Madrid
Tel: (1) 431-3399
Fax: (1) 575-3998
http://www.tsai.es/mprensa

Mundi-Prensa Barcelona
Consell de Cent, 391
08009 Barcelona
Tel: (3) 488-3009
Fax: (3) 487-7659

SRI LANKA, THE MALDIVES
Lake House Bookshop
P.O. Box 244
100, Sir Chittampalam A. Gardiner Mawatha
Colombo 2
Tel: (1) 32105
Fax: (1) 432104

SWEDEN
Fritzes Customer Service
Regeringsgaton 12
S-106 47 Stockholm
Tel: (8) 690 90 90
Fax: (8) 21 47 77

Wennergren-Williams AB
P. O. Box 1305
S-171 25 Solna
Tel: (8) 705-97-50
Fax: (8) 27-00-71

SWITZERLAND
Librairie Payot
Service Institutionnel
Côtes-de-Montbenon 30
1002 Lausanne
Tel: (021)-341-3229
Fax: (021)-341-3235

Van Diemen Editions Techniq
Ch. de Lacuez 41
CH1807 Blonay
Tel: (021) 943 2673
Fax: (021) 943 3605

TANZANIA
Oxford University Press
Maktaba Street
PO Box 5299
Dar es Salaam
Tel: (51) 29209
Fax: (51) 46822

THAILAND
Central Books Distribution
306 Silom Road
Bangkok
Tel: (2) 235-5400
Fax: (2) 237-8321

TRINIDAD & TOBAGO, JAM.
Systematics Studies Unit
#9 Watts Street
Curepe
Trinidad, West Indies
Tel: 809-662-5654
Fax: 809-662-5654

UGANDA
Gustro Ltd.
Madhvani Building
PO Box 9997
Plot 16/4 Jinja Rd.
Kampala
Tel/Fax: (41) 254763

UNITED KINGDOM
Microinfo Ltd.
P.O. Box 3
Alton, Hampshire GU34 2PG
England
Tel: (1420) 86848
Fax: (1420) 89889

ZAMBIA
University Bookshop
Great East Road Campus
P.O. Box 32379
Lusaka
Tel: (1) 213221 Ext. 482

ZIMBABWE
Longman Zimbabwe (Pte.)Ltd
Tourle Road, Ardbennie
P.O. Box ST125
Southerton
Harare
Tel: (4) 621617
Fax: (4) 621670